To Cathy,

Best of Wishes

[signature] BPM

October 1998

# BELIEVE NO ONE

# BELIEVE NO ONE

## Roy Herridge
*with*
## *Brian Hilliard*

Little, Brown and Company

A *Little, Brown* book

First published in Great Britain in 1993
by Little, Brown and Company

Copyright © Roy Herridge 1993

The moral right of the author has been asserted

A CIP catalogue record for this book
is available from the British Library.

Typeset by Hewer Text Composition Services, Edinburgh

Printed and bound in Great Britain by
BPCC Hazell Books Ltd
Member of BPCC Ltd

ISBN 0 316 90563 1

Little, Brown and Company (UK) Limited
165 Great Dover Street
London SE1 4YA

ACCEPT NOTHING BELIEVE NO ONE

CONFIRM EVERYTHING

Traditional Police advice

# Contents

# Acknowledgements

This is not a book that has been written for personal glorification. This is the only way I have of thanking the many police officers, young and old, of high and low rank who over the years have pulled together to form the excellent teams with which I have had the privilege of working. Many of the crimes that I have investigated have been solved by very junior members of the squads concerned; unfortunately only the senior members have received the subsequent praise. I hope that I have been able, throughout my service to make sure that praise and commendation have always reached those who really deserve it.

I would also like also to thank all those members of the media who have helped in many investigations, often ensuring an extremely quick solution to crimes that might have gone unresolved for long periods. They have made my lot and that of my officers far easier.

Finally and most importantly I want to thank the families and friends of many victims as well as the many members of the general public who have done their utmost to help us all to bring many violent despicable offenders to justice.

Quality of service is the new police objective. My contribution to that concept would be to encourage every officer to see some good in everyone – witness or suspect – with whom he or she deals, and to care about the little man. Police are generally tough and resilient; we often see the worst in individuals and we will never give up on our investigations of murder, rape, robbery and many other

very violent crimes. But we must not close our eyes
to the possibility of there being some good in those responsible. I discovered a long time ago that there is some good
in everyone.

Roy Herridge QPM

# A Failure Of Justice

At 9.00 a.m. on February 2, 1987, I was driving to the Old Bailey with the victim of the worst rape I have ever investigated. Eight hours later I drove back with her, stunned and angry that the most important court in the land had demonstrated that her hour-long ordeal was of less significance than the theft of a video-recorder, some jewellery and a handful of credit cards.

Jill Saward had been raped, buggered, and degraded, yet based on what the judge said when sentencing, I had the impression that he thought it had not been so bad for her. She had been stripped and dragged from room to room by two men. One of them was sentenced to three years for the rape, and five years for theft of property. The other, the principal rapist, was sentenced to five years for each offence. The sentences must have reflected the judge's view of the relative seriousness of each.

The Old Bailey to me, and, I think, to most people, is the symbol of justice. I've been there fifty or more times. I haven't won every case. I haven't always been happy about the juries, but I've never come away feeling that something was desperately wrong with the system. I've never gone wanting vengeance. But never before or since have I felt the deep cold anger of that dismal February day, anger at the way the most famous court in the world could treat the victim of one of the most perverted crimes I had ever dealt with. I was not alone. This was also the feeling of the general public at the outcome of the case. The world's press gave the verdicts wide publicity and the editorials of the majority of the papers were critical of the criminal justice system.

It's out of character for me to be angry. I'm normally very calm. I suppose some people would see me almost as insensitive. As a young copper I learned quickly that anger clouds your judgement, it messes up an investigation. It makes you follow the wrong leads, or ignore inconvenient evidence. If you get angry, you lose the clear mind that anyone needs if they want to learn the truth. As Mr Justice Leonard made his own sentiments clear, I had wanted to bang the Old Bailey table in front of me, and say to him coldly and clearly, 'What about her?' I wanted someone to tell the listening reporters that the two men in the dock were the most evil I had come across in thirty years of policing, but here was a judge speaking of passing a sentence which would not keep a 22-year-old man in prison 'for a disproportionate length of time'; a judge who, from what he said, I thought was showing more concern for the future of the rapist than for the past and present of the victim.

Detective Superintendents are not paid to give way to their feelings. In fact Detective Superintendents are better off without feelings, so that day I bit my tongue, gripped the edge of the chair, and wondered what I could say to Jill in defence of the Criminal Justice system of which I had been so proud. If I was angry what must she have been feeling? I with twenty-five years' service could also see my feelings were shared by my younger colleagues on the team which had ensured the success of the investigation from the very outset.

The Ealing Vicarage rape in which Jill Saward had been the principal victim had made the front pages of the world's newspapers less than a year before. Three men forced their way into St Mary's Vicarage in the middle of the day. One of them raped, buggered, and bound the 21-year-old daughter of the vicar while a second looked on, and then forced her to fellate him. They kicked her boyfriend unconscious, and fractured her father's skull by striking him full force with the face of a cricket bat. They left the vicarage taking about £2,000 of property, and were arrested within a week. I'll cover the investigation into that case later in this book, but first I need to deal with the anger, depression, even the disillusionment, we experienced on the day of the trial.

I can talk about 'we' because I've always, when it has been possible, treated the victims in my cases as part of the prosecution team. Jill Saward could have been one of my own daughters. She and all victims of crime deserve to be treated as their parents, friends and relatives would want them to be treated. Too often, victims are treated as the least important part of a prosecution.

Jill Saward was, and is, a very strong character. She had not gone to pieces during the disgusting hour-long perverted orgy carried out at knife-point, knowing that the slightest sign of resistance could result in her own death, and almost inevitably the deaths of her father and boyfriend. Her first thought when she was free, was to assist them. But the police officers who interviewed her, and kept in contact with her between the time of the offences and the day of the Old Bailey trial while admiring her presence of mind, were in no doubt about how much she had suffered physically and mentally, and how much those sufferings were added to by the long wait between the arrests of her attackers and the subsequent trial. Her ordeal had not stopped when her attackers were arrested; her natural feelings of satisfaction at the arrest were quickly replaced by the fear that sometime in the future she was going to have to describe in detail everything that had happened to her to a courtroom full of strangers.

When we knew that the case was due for hearing at the Old Bailey, I arranged for Jill to be taken there for a day so that she would not feel strange when she came to give evidence. She sat in some of the courts and heard defence lawyers attacking victims and prosecution witnesses as if they were accused of crime, treating them as liars, as people prone to exaggeration. We warned Jill that in spite of the horrors she had undergone, she might still be treated in the same way, presented to the court as a liar, or as a woman of loose morals.

Although she knew that all the men concerned had been arrested, and had all admitted most of the offences, she knew that this did not automatically mean that she would not be required to give evidence.

'I don't understand this, Roy,' she told me, when I was explaining the procedure to her. 'You've arrested them. They've told you what they did. They've signed statements. Their solicitors know all about it. How can they plead not guilty?'

'I know it sounds silly,' I told her, 'but even with a date fixed for the trial, the defence don't have to tell the court what they're going to do. I don't think it will happen in this case, but sometimes defence lawyers hang on until the last minute hoping that an important witness will go on holiday or get taken ill, or just lose confidence because of the long wait.'

It's a bit hard to tell someone like Jill, who is living through a private sort of hell of which the rape is only the beginning, it's a bit hard to tell her that she might have to spend two days in the witness box, giving her own evidence and being cross-examined on it by separate lawyers acting for each of the defendants who are going to suggest that she was lying. And how much harder it was going to be for Jill, who was so sexually inexperienced at the time of the rape that the officers who first interviewed her had to explain some of the terms and words used to describe what happened to her.

So we drove to the Old Bailey from the vicarage on the first day of the trial. Besides Jill, there was Julie McCafferty, the woman Detective Constable who had acted as a friend to Jill; she had shown her round the Old Bailey and explained the procedures to her; and John Kelly, the DS who was office manager on the investigation, assisting me with paperwork. We were all tense. Jill was worrying about remembering the details in her statements. Which man had the tattoo on his hand? Who had the disfigurement on his thigh? At what stage did someone try to get her to drink vodka?

'Will I be able to look at my statement again?' she asked. 'I'm frightened about my mind going blank.'

'Course you can look at your statement. But don't worry, Jill, you're going to be all right. If you make a mistake, don't be afraid of admitting it. Everybody makes mistakes in court, even judges.'

We didn't know just how right I would be proved to be. We were tense in our own ways. We all knew how easily cases can fall apart in a major trial: a technical error, a missing statement or photograph, a failure to serve all the required documents; any of these mistakes could result in the case being thrown out, the months of patient investigation counting for nothing. We knew how easily the most reliable witnesses, and Jill was very reliable, how easily the defence can bully them into panic and contradiction.

Jill had other worries. This was going to be the first occasion since the rape that she would see the men who had been responsible for her ordeal. I had warned her that they had changed their appearances before they were arrested, and that it would be hard for her to recognise them. She listened and took it all in as calmly as she could. She had also broken up with David Kerr, her boyfriend at the time of the rape; this would be the first time for months that she would be meeting him.

She really was under more stress than anyone should be expected to handle, and yet she would be required to give evidence calmly and clearly. I think that one of her many qualities is a sense of public duty, and that part of the reason for her maintaining her self control was that we were depending on her. She was certainly not thinking about herself.

On the way I tried to keep the conversation going with remarks about the parts of London we were going through, and Jill responded readily, but we all knew we were hiding our fears on Jill's behalf, and that she was hiding her own fears to make it easier for us.

When we arrived at the Old Bailey, there was still a trial

to be finished in the court in which our case was due to be heard, so our first problem was to find a private room for Jill. We couldn't leave her to sit in the public parts of the building. The press would have found her in seconds. So there was another delay for her, another postponement of the crisis that had been building up for ten months. It was two hours before we heard that her attackers were admitting all the offences. So around about noon on February 2, 1987, I took Jill into court, to see justice done in the case of the Ealing Vicarage Rape.

I've thought about this since. Our courts are not designed to help the victims. The judge sits above the rest in his red robes; barristers, their clerks, and solicitors sit facing him, talking and swapping jokes with each other. They might be on opposite sides, but they are all members of one club. Then there is a jury, its members sitting prominently in their own place, and the prisoner has his or her own space in the dock, even the company of friends when there is more than one defendant.

But the victim is on his or her own; the person for whom the whole trial has been arranged, has no special place. The victim sits on a bench outside the court, is called into the witness box, and when he or she has given evidence, is expected to go home quietly, and let the court get on with its business. So the only place I could find for Jill was a small seating area left in the court for VIPs who might drop in to watch a particular trial. From there she could just see Martin McCall, the man who had stripped and raped her, and Christopher Byrne who had forced her into oral sex.

When the prosecuting lawyer started to outline the facts of the case, he referred to 'Jill' as 'Jennifer'. I could see this was annoying her, and passed a message to counsel to have him use the proper name. It must have made Jill feel that she was little more than letters on a page, a word without personality. The defence lawyers then spoke, asking for consideration for their clients because they had pleaded guilty and spared Jill the trauma of having to go in the witness box. No word about the trauma she had suffered during the time it had taken the case to come to trial. It was almost as if they were doing her a favour.

And no one was told that McCall had in fact beaten up his fellow defendant Christopher Byrne, and Byrne's mother, to prevent their giving evidence against him. He had also apparently beaten up Andrew Byrne who had taken a small part in the burglary, beaten him up so badly, that later in prison he collapsed and was taken to hospital and was found unfit to stand trial. (Andrew became progressively disabled and died in hospital in December 1990.)

So that was the end of that. The judge had to try a third man only for the thefts from the vicarage the next day. It seemed likely that he would sentence all the defendants at the same time. I was turning round to Jill to tell her to wait for me to take her out of court by a rear entrance. Otherwise she would be swamped by the reporters who were even now leaving the press desks to get in position for her leaving court. But Mr Justice Leonard had not finished. He indicated that he was going to sentence the rapists immediately.

Although Jill had been subjected to a variety of sexual attacks, they were all dealt with under one single charge of rape. The burglary charges listed £2,000 worth of property and included the assaults on the two men. We were expecting McCall to receive a minimum of fifteen years for the rape, perhaps even life imprisonment. But Mr Justice Leonard, commenting on the horror of the offence said that he felt Jill's trauma 'had not been so great'.

Not so great? Stripped and raped in one room, buggered in another, forced into other perverted acts at knife-point while she could hear her father and boyfriend being kicked and beaten. Not so great? What would his Lordship have considered really traumatic? Jill's hands were clenched white. I was too shocked and too ashamed to look at her face.

The judge's voice went on. 'I cannot possibly pass a sentence which adequately reflects the horror . . . otherwise you would be in prison for a disproportionate period for a 22-year-old man.' A disproportionate time? What about the prison in which Jill had been living for the last eleven months and from which she might never escape, the prison created by the fear and memory of what happened to her in her own home. Mr Justice Leonard gave McCall five years for the rape, and five years for the burglary. Byrne was also given five years for the burglary, and only three years for the rape.

There were murmurs from the press bench. Experienced reporters were asking each other if they had misheard the sentences. The defence team put their heads down, careful to conceal any satisfaction they might have felt at a sentence which had really gone in their favour. There had been recent guidelines on sentencing indicating that there should be longer sentences if the rape was carried out in the victim's home, or if more than one man was involved. Too late now to say anything. Only years of training and discipline stopped me jumping to my feet.

'Is this right?' I felt like shouting. 'What are you playing at? What are you doing to this girl?' Perhaps he would clear the court and have a few words of sympathy for Jill, express the gratitude of the Criminal Justice System for her help and co-operation. But that didn't happen.

'What about her?' I wanted to shout. 'You're going onto the next case, and she's now got to live with the thought that she's worth less than £2,000.' The court emptied. I couldn't speak. Jill herself was dumb with shock. Somehow, we got her back to the car and started the drive back to Ealing in silence. Then the anger took over. The three of us were almost shouting with rage. What a waste of time. What an insult to Jill. What sort of signal would it send to the next rapist? We stopped, aware of Jill's own unspoken anger, but a few minutes later, Julie started again.

'Look Jill, I don't know what you feel like, but I just want to lie down and die. It's all so unjust. All this time. All you've been through, and we know it doesn't go away just because the case is over, but justice? You call that justice? Theft treated more seriously than rape?' She was near tears. And that's how it went on until we dropped Jill back at the vicarage. I don't think I've ever been as angry before, or since. I have dealt with men who have beaten their wives, a child starved to death, the needless murder of an 80-year-old spinster, a sixteen-stone youth who used a knuckleduster to knock down a five-stone elderly widow, but I've never felt the anger that I felt that February day when Jill Saward's virginity was dismissed as of less value than a handful of credit cards.

I spent an hour sitting alone in my office that night wondering if I wanted to go on with this job I had enjoyed for twenty-five years. Then an idle remark that I heard on my way out of the Old Bailey reminded me of how it had all started.

A group of Americans were standing on the pavement having just come out of the public gallery entrance. As I walked past, angry, depressed, frustrated, I heard one of the women say, 'Well, that was sure one swell experience. Now we've got to meet up with Sidney and Dee at that hotel near Tower Bridge. Young man,' she asked one of the officers with me, 'can you tell me where Tower Bridge is?'

I could tell her where Tower Bridge was. Tower Bridge was where I had joined the police twenty-five years before.

# Learning The ABC

I was 19 years old, on my own as a policeman for the very first time. It was two o'clock in the morning and it was raining. I hadn't even learned the first rule of coppering: 'Always have somewhere to get out of the rain.' Rule two said that you should know somewhere you can get a cup of tea; I hadn't learned that either. At 19 I didn't know the meaning of disillusionment, but I know now that's what I was feeling that morning. I'd come on at 10.00 p.m. the night before, certain that I'd be involved in half a dozen scraps outside the Tower Bridge pubs which were then fairly rough. Most of them have now been replaced by winebars, or pubs that sell these beers that need a slice of lime to give them some taste.

But no. The pubs emptied promptly at 10.30 p.m.

'Night, mate,' the sober customers called to me, and then the streets were empty. OK, now was the time to concentrate on the smash and grabs. In 1957, criminals were still unsophisticated enough to drive up to the front of a television shop, throw a brick through the window, and roar off with half a dozen sets. Old coppers had told me that this sort of crime usually takes place around midnight, as old-time crooks tell young villains that midnight's the time when all the coppers are back at the nick dealing with the drunks picked up when the pubs turned out at 11.00 p.m.

Well, this night the young villains were ignoring all this good advice, and staying at home. All right, I wasn't proud. I'd settle for a burglar. The thing to do, so the old coppers said, was to hide round the back of some shops or offices, have a crafty smoke, and more than likely you'd hear the sound of breaking glass, and the thief would step into your arms. Well, I didn't smoke, but I didn't think that villains would take objection to my abstinence, so I hid away for an hour seeing nothing but a cat, and hearing nothing but a woman giggle before a window was closed.

Grub time, or to give it the official name, refreshments, was at 1.00 a.m. I got through my sandwiches as quickly as possible. Nobody had made any arrests that night but they didn't seem too worried about this stain on their record. No one else was hurrying to go out. I was back on the streets well before time, checked the shops, had a look at the locks on a couple of warehouses, and began to wonder how I was going to pass the next four hours. And it started to rain. That warm soggy August rain that gets down the back of your collar and through the laceholes of your boots. Then I saw the van.

Now I'd been shown how to stop cars and vans by other officers.

'Give 'em plenty of time to see you. Make sure they see you, and then make certain you've got room to jump out of the way because they won't have seen you.'

I stepped into the middle of the road, shone my torch, put up my hand in the approved stop sign, and it all worked perfectly. He stopped, wound down his window and peered out at me. He was a small bald-headed man, about fifty years old. He had a mac on over his overalls, and looked as if he was coming home after a hard day.

'Mornin' Guv. Anything wrong? My lights dodgy?'

'No sir. Your lights are OK. Just a routine check. Can you tell me what you've got in the van?' Not that I really needed to ask. It was one of the old A35 vans, and you could see into the back from the driver's seat.

'Nothing at all, Guv. Just coming back from Smithfield. Nothing at all.'

'So what are those two bags?'

'Bags? Oh them. Sorry Guv. Thought you was checking

for nicked gear. Them's golf-clubs. One set's mine and one's Harry Smith's. We had a round this afternoon on the public course in Swanley. Old Harry broke a hundred for the first time. He's got a bit pissed and didn't go into work, so I looked after the clubs and did half a shift at Smithfield. Now I'm off home for a well-earned kip.'

Nice chap. Not at all upset at being stopped on his way home. Even showed me his driving licence.

'Night, Sir. Sorry to have stopped you.'

And that was it until 6.00 a.m. Of course it carried on raining.

You can guess what happened then. Came on at 10.00 the next night. Section Sergeant reads through the list of stolen cars, local villains wanted, a couple of breakings that we missed during the night.

'And there's one here from Kent. Someone broke into the shop at Swanley Golf Club and helped themselves to a couple of bags of their best clubs. Not the sort of thing that's likely to end up on this manor. Still you never know.' I kept it to myself. I wasn't going to let the rest know how easily I had been fooled. But I did know where the van owner lived. He'd shown me his driving licence. Before I had gone off duty the night before, I had checked the block of flats and had seen the A35 in the car park. At 10.05 p.m. I was knocking on his door. He answered almost straight away.

'Evenin' Officer. Something the matter? Not the poor old lady downstairs is it? Been expectin' her to pop off for some time.'

'No, it's not the old lady. It's those clubs. Where are they?'

'Clubs, Officer? Don't follow you. Sort of offensive weapons you talking about. What's going on then?'

'I stopped you at three o'clock this morning on your way back from Smithfield, and you had two sets of golf-clubs in the back of your van.'

'Me? Golf-clubs? Smithfield? Three o'clock this morning? Here, Mildred, come and listen to this.' Mildred came out in her curlers, accompanied by her friend from next door, and her friend's husband. I was making a big mistake. George didn't work at Smithfield. Never played golf in his life. Wouldn't know a golf bat or club or whatever from one of those tennis racquets. As for three o'clock this morning . . . Well the four of them had been having a quick cocoa together last night.

'Bit of a gossip. The way you do. We're old friends . . .' And George had come all over tired so he'd gone off to bed early, and the friend from next door suffers with her nerves and was awake all night and would have heard anyone come in or out. I was, of course, very welcome to search the flat for these golf things, you've got to do your job after all, but you can see how small it is, and you couldn't hide anything like golf-clubs. Four pairs of eyes stared innocently at me. Four cunning minds were congratulating themselves on getting the story right. I knew I was beaten, this time.

'Good-night,' I said, 'Sorry you've been troubled.' No they weren't in the van either. I must have stopped him a dozen times after that. He was always very cheerful and courteous. But he never ever had anything in the back of the van again. At least he taught me the copper's ABC. Accept nothing. Believe no one. Check on everything. Terrible thing to happen to a young man, but I've never believed anyone from that day. I've used the ABC with great success throughout my service, and handed it onto others that I worked with. I hope it's been as useful to them.

# The Little Prisoner

The little girl did not know how long she had been locked in the room. If she thought very hard about it she could remember being out in the sunshine, but it wasn't sunshine now, it was cold and dark nearly all the time. At 4 years old, she had little sense of time, and the single window in the room, a narrow slot four feet above her head, was her only means of telling if it was night or day. She could remember screaming and banging at the locked door, but that was a long time ago; perhaps it was yesterday, or before yesterday. A 4-year-old does not find it easy to think about time.

She did remember that when she had screamed, no one came, but she also remembered that sometimes her new daddy would open the door, and give her a biscuit, or a piece of bread. Then he would lock it again. Yesterday or the time before that, she had given up pulling at the door handle. It was never going to open. Sometimes it had moved slightly and then she had pulled harder, hanging onto the handle until she had slipped exhausted to the ground. Sometimes when it moved she had pushed it to and fro without getting it open.

The little girl was being starved to death. She was not old enough to realise that. The first pains of hunger and thirst had become confused with the penetrating cold. There was no heating in the room, and she had only a T-shirt to cover her. She could no longer think. Some animal instinct dragged her from the dirty double mattress to the door handle and back again. But the journeys to the door became fewer and fewer. A long time ago, yesterday, or in the time before yesterday, she had been able to hear her baby brother crying. She could hear the television, and her new daddy talking to mummy. She could hear the front door open and close. But now, she no longer reacted to sounds. Perhaps there was no one there. Perhaps they had all gone away. Then she would hear the baby cry, but she stayed lying on the mattress, with only a dim spark of memory keeping her alive.

Sometimes when there was light through the window, she had looked for food in the corners of the room. Besides the mattress, there were some car tyres, bits of wire and cable, a box of old car parts, but nothing to eat. One day she discovered that the wallpaper could be pulled easily from the wall. She tore strips off, and tried to eat them. The paper was nice to suck because it was damp, but she was no longer strong enough to chew and swallow it.

One day, of course, she died. The expectation that someone might open the door, the memory of what it had been like to play with other children, the hidden hope that her mother would help her, all flickered out. She was too weak to stand, too dazed to think. She did not so much die, as simply stop living. Already wasted to half her natural weight, her body began to shrink. In the cold unlit room, it was difficult to see the corpse.

In the flat outside the room, the little girl's mother had another baby, and her new father continued to work on the car that occupied most of his attention. The little prisoner's birthday passed. Christmas came, and carollers sang 'O Little Town of Bethlehem' ten feet away from the shadow-like corpse. Then it was New Year, and the father and mother who had starved the little girl to death wished each other the compliments of the season. On January 23, 1985, a police woman broke open the door of the cold dark room and found what was left of Heidi Koseda.

I find it hard to say which was the worst aspect of the Heidi Koseda murder. She didn't die by neglect but as the result of a deliberate decision not to feed her. No one knows, or is ever likely to know, just when she died or how long she had been locked away. But perhaps the most horrifying fact is that the NSPCC inspector responsible for seeing and reporting on Heidi, failed to visit the flat, and made a false report saying that he had seen her alive and well at a time when he could have saved her.

We didn't become involved with Heidi's family until just after Christmas in 1984. A health visitor had reported her concern over Mrs Koseda's two other children, James, who was then 15 months old, and Lisa, born in December. Police went to the flat with a search warrant to allow the health visitor access to the children. They were in reasonable health, and the parents told the health visitor and the police that Heidi was staying with friends. They explained that one bedroom was kept closed because it was being treated with chemicals for dampness and they didn't want the little boy to go in there.

There was a broom across the door jammed behind the handle making it impossible to open from without or within. The police and health visitor left without any reason to suspect that Heidi's body was behind the locked door.

A month later, Steve Rogers, a Detective Sergeant, accompanied by health visitors, used his skill and knowledge to gain entry to the house and force open the door. He found the poor pathetic carcass of a child.

When we began our grim and sad investigation into Heidi's murder, we had to work backwards to establish when she had last been seen. That necessitated an examination of her family's history.

Heidi lived with her mother and stepfather in a council flat in Hayes, a west London suburb just north of Heathrow Airport. Rosemary Koseda married in 1978, and gave birth to Heidi in December, 1980. Her husband, Henryk, left her two years later, and she almost immediately took up a relationship with a childhood friend, Nicholas Price, who moved in with her. Rosemary was of very low intelligence, and Price was not much brighter. He had a certain self-protective cunning, and boasted of the fights that he had won and the petty crimes he had committed. She was so immature that on the day of her wedding she was found kissing a former boyfriend outside the church. Price had little trouble dominating her, and she relied completely on his judgement in all things. When Rosemary's mother refused to lend him money, he forbade Rosemary to visit her or ask her to their flat, and Rosemary obeyed him.

Nicholas and Rosemary were unemployed. They begged constantly from their neighbours for food, cigarettes, money. Their rent and other bills were paid by the DHSS, and their benefit payments amounting to £100 a week were supplemented by Price's work on neighbours' cars. He himself admitted that this averaged about £20 a week, so it was possibly much more. Even so, £20 is a considerable sum to a family which claimed there was not enough money to feed one particular child.

Our first problem was to find the last day on which anyone had seen Heidi outside the flat. The best we could do was a neighbour who thought she had seen Heidi in September, 1984, while the most positive evidence placed her with other children in July. A Miss Martin, who had moved into the flat below Koseda and Price in August had never seen Heidi, although she knew of her existence from talking to neighbours. Rather bravely, for a stranger moving into a block of flats, conscious that she could be branded a busybody, she phoned the NSPCC at the beginning of September.

She told them that she had never seen Heidi, but that the little boy James had a bruise on his face. She had also heard screaming from the flat above her, and had heard a curious sound from one of the bedrooms, a sort of muted banging as if someone was opening and closing a door quietly and repeatedly.

There was no response from the NSPCC. Miss Martin phoned again in October, November, and December, without their taking any action. However, a social worker visited the flat early in September, and found the family outside, gathered round the car that Price was spending his money on. Neighbours said that Rosemary's principal occupation seemed to be sitting on the front steps of the flats watching Nick work on his car. The social worker thought that James looked healthy and cared for, and asked about Heidi.

'Fast asleep upstairs,' Price told her. 'Having a good kip. She's OK.' Heidi, at that time, was locked up in the room in which she would eventually die.

In December, the health authority's interest in the family was renewed. Rosemary had a baby. She had told neighbours who had asked that she was just getting very fat, she wasn't pregnant. She tried to have the baby without assistance, but Price had to call an ambulance to the flat. A week later when the birth had not been registered, a health visitor called at the flat. She could not get an answer. She tried two or three further times, and eventually applied for a warrant to enter to see if the child was well. Two days after Christmas, she went to the flat with the warrant and two uniformed police officers. Price answered the door.

'What you lot want then?' He was told clearly, and shown the warrant.

'Kid's OK,' he told them. 'No need to disturb her. Lot of people tramping round. Disturb her.' The police inspector made it clear they were coming in, and Price stood aside. Lisa, the baby, was well, although the flat was dirty. The family appeared to be living in one room. Neither Rosemary nor Price appeared to have washed for several days. A bedroom door was closed with a broom across the door frame and jammed behind the handle.

'Sort of damp in there,' explained Price. 'Got this chemical stuff to cure it. Got to keep the little boy out. Little bugger'd be in there in no time.'

'What about your other little girl. Heidi?'

'Oh, she's OK. She's all right. Don't have to worry about her.'

'Where is she?'

This time Rosemary answered. 'She's stopping with friends.

They looked after her when I was having the baby. She's fine.'

Price joined in. 'Yes. That's right. She's over in Hounslow. Some mates over there. One of these Polish names, you know, bit hard to pronounce. But I know where she is. She's quite safe. Got her down to go to school after the holiday.'

So the police and the health visitor left. Strictly, their warrant only allowed them to look for Lisa, and having found her, they had no rights to search any further.

During the next two weeks, Doreen Braybrook, a local social worker, tried to see Heidi twice. The second visit was at the urging of Heidi's grandmother who was becoming increasingly worried about not hearing anything about the child. On January 15, yet another health visitor saw Mrs Koseda but could not get her to answer questions about Heidi, and finally on January 23, one of my Detective Sergeants, Stephen Rogers, and a WPC went to the flat again. Price was on his own, and gave confused answers about where Heidi was. DS Rogers, convinced that something had happened to the girl, arrested him. At the police station, Price said firmly that Heidi was with friends, and offered to bring her to the station the following day.

The two officers then went back to the flat. Rosemary Koseda had returned with the other two children.

'No, don't know where she is. Nick knows. All her clothes are gone anyway.' The officers searched the flat, breaking open the door of the bedroom, and found Heidi, dead, emaciated, lying on her back, her eyes almost invisible in their sockets. Rosemary was arrested and taken to the same police station as Price. The smell in the room in which Heidi had been slowly starved to death was so vile that one of the officers vomited in the street.

I saw Price at about 8.30 p.m. after his arrest. He admitted that he knew that Heidi had died. I asked when she had died.

'Don't know, mate.' He sounded as concerned as a man

who didn't know the time of the next bus. 'Don't know, mate'. The implication being that it was nothing to do with him. 'I put her in the back room. We weren't eating ourselves. I didn't feed her at all and she died in about three weeks.'

He said he was able to feed the other child, James, because they had a 'stock of milk' in the flat, most of which he had been given 'by a stranger in a pub'. He had never heard her cry, and he had never hit her. He did go into the room and check her a couple of times, but he could not remember whether or not she was conscious. Sometime in November he told his wife that Heidi had died. But he did not do anything else about it.

Rosemary told us that she had accepted Price's story that Heidi was with friends, and had never gone into the bedroom. We put it to her quite simply, 'You have not seen your daughter for three months or more. You don't know the names of the people she is staying with, or where she is staying. You have not slept in your own bedroom since Heidi left home, and you have never been into that bedroom since she left.'

'Yes,' she said. 'I never went in the bedroom because it was damp.'

I saw Price again the next morning with David Lamper, the Chief Superintendent in charge of the case.

'I told you that we didn't have enough money to feed her. But the truth is she had a lot of puppy fat, and she kept asking for spaghetti bolognaise, but she was getting thinner all the time and then she was eating. She hadn't eaten anything for ten days before I put her in the room. But when it comes time for her to come out of the room, she wouldn't come out, and she wouldn't eat nothing.'

When Rosemary was interviewed she claimed that Heidi had been put in the bedroom so that she could get used to sleeping alone. She did not admit starving the child until she was told that Price had said that they had both planned it.

These were routine interviews about a very nasty murder. Both Price and Rosemary were almost subnormal. Neither of them seemed to appreciate the seriousness of the offence when they were charged, and Price's attitude throughout was almost one of unconcern, a sort of 'this has nothing to do with me'. There is little point in getting angry with people like this, or even showing how much you detest them. Better just to get on with the job, get the evidence together, and try to put the dead child out of your mind. But, although the parents were admitting that they had caused the child's death, we had to provide the court with the evidence that would allow the jury to decide if they had caused Heidi's death deliberately, or just through stupid neglect. So as Price had claimed at one point that there was not enough money to buy food for Heidi, we had to show what he had spent his money on.

He had been receiving about £53 social security and milk tokens, while Rosemary drew child benefits. His rent was being paid, and the DHSS was also repaying about £1,000 worth of debts. Price denied that he had been selling the milk tokens, but admitted that he earned about £20 a week doing car repairs.

'So does all the money go on buying food for the family?'

'Yes, every penny. It's not enough. We weren't eating ourselves. So I put her in the back room. The council wouldn't give us any money for food and we didn't have the money to feed her, so that's why we didn't give her no food.'

'This £20. Did you spend that on food?'

'Oh no. I worked for that, mate.' He was genuinely surprised at my question. 'That was mine. It was my fag money. Fag money and beer money.'

That's the nearest I've ever come to hitting a prisoner. The hardest it has ever been for me to control my temper. He'd starved a 4-year-old child to death, but had become indignant at the thought that he should have given up his cigarette money to buy her food. I stood up, and walked out of the interview room. It took me more than ten minutes to calm down and go back to continue to question him. He claimed that he had an outstanding electricity bill for £60 which had contributed to his inability to feed Heidi. When I checked later, I found that the bill had been presented in November, probably after Heidi had died.

Yet he was still able to say, 'I loved her like my own child.' He admitted that he and Rosemary had agreed to lock Heidi away and not feed her. He kept changing his reasons for doing so, but whatever the explanation, he agreed that he and his wife had left the child in the room to die.

'She used to cry a bit, sometimes, but that stopped.'

Nine months later he was sentenced to life imprisonment for murder; Rosemary Koseda, who had become more disturbed, was sent for hospital treatment.

The NSPCC had become involved in the early autumn. I've worked with the NSPCC before, and know just how dedicated its officers are. But the Koseda case was an exception. Lorraine Martin, the downstairs neighbour, had told the NSPCC about her fears for Heidi. The inquiry was allocated to one of their inspectors, Marcus Colquhoun, early in September. In our efforts to find the last person to see Heidi, we interviewed him. His notes showed that he had visited Heidi on September 7. She had been well, as had her brother. They were both on single beds in the same room. Dave Lamper, looking quickly through the statement, thought this a bit odd. When he had visited the flat after the arrests there had been no single beds there.

Two days after the arrests, on a Sunday, there was a call from the NSPCC to the incident room. Colquhoun had admitted that he had never visited Heidi. He had put false entries in his files. He had also admitted that he had not followed up a second call from Miss Martin in October. He made a full statement admitting his errors on January 28, and was dismissed from the NSPCC. After leaving the meeting, he drove away and was involved in a crash that wrecked his car. No proceedings were ever taken against him, as he had not committed any criminal offence.

The only other facts I know about the death of Heidi

Koseda come from the pathologist's report. She had died about two months before she was found, which would make it about the middle of November. Deprived completely of food and water, it would have taken her three days to die. She was not ill, she had no diseases, she was a perfectly healthy child until her parents locked her in a room and starved her to death. As for the door of the room in which she had been kept prisoner, there were indentations on the frame where the broom handle holding it closed had been forced against the wood. The broom handle wedged behind the door handle was bent. It looked as if someone inside the room had been constantly pulling the door, trying to open it. Each pull would mean that the door would open a fraction of an inch before the pressure of the broom forced it shut again. Every pull meant that the broom handle moved very slightly and made a fresh indentation. Someone had pulled at that door many, many times.

# Most Unreliable Evidence

Some villains are just that, villains, but others; well, you meet one or two that it's hard to dislike. 'Cheeky monkeys' we used to call them. I still smile when I think about two in particular, although at the time I was not over-fond of them for the risks I had to take chasing them. It was some years before I joined the CID, in 1964. I was driving the area car at Tower Bridge – Mike One. The car was the old Wolseley 690, almost the traditional police car, possibly the best and most appropriate car the police service ever had. About midnight there was a call about a white Jaguar which had been involved in an armed robbery at Deptford, about ten miles away. Two black men had threatened a garage attendant with a sawn-off shotgun and taken the contents of the till. The attendant may have been frightened but he *did* have the presence of mind to take down the index number of the Jaguar; let's say it was ABC 123.

Well, I was in a turning off the Old Kent Road when I saw the Jaguar hurtling past, or rather I saw a white Jaguar with two black men in the front; but it had a different index number. It was worth a pull. In traditional police jargon, 'a chase ensued'. When you come to give evidence about the car chase, you might describe the beginning and end, and some of the speeds at which you travelled, but no one ever hears of the mixture of fear, exhilaration, impatience and determination that takes over even the most experienced driver, not to speak of the concentration and confusion that overtakes most radio operators and makes them forget that his listeners cannot see what he sees.

'He's turned left, just missed that Morris on the corner. Look out, there's a zebra crossing, the lights are red, he's gone right again— ' And that is broken up by the impatient interruptions from other operators. 'For Christ's sake. Tell us where you are!'

Well, this chase was no different. I stayed behind him at speeds that varied from 30mph to 70mph. No point in attempting to overtake. Other cars would be coming towards us and eventually he'd be blocked in. So that's the way it was until we got to Tower Bridge itself where a line of police cars blocked off every exit. As the Jaguar made a sharp right to try some route to get away, I noticed that something was thrown out of the passenger side. The Jaguar screeched to a halt, the driver and his passenger were pulled out without a great deal of politeness.

'Hold on! Hold on!' yelled the driver.

'You've got it wrong,' shouted his passenger from the other side. We took them to Tower Bridge Police Station, put them in the charge room, and asked them to explain how they came to be in a stolen car, with the money stolen from a garage in Deptford, having thrown two sawn-off shotguns out of the car.

'Look, you just ain't going to believe this,' said the driver, 'but I swear on my baby's life that this is the way it was. Like, Kelvin here, and me, we was walking along by Clapham Common, and we see this white Jag with the doors open. Now there ain't too many white Jags round Clapham Common, so we just took a look. Know what I mean? Didn't get in or nothing. So then we see these guns on the back seat. Kelvin and me, we look at each other, and we both got the same thought. What if some kid got hold of the guns. Obviously some robber's motor. Thing to do is hand it over to the law quick as we could. So we decided we'd take it to Brixton nick.'

'But when we saw you you were nowhere near Brixton.'

'You're right. You're right. Trouble is Kelvin ain't too good on geography, so we got lost.'

'That why you turned up in Deptford?'

'Deptford? Don't know no Deptford, but we could have been there. We got so lost that Kelvin said to go to a garage and ask where we was. Kelvin goes to the man at the till to ask where we was. I took out one of these guns to look at it in the light. Could have been one of these imitations. Don't want to go into no Brixton nick giving them some shit about dangerous firearms when all we got is a couple of toys. That's when this very weird thing happened. This young dude at the garage, Kelvin don't even get a chance to speak to him, he just comes out with a cash box and throws it into the back of the motor. Kelvin and me see something funny going on, so we just drove off. We going to take the cash to Brixton as well. Trouble is we still don't know where we are. Then we got more problems. This car coming up real fast behind us, and nowhere to pull over to let it get past. Then we see it's a police car, and Kelvin gets a bit scared.

'"Could be in trouble if they find them guns," he says. So we throw them out the window. Then we see all the police cars, so we stop.'

There was quite a crowd in the charge room by now, and no one said anything. I think we were all just struck dumb by such a stupid story. It was the night duty DS who spoke up.

'You know,' he said, 'there are juries who'll swallow that one.' No one contradicted him. Then I spotted the weak link.

'Let's get this right,' I said to them. 'You find this car in Clapham. You get lost on the way to Brixton. You end up in Deptford, and for no reason at all some garage attendant throws his night's takings into your motor. Is that what you're saying?'

'Absolutely, Officer. You got it exact. Sounds weird but that's exactly the way it was.'

'So tell me this. This garage attendant says the car that robbed him was ABC 123. When we stopped you, you had a different number on the car. So why change the plates if you're taking the motor back to Brixton?'

The driver looked at Kelvin. Kelvin looked at the driver. They had no answer to that. We also pointed out that the number that the garage attendant had taken was on the set of plates found in the car with electrical tape attached; they had obviously been taped over the original registration of the car solely for the robbery and then taken off before we saw the car. The driver looked at Kelvin again, Kelvin looked at the driver. Again they couldn't think of an answer.

They hadn't thought of an answer when they came up for trial; to their lawyer's disgust, they stuck to the story they had told us. The jury didn't wear it either, they got four years apiece. I'm sure that a smile must have crossed my face while they were giving evidence, and when I looked at the jury, I'm also sure that some of them were smiling too.

# Call Me John

Ian Erskine left the Bank of England at 6.00 p.m. on Friday December 15, 1989. In March of the following year his body was found 100 miles away in a Cambridgeshire river. We have a very good idea of what happened in those three months, but the man who really knows, the man who, we are certain, killed Ian, will never be arrested for it.

Ian left the bank at 6.00 p.m. wearing a good grey suit and dark overcoat, using his season ticket to travel on the central line to Holland Park. He was a wealthy man of independent means, but found that the tube was the quickest, if not the most comfortable way to travel across London. That Friday the train would have been packed with office workers preoccupied with Christmas plans, perhaps on their way to or from office parties; some of them already starting extended Christmas holidays. On its way through the West End the train would have become unbearably overcrowded with Christmas shoppers, but no one noticed Ian, or if they did they never responded to our appeals to hear from anyone who had seen him on that journey. We are convinced he travelled alone, but we could be wrong.

Just before 7.00 p.m., he let himself into his basement flat in Norland Square, off Holland Park Avenue, unfastening the three deadlocks and turning off the alarm, essential equipment in an area with a high burglary rate. In a store room next to his flat, he kept an extensive wine cellar, but this evening he ignored his wine collection, and almost as soon as he had closed his door behind him, started to drink bottled beer. He moved nervously round the untidy flat, waiting for an expected caller. Then there was a knock on the door. He opened it to a white man, five foot eleven inches tall, fair-haired with a beard, wearing a green camouflage jacket. It was a man whom Ian knew as 'The Rhodesian', or John from Surbiton, the man who was about to kill him.

'Come in, John,' Ian welcomed him, 'I've been looking forward to this.'

'The Rhodesian' had been to Ian's flat before and knew exactly what Ian wanted of him. Both men moved in a world in which what followed required no payment of fees, no explanation. Each was achieving his own peculiar form of sexual satisfaction. While Ian went to his bedroom to undress, his visitor took a home-made folding bench from a hall cupboard and erected it among the antique furniture of the dining-room. The bench, which Ian had made himself, was about two feet high, three feet long and eighteen inches wide. The folding legs had handcuffs attached at the front and chains at the rear. By the time the table was in place, Ian had come back to the room naked except for a pair of socks. He was going to be here for some time, and knew from experience that his feet would get cold and detract from his anticipated enjoyment. He handed one of his expensive handkerchiefs to 'John' and knelt in front of the bench.

Without speaking, 'The Rhodesian' pushed him forward and fastened the handcuffs round his wrists, then secured the chains round Ian's thighs, and buckled a wide belt under the bench and around his back. Ian was almost immobilised. 'The Rhodesians'' next move was to put a leather hood over Ian's head; Ian expected him to do so, and did not struggle or protest. The hood had two breathing holes only; Ian could see nothing. He stayed immobilised, kneeling on the floor, waiting for the next move. 'The Rhodesian' returned from the bathroom with a wet towel which he spread over Ian's back and buttocks. Then he began to beat him with one of a number of thick canes. He took his time, striking regularly and deliberately, knowing that the wet towel would prevent the canes marking Ian's body. His art lay in not tiring himself out. Ian had complained previously that after 200 strokes most beaters were too tired to carry on.

Half-way through the beating, 'The Rhodesian' paused and fastened the handkerchief which Ian had given him round the latter's throat. He had tied two carefully placed knots in the handkerchief, to lie against the carotid arteries on either side of Ian's neck. Watching him carefully, 'The Rhodesian' knotted the handkerchief carefully at the back, ensuring that the two front knots were pressing against the arteries but not restricting them. Both men knew of the heightened sexual sensations that this would cause. The beating continued. Almost thirty minutes had passed, when 'The Rhodesian' noticed that Ian was no longer flinching as the cane struck the towel across his back.

'You OK?' There was no answer. 'The Rhodesian' knelt beside Ian and pulled the hood from his head. His eyes were open, but lifeless. It was impossible to see if he had been suffocated by the hood, or if the flow of blood to his brain had been cut off by the handkerchief. He was almost certainly dead. 'The Rhodesian' unfastened the body quickly, laid it on its back and immediately and expertly administered cardiac massage and the kiss of life. He was a man used to death and violence, and did not panic. But after fifteen minutes, it was clear that Ian would not recover. 'The Rhodesian' sat in one of Ian's leather armchairs, and thought carefully through his next moves. He was certain that Ian, having made this arrangement with him, would not be having any visitors during the evening, and was unlikely to have any plans for the weekend. He had two days in which to act. He knew that rigor mortis would set in fairly quickly because of Ian's physical exertions, but would have passed within twenty-four hours. If he wanted to do anything with the body, he would need to act immediately, or wait until the next day, when it would become easier to handle. He lifted the body into the bedroom, restored the whipping bench to its hall cupboard and replaced the canes in a drawer in the bedroom. Then he began to go through Ian's wallet and personal papers.

As I said, this is what we think happened. The death might have been accidental, but the Rhodesian's subsequent actions gave some indication that he might have intended to kill Ian. But we learned enough about Ian to be fairly certain that this is how he died. It's fairly rare for the circumstances of any murder to be known in the fullest detail. Even when the murderer confesses, police cannot be certain that he, or she, has remembered every detail.

Ian Erskine did not become of interest to the police until December 23, a week after his probable death, when a Bank of England senior security officer reported him as a missing person to Notting Hill Police Station. There had been some concern at the Bank on Monday, December 18 when Ian had neither turned up, nor had phoned in with an explanation. During the week, a colleague and friend of Ian, who knew of his sexual background, called at his flat, getting keys from a neighbour. She found the curtains drawn and a hall light on at 3.30 p.m., but noticed that only one of the three front locks was secured. Several other friends made similar inquiries. The Bank also phoned Ian's mother who was unable to tell them where her son was.

On Saturday, December 23, Mrs Erskine, knowing that her son should have arrived at her Edinburgh house for the Christmas holiday, phoned a friend, Robert McGregor, asking him to search Ian's flat to see if he could find a reason for his absence. Mr McGregor went to Norland Square, searched thoroughly, and then told Bank security officers, who officially reported Ian as a missing person at Notting Hill Police Station.

Dozens of persons are reported as missing every day in London. It is fair to say that some reports are given less priority than others. A wife who appears to have absconded with a lover, a lodger who owes rent, a discontented teenager, all have to be investigated, but a senior Bank of England official with known homosexual connections merits something more than a routine inquiry, particularly in view of one other disturbing feature. Ian had never been known as a tidy person, and his flat usually had unwashed dishes, open books, records without covers, but everyone who knew Ian and who had visited the flat since he was last seen alive commented on its unusual tidiness. There were no signs at all of any struggle. We also found very quickly that Ian's neighbour had assumed he was there all weekend because she had heard the sounds of music and vacuuming during the Saturday and Sunday. Other friends however, had rung Ian frequently without having the phone answered.

On the December 28, the flat at Norland Square was searched thoroughly by a team lead by Detective Inspector Laurie Vanner on the assumption that Ian's disappearance was connected to his work at the Bank of England. Nothing appeared out of place in the flat, the corporal punishment equipment was found, but not removed. Of much more significance was what was not found. It was clear that Ian Erskine had three bank accounts, but there was no trace of credit cards or cheque books in the flat. A later search showed that other articles, including a pair of silver candlesticks, had been stolen, but initially we were concerned only with cheques and credit cards. At the same time we checked on Ian's working and social background.

Ian was an economics researcher at the Bank of England, recognised as having great potential, but prevented from rising to the most senior posts in the Bank because of his declared homosexuality. He was 44 years old, and had worked at the Bank of England since leaving Oxford. He had private means, a salary of £40,000, a very low mortgage, and no emotional or close family responsibilities. In 1984, during positive vetting for a senior appointment, he had been quite open about his sexual orientation. Unfortunately his honesty may well have halted his career. He was moved sideways. This may have caused great bitterness in a talented and committed employee, but his colleagues, many of whom knew of his homosexuality, saw no signs of that bitterness affecting his work relationships.

In the same year he found that he was an HIV carrier, having contracted the infection from his only close lover, Andy Tooth, who was to die of AIDS in 1986. From then on Ian had regular medical checks, and on the day before he disappeared, had been told that his condition was stable. On December 15, Ian Erskine had every reason to be cheerful. Freed of health worries, with Christmas approaching, which he had planned to spend with his mother in Scotland, he seemingly went home to spend what for him promised to be a thoroughly enjoyable evening which he had planned carefully for weeks before.

Ian had taken up the sexual deviancy of corporal punishment after the death of Andy. For four or five years he cruised the pubs and clubs which then catered for this particular fancy, wearing a black and white handkerchief protruding from a back pocket, the underground signal for a gay person who enjoyed being beaten. He advertised openly in gay magazines for partners to beat him. 'Fit young bloke requires a good thrashing. Seeks straight males willing to oblige. Canes provided. Private place. Absolute discretion.' Ian's was a particularly specific requirement; he wanted a heterosexual who enjoyed beating other men but with whom there could be no emotional or physical involvement. He made no secret of this particular taste to other homosexual friends, and indeed complained often that most of those who answered his adverts tired of beating him before he wanted them to stop. 'Except for "The Rhodesian",' he told his friends. We also found an explanation for the two empty beer bottles found in his flat. Ian had told friends that he had discovered that drinking a couple of pints of beer inhibited the pain caused by beating; he could endure the pain longer than his partners had the strength to continue to beat him.

When we started our inquiries about the missing cheque books and credit cards, we quickly found that three of his

cheques had been presented with forged signatures around
Victoria Station on December 16, the Saturday after he
had last been seen at the Bank. His Access card had been
used twice. Two days later there were two more Access
transactions. On December 19, 20, and 21 more cheques
were passed and the Access card used twice to purchase
heterosexual pornography. (Those purchases became more
significant when it was deduced the pornography was being
bought by someone who normally had no access to such
material.) The card had also been used to hire a car on
Monday 18. That car was returned on the 21st showing
an extra 240 miles. The man who had hired the car had
certainly not been Ian. It was becoming clear that Ian had
been murdered.

There were no more transactions until January 8. We were
thus faced with the possibility that whoever was using Ian's
cards had spent some time abroad, particularly as one of the
earlier Access withdrawals had been in guilders and dollars.
On the 8th another £500 was withdrawn and used to purchase
a return ticket to Amsterdam. During the next two days the
card was used to buy more heterosexual pornography in
Amsterdam. But by then the card had been logged as stolen,
and on January 10 it was seized when the holder tried to use
it to buy a leather jacket.

We were unhappy at the bureaucracy that was preventing
us being told of the fraudulent use of the cheques and cards
as soon as they occurred. We were notified of the transactions
two or three days later. Our unhappiness was increased when
we were told that Access in the UK had been unaware that
the card had been seized in Amsterdam. Unhappiness was
not the word when we finally heard that Access had then
lost the card. The Amsterdam police too were being casual
in attempts to trace the suspect's movements, and when we
finally sent over one of our own officers the trail was cold.

But we did have one very good lead. The Guy Salmon
executive who had hired the car to the man pretending to
be Ian Erskine had talked to him for almost half an hour

while they prepared the hire documents. He described him as white, five foot eleven, round about thirty, dark brown hair, full beard. 'Not a London accent,' he told us. The customer was wearing a green combat jacket and blue jeans, and gave the impression of being a police officer. His demeanour, direct manner, and positive approach made the man from the car hire firm think that his client was a man used to being in charge of events. We seized the car, and forensically examined it, without finding anything to indicate it might have been used to take away Ian's body. At that stage, in mid-January, we were convinced that Ian Erskine had been murdered, and his body removed from his flat.

Another lead of which we had great hopes but of which nothing came was a limited edition Seiko watch, which had been bought in one of the Access transactions. The watch was one of only 3,500 made, and was one of the only 350 which had been imported into the UK. Despite extensive publicity we never found anyone who remembered seeing anyone with it. It may have been a coincidence, but the man using Ian's card bought the watch on the day it was advertised in the *Daily Telegraph*. Was he then a Conservative *Telegraph* reader? There was another lead, albeit a negative one. The case was fully featured on the BBC's *Crimewatch UK*, but we had no calls at all from the programme about the killer's possible identity. Was he perhaps a foreigner, with no friends or relatives in this country, no one close enough to him to even think he might be a suspect? This was a most unusual result for the programme, especially with the very detailed description we had.

A full forensic examination of Ian's flat produced a number of fingerprints, but a much clearer indication that many surfaces had been wiped clean. The bed sheets were heavily marked with semen which had to be subjected to DNA tests to determine from how many sources it had come. Some was certain to be Erskine's. If there were second samples they may have come from the murderer. If he was ever traced they would link him to Ian's flat, but would not provide evidence of the killing.

But while part of the investigation was concentrating on tracing every purchase made by the missing cheques and credit cards, a second team was researching Ian's particular life style. Homosexuals of all kinds (and we quickly became aware of the many varieties of homosexual behaviour) are wary of police. Even though the great majority still live well inside the law, there is an understandable paranoia about being questioned by the police, and having to confess to a life style which is perhaps being successfully hidden from friends, workmates, even family. Laurie Vanner, the Detective Inspector who undertook the investigation into Ian's background, put up with the mickey taking of his colleagues, and established a rapport with many homosexuals, who, once assured of his sincerity, revealed the hidden world in which Ian moved.

Laurie was told about the London Boxing and Wrestling Club which catered for gay athletes. There was certainly some serious sporting competition, but there was also the opportunity to wrestle naked or oiled, preferences which were indicated by code letters in the membership register. This naturally attracted men who were more interested in sex than sport. Ian Erskine had been on the club committee and attended regularly. The LBWC became of more interest when it was found that a former member, a good friend of Ian's had also been murdered, twelve months previously. John Hudspith, the victim, had died as the result of a ferocious battering on Hampstead Heath, a beating sought and voluntarily endured. Ian's death had brought the club to an end.

Laurie was also told of an SM (Sado-masochistic) information exchange in Cowcross Street that Ian had used, the Back Street Club in Mile End, an occasional club which met at the London Apprentice in Old Street and the Mother Blackcap in Camden Town. Each of them were recognised meeting places for homosexuals of all tastes. At each of them the regulars remembered Ian as a loner, always in the standard SM uniform of motor cycle leathers, with his black and white handkerchief proclaiming his desires.

Laurie's attention was also drawn to five gay papers that carried explicit personal ads, and as many contact sheets, carrying coded details of bizarre sexual perversions with requests for partners to join in them. But the most productive magazine for such contacts turned out to be the five times a week publication *Loot*, which combined sexual requests with flats to let, and videos for sale.

Laurie traced half a dozen people who had spoken to Ian before December 15. One of them, Richard, told him that Ian had been contacted by a man he had first met through a contact magazine, a man he knew as John from Surbiton or 'The Rhodesian', who was coming to see him on the Friday night. Richard himself became a momentary suspect when it was found that he was also the last person to see John Hudspith alive before the latter had been murdered a year before Ian. (This man had been beaten to death on Hampstead Heath, not by gay bashers, but by other homosexuals who had agreed to beat him up, and who had been taunted by Hudspith with such remarks as, 'Is this the best you can do? Harder. I can hardly feel anything.') Another friend was told in a phone call of 'The Rhodesian's visit. This friend confirmed that Ian had met 'The Rhodesian' a year earlier, had been beaten by him several times, and that 'The Rhodesian' had been in the Rhodesian army during UDI.

Ian had a third life as a music lover, a wine buff, and an opera lover. Most people who met him in that world knew nothing of his sexual life, and were cultural acquaintances rather than close friends. There was little in those relationships which indicated that there were connections with Ian's disappearance. The most likely contacts were those who confirmed that Ian liked to be beaten, that he preferred 'The Rhodesian' to anyone else, because he could go on beating him longer, and that 'The Rhodesian' was expected at Ian's

on December 15. It also became clear that Ian's first contact
with 'The Rhodesian' had been through an advertisement,
and that their subsequent meetings had all been the result of
his being contacted by 'The Rhodesian'. Ian's friends knew
that he had no way of contacting 'The Rhodesian' himself.

At last, on March 25, a Sunday, Ian Erskine's body was
found in the River Cam at Upware. Although it is only
ten miles from Cambridge, Upware is a deserted corner of
the fens with only a large pub used by boatmen to give it
significance. Two men mooring their boat in the dusk on
that March evening saw a large plastic parcel caught in the
branches of a riverside tree. They looked, and found Ian's
naked body wrapped in three dustbin liners fastened with
insulation tape. At that time, of course, it was just a body in
the river. There was nothing to link it to a three-month-old
disappearance in London.

The post-mortem examination next day at Addenbroke's
hospital noted that the body was naked except for white
socks. There was a knotted handkerchief round the neck
and a wide mark across the middle of the back and both
sides. There were splinters of wood, perhaps from a cane
in the flesh of the back. The pathologist thought at first that
the body could not have been long in the water, but changed
his opinion on finding that the low water temperature might
have preserved the body for months. The same day, the body
was identified as that of Ian. The cause of death was given as
asphyxia, but the state of the body precluded any findings on
how it might have been caused.

Back tracking with the Cambridgeshire CID, we found
that the black plastic bag had been seen higher up the river
as early as December 23. There had been half a dozen other
sightings, including one by a young boy who was convinced
that he had seen a body, but had not been listened to.

There was now a niggle in the mind of the investigation
team. All the inquiries showed that Ian had been expecting
'The Rhodesian', and that this man would have bound and

beaten Ian. Ian's body had been put into the river before Christmas. Now the steps leading from Ian's flat to the street were quite steep. It would have required a very fit and determined man to carry a body up the steps by himself. Were we looking for two men?

The search widened. I decided that all the pubs, all the people, all the contacts listed in Ian's diaries and letters had to be eliminated, if only to find someone who could not be traced. But the more people we spoke to, the more we became convinced that the man that Ian had introduced to a friend as John from Surbiton and to others as 'The Rhodesian' was the only real suspect. Laurie Vanner, working hard at overcoming the prejudices of the homosexual community, persuaded two or three of the managers of pubs they used, to display a picture of Ian and a photofit of 'The Rhodesian' to see if anyone could remember seeing them together.

'No wonder they don't think we're interested in what happens to them,' Laurie told me at this stage of the investigation.

'Come on Laurie, we're doing everything we can on this one. They must see that.'

Laurie took his time before answering.

'It's like this, Guv. In some of these pubs, they've got a sort of "Killer's Corner". There's quite a few pictures of blokes like Ian.'

'Few, perhaps. Can't be that many.'

'Would you believe forty? That's right. Forty unsolved gay murders. Not unsolved through want of trying, just through want of information.'

Laurie was right. The record showed there were forty such murders, not one of them had anything in common with Ian's murder, other than each victim was a gay man, and in each police had never been able to trace the suspect.

There were more and more reports that referred to 'The Rhodesian'. He had been seen at Ian's flat, seen in his company. His description varied, but most of them matched the man who had hired the car with Ian's Access card. Ian had often spoken of him, and his background in the police in South Africa. But what part of the police? The British South African Police? The South African Police? The Selous Scouts? Even the SAS? Or was that all a cover? We found that men in Ian's world enjoyed role playing. They would pretend to a more violent background to give more pleasure to the victim, or the victim himself would enhance the background of a beater to add to his own reputation in the SM and CP world. A story in the *Observer* brought another witness who knew a gay Rhodesian who enjoyed inflicting violence during sex. The witness, a former boyfriend of the suspect, spoke to us by phone, but would not agree to be interviewed face to face.

We made inquiries in South Africa and Zimbabwe. A number of people there recognised and put a name to the photofit. The man was interviewed but could not be linked to the murder.

At the end of 1990 we had to finish the investigation leaving the file open. I still wonder if we did everything we could. The three plastic bags in which Ian's body was wrapped were made by Sainsbury's and sold all over the country. I don't think they had been in Ian's flat at the time of his death. He had plastic bin liners of a smaller pattern. Should I have put posters up in Sainsbury's asking if anyone had remembered selling plastic bags to a man like 'The Rhodesian'? Did we really make all the inquiries we could into that very small circle of heterosexuals who moved on the edge of the homosexual world? The few people who had met 'The Rhodesian' were convinced that he was not gay. And what had happened to the Access card lost by that firm? It must have had a dozen of the suspect's fingerprints on its glossy surface.

Most of all, was it a murder? I think, at the very best, that 'The Rhodesian' was prepared for Ian to die. He knew that he would have been identified as Ian's last visitor and was confident enough to go on a controlled spending spree immediately after the death. He was collected enough to hire a car calmly to take the body to a deserted fen. (At least we presume that is why the car was hired. The 240 miles on the clock would have accounted for the journey to Upware and back. The purchases made in central London at that period made it unlikely that the car was being used for local motoring.)

'The Rhodesian' took his time cleaning and tidying Ian's flat to give the impression that Ian had gone away for Christmas. He presumably knew he was leaving the country and therefore would not be around to be identified by the few gays who had seen him.

I've heard people say about Ian, 'Serves him right. If he took risks like that, he must have expected someday that someone would kill him.'

It does seem extraordinary that anyone would voluntarily allow himself to be made completely helpless, but it's what he and a very small number of other reasonable and intelligent people choose to do, and he didn't deserve to die for it.

I know that the team working on this and many of the other unsolved killings would have given their eye teeth to solve them, not only for the sake of arresting the offender, not only for self satisfaction, but for the family and the friends of the victims for whom each and every officer has great sympathy. None of us will show any bias against whatever way of life the victim wishes to lead. Our single consideration is to do the job to the best of our ability, solve the crime, and bring the offenders to justice.

# The Man With The Gun

Keenan, Michael James Keenan. I came across him when I was in a Q car at Notting Hill. I don't know how Q cars got that name; they were unmarked cars manned by two or three detectives. They patrolled in the same way as their uniformed colleagues, but just dealt with crime. Don't know either how Keenan came to be a criminal. He was a head teacher once. When our paths crossed we were both driving along Bishops Bridge Road in Paddington. My driver and I had no particular work in mind and I noticed the Avis sticker on the car in front of us. The sticker is a fleet number which Avis places between the figures and numbers of the index plate, and it identifies the vehicle immediately as a hire car.

Now, hired cars are usually driven with some sort of purpose. Businessmen in a strange town hurrying to a meeting. Tourists finding their way round the sights. Anyone whose own car has broken down, and who is faced with the expense and necessity of hiring another one. There's something about the body language. Some sign of anxiety. I'd never be able to describe exactly what it was, but there was a gesture, a movement, something about the man in front which said, this might be a hired car, but I don't fall into your category of typical hire car drivers. This might sound very airy-fairy to you, but, just as some people can pick horses better than others, some policemen and women can pick up a reason for suspicion that can never be explained to their most hardworking and committed colleague. This intuition, this almost unconscious matrix of behaviour principles, has been of the greatest help to me in every rank from Constable to Superintendent.

★ ★ ★

To digress for a moment, the best example I ever saw of this police sixth sense was in the Bayswater Road one Friday evening about 6.00 p.m. The pavements were crowded and the rain was bucketing down. I was driving back to the station when the PC with me said, 'Hang on a minute, Skip. Want a word with this bloke.'

I don't know how he could have even distinguished a male from a female on the pavement. It was wet, the car windows were beginning to steam, and everyone outside was head down, trying to get home and dry as quickly as possible. So he was out of the car, and had gathered a man coming towards us by the arm and had taken him into a shop doorway before I could ask what was going on. Within seconds he brought him back into the car.

'Nicked him for possession of what looks like heroin, Skip,' he said, handing over a plastic bag of white powder. It did turn out to be heroin, about £2,000 worth.

'What made you pick him out?' I asked the PC afterwards.

'Don't really know,' he said. 'Just something about him. Probably no more than his looking around him all the time. Everyone else was concerned to get out of the rain. He was concerned about who might be watching him.'

So on the basis that it's always safer to check someone that you're not sure about we decided to stop the man in the Avis car. None of that bells and siren business. When he stopped at traffic lights, I got out, produced my warrant card and tapped on his window.

'Sorry to have stopped you, Sir. Just a routine check. Is this your car?' I know this sounds like someone just out of Training School, but I've always been polite in speaking to people. I don't think there's anything to gain by being rude and aggressive, you learn more and get quicker results if you don't upset whoever you're talking to. So I was polite. And so was he.

'Yes, it's my own car, Officer. Had it a couple of months.' So he was lying; this was a hire car. But why was he lying?

There was a camera on the back seat. Had he nicked that as well as the car?

'That your camera, Sir? Mind if I have a look at it?'

'Not at all officer. Help yourself.' Still polite and pleasant. He opened his door as if to get out to help me. As he stepped out, he reached inside his jacket, and there I was, looking down the barrel of a revolver. When it's that near to your face the barrel looks the size of a manhole, and the trigger finger looks as steady as half-set jelly. I'm not a hero, so I stepped back.

'Just stay where you are, and you won't get hurt,' he said, and ran off up the street. Jim Yates, the Q car driver had seen it all, and tried to make a U-turn to pick me up to chase after him, but he ran into the kerb and stalled the engine. I took off after chummy, and caught up with him at the next corner. He stopped and pointed the gun at me again. It looked bigger than ever, a cannon. He couldn't miss from that range.

'I'm warning you, copper. I don't want to shoot, so don't make me.'

While he was pointing the gun at me he was in charge. I stood still. He ran off again, round a corner. Don't ask me what it is that makes a perfectly sane policeman run after a man with a gun who has twice threatened to shoot him. It's not bravery, it's more like indignation that anyone should dare to think they can pull something like that.

So I ran round the corner and there he was with the gun raised to shoulder height, about six feet away from me.

'Out of the way. Try to stop me and I'll shoot.' I ducked to knee height and dived at him. I'm not the most athletic of men, but I am heavy and I'd judged the dive to perfection. I knocked him flat and he dropped the gun. For a moment it began to look like one of those film scenes where the goody and the baddy are both reaching for the gun that's two feet out of reach. Luckily there was a civic minded bystander, Nigel Beaumont. I called out to him that I was a police officer.

'Get hold of that gun, quickly,' I yelled. He did, and I was able to concentrate on holding on to Keenan.

By now, of course there were plenty of police about. Cars zipping up and down looking for me, sirens going. PCs running round the corner. A vicar stopped opposite where I was holding Keenan on the pavement and Nigel Beaumont was hanging on to the revolver. The vicar looked at us, looked at the cars, and the uniformed officers who were now running towards us.

'Goodness me,' he exclaimed, 'you must be making *The Sweeney*. How exciting! Which one are you? When will it be on?' Someone told him in very unvicarish language that this was not television, and he went off, obviously feeling cheated that he had had to put up with the real thing, and not the glamour of the box.

It was my turn to feel cheated when we got to the Old Bailey. Keenan was wanted for a string of offences including jumping bail in Essex, stealing cheques, false pretences and the odd burglary. He pleaded guilty to all of the offences but not guilty to using a firearm with intent to resist arrest. His counsel said that he had never pointed a gun at me. Three times, he claimed, Keenan had tried to hand it to me, and three times I had jumped at him, and he had been so frightened that he ran off. He didn't want to throw the gun down in case it was left behind in the chase and a child might pick it up. He tried the same line with Nigel Beaumont after he had given his evidence.

'Now, Mr Beaumont, I suggest that what you saw was my client with the revolver in the palm of his hand offering it to Mr Herridge. Naturally it was an alarming sight, and quite understandably you thought that he was pointing the gun at the officer.'

'No, I was not mistaken. I saw the gun being pointed at Mr Herridge.'

'I see. But is there not just the possibility that my client had the gun in his hand offering it to the officer? He wanted to surrender it. Was he not trying to hand it over?'

'He was pointing it. He was pointing it directly at Mr Herridge. He was not trying to hand it over.'

'Now, Mr Beaumont, I don't expect you have had much experience with guns. Are you sure you can distinguish between a gun that is being pointed, and one that is being offered, surrendered? If you have not had much to do with guns, and were perhaps understandably alarmed, you could easily confuse the two actions. It would be quite understandable for a layman to make an honest mistake, following your initial alarm at seeing this pistol.'

'I don't think I made a mistake. I do not think I can be described as a layman in the matter of firearms. I am a gunmaker by profession. My father is a director of Purdey [the Royal Gunmakers]. I have used guns of all sorts since the age of 12. I know when a gun is being pointed, and that gun was being pointed.'

That was about it. I've become used to being called a liar in the witness box, and I wonder if Nigel Beaumont had not turned up, I wonder if the jury would have believed me. Still, being disbelieved is something you have to get used to. Keenan was sentenced to imprisonment.

At the end of the trial, Nigel Beaumont was commended by the judge and awarded £50 from the Bow Street Reward Fund for his public spirited action and bravery. I was enormously pleased when the trial judge gave him this public recognition, and I'm sure that he treasures the moment as much as the later occasion when his bravery was recognised in a certificate from the Sheriff of London. All I could give him was my heartfelt gratitude, and whenever I think of him I still say a silent 'Thanks, Nigel'.

One more thing. Keenan had described himself as a teacher. In fact, a head of year at a school in Dublin. I wonder why he gave up a perfectly respectable profession. Perhaps the money wasn't that good, or perhaps the risky life of a thief was preferable to facing dozens of nasty kids every day.

# Sunday In Southall

Most of us stay late in bed on Sunday mornings. Even on a morning as summery as it was on June 12, 1988, we would have been tempted to mutter, 'Looks like a really nice day. We should go out somewhere,' before turning over and stealing another half-hour's sleep. But in Southall, well before 6.00 a.m. the Bhattis had started their day. Yaqoob Bhatti left his house in Orchard Avenue shortly after 5.00 a.m. to travel to Heathrow where he worked as an aircraft cleaner. He had taken his wife, Pushpa, a cup of tea, knowing that she would also be up soon. They had been married for twenty-two years, and had three sons, the eldest of whom was at university. The two younger ones did not share their parents' willingness to be up and about, and stayed asleep.

Mrs Bhatti, then aged 53, was well known, and highly respected. She taught at a local school, was a regular attender at the local C. of E. church, where she was a member of the parish council, and president of the local Asian Christian Fellowship. She was the type of woman of whom you could say, 'She's a real credit to the community.'

On this Sunday morning she followed a custom of the people of northern India where she had been born, and rose early to watch the morning sun. Southall does not sound a likely place for such an activity, but Mrs Bhatti lived close to Southall Park – eleven acres of playing pitches, trees, and bushes. Not exactly countryside, but enough of a open space, especially at 6.00 a.m. on a summer morning to give the illusion that it was far from the traffic of the Uxbridge Road, and to allow the sun to be seen in an atmosphere of calm which, whatever your religious beliefs, must be of help to the human spirit.

Southall Park has a number of official entrances, linked by formal paths, but locals using the park to cross to other parts of Southall had created a number of unofficial entrances linked by well-trodden short cuts. Pushpa Bhatti knew that she would be able to walk into the park even if the keepers had not opened the gates. She was in the park just before 6.00 a.m. At about 5.50 a.m. she was seen walking past Southall Police Station, which is almost opposite the park entrance, by a fellow church member. He noticed that she was wearing headphones and carrying a personal stereo, and assumed she was listening to material for a forthcoming theological examination he knew that she was about to sit. She was in fact listening to organ music.

So Pushpa Bhatti walked into Southall Park, looking towards the sun, and cut off from other sounds by the church music on her headphones. Only fifty yards away from the police station, inside the park there is a large overgrown holly bush, large enough for a man to stand inside without being seen. As Mrs Bhatti passed the bush, Michael Ogiste, a 19-year-old black youth was waiting there. Although only 19 years old, he was extremely powerful. Some months later when he was arrested, it took seven policemen to get him into a cell. At 6.00 a.m. on this bright June morning there was no one to protect Mrs Bhatti from him.

He leapt from the bush, dragged the suddenly terrified woman back into it, smashed her in the face repeatedly with a broken bottle, tore off her skirt and underclothes, attempted to rape her, strangled her with his hands, and finally ejaculated over her dying face. Then he grabbed her handbag, pulled two gold bracelets from her wrist, and walked away looking through the handbag and throwing away letters and other papers in which he had no interest. It was as quick as that. Murder usually doesn't take long. Mrs Bhatti's violation and death was a matter of a few minutes. Her body lay undiscovered in the holly bush until the evening.

Mrs Bhatti's disappearance did not become a matter of concern to her family until her husband returned from his work at Heathrow. Her two sons had noticed that their mother was not in the house when they eventually got up, but had assumed that she was out busy with church matters. Yaqoob Bhatti, however, recognised that his wife would not break her routine without letting him know. He began to phone friends, fellow church-goers, neighbours, trying to find where his wife was. At 5.30 p.m. he was alarmed enough to go to Southall Police Station to report her as a missing person. The forms were still being completed when a man ran into the station.

'In the park, just over there, the bush, there's a body. A lady. She looks as if she's dead. I think she's been hit with something.'

Mrs Bhatti had first been found by two local characters, Shantilal Patel and Roy Connolly. They were the sort of men who always appear slightly drunk, affable rather than aggressive. They had spent lunchtime, as they had spent many other lunchtimes, drinking in the nearby Red Lion. Then they had gone to sit on the bench near the holly bush to talk to each other and to any passer-by who cared to join in their conversation. Shantilal went to the bush to relieve himself, standing well inside and out of view of other people using the park. As he was about to open his flies he became aware of the body a few feet away from him. He ran from the bush calling to his friend. Roy, not sure if Shantilal was telling the truth or suffering from some drunken delusion, went into the bush himself. Seconds later he was back with his friend, confused, but certain that they had to do something. But who would take any notice of them? This needed a more respectable, more responsible citizen to take the necessary action.

'Mister? Sorry to stop you, Mister. In the bush there. A lady, dead by the look of it. Someone should tell the police.' This mister was a 25-year-old civil servant who checked that there was a body, and then sprinted the fifty yards to Southall Police Station, where he blurted out his discovery to the sergeant patiently taking down the details of Mr Bhatti's missing wife.

Two uniform officers and two detectives went to the bush almost immediately. They could see Mrs Bhatti's body from the edge of the bush, with the legs apart and clothing scattered around. Wisely they made no attempt to examine the body. If this woman had been killed, she would have been in immediate contact with her killer, and the traces of that contact would be in the immediate vicinity of the body. Any careless step could destroy vital evidence.

By the time I got to the scene just after 7.00 p.m. (I was the senior officer on call under a system in which one senior detective has to stay within reach of a phone on a Sunday in case of any emergency such as this), a photographer, a Scenes of Crime officer, and a forensic scientist had already been called to the park. The park had been partially closed to the public by uniformed officers brought in from surrounding stations, and the holly bush was screened off and floodlit. I called out a forensic pathologist, Dr Susan Clayden, to examine the body before it was moved. Even the most careful of undertakers and mortuary attendants may mark a body before a full post-mortem can take place, and I feel it essential that any subsequent court should have the fullest possible knowledge of the condition of the body before it is moved. In some cases of asphyxia, for instance, the only signs of violence might be slight bruising to the victim's nose. Unless those signs have been noted before the removal of the body, how can we subsequently answer a defence challenge that the bruising had occurred in the undertaker's van, or at the mortuary?

In the meantime, poor Mr Bhatti had to be told that we were certain that the dead woman was his missing wife, but that he would be unable to see the body until the next day. It was part of the process that Mrs Bhatti's body would not be cleaned or dressed properly until the post-mortem had been completed and all the forensic and other evidence available from the state of the body and of the clothing had been secured. It would have been enormously distressing for Mr Bhatti to see his wife in the condition in which she was found. The post-mortem on Monday morning showed that although there was sperm in Mrs Bhatti's mouth, there was none in her vagina, although all the signs had pointed to an attempt at rape.

In the next five weeks we took 600 statements as the result of 1,300 incident actions. These are messages relating to the murder inquiry which were either direct calls from members of the public offering evidence, or actions initiated by police officers on the basis of their own inquiries. We also stopped 1,200 cars in the area of the park to ask the drivers if they remembered anything about the morning of June 12. We heard hardly anything worthwhile. The only information of any value would have just about covered a single A4 page.

About 6.30 a.m. on the morning of the murder, a workman in Uxbridge Road spoke to a West Indian man who wanted to know the nearest shop. He describes the man as 'sweating' and put his age at about 40. A few minutes later a West Indian with bruising to the knuckles of his left hand, which was wrapped in a blue handkerchief, took a minicab from a road near the park to a nearby industrial estate. When we later made inquiries at the estate, we could find no one who matched the description of the minicab passenger.

Some of Mrs Bhatti's correspondence was found by a park keeper about an hour after her murder and hours before her body was discovered. It was four days before the keeper realised the significance of the property and handed it over to police. Mrs Bhatti's handbag was found at the back of the Red Lion on the evening following her murder. During the time that Mrs Bhatti's body lay in the middle of the holly bush, we found one man who had gone into the bush to relieve himself without seeing the body, and a second who had changed into football kit and thought the body to be a discarded tailor's dummy. And that was the extent of our success in the search for the murderer.

We traced everyone who had used the park on Saturday evening and Sunday. The idea was to list the joggers, the dog owners, the people using short cuts, the parents with children, anyone who had been seen in the park during that time in the hope that the regulars would be able to describe each other, and from their statements we might isolate a stranger, a possible suspect. We learned at a very early stage that many of the regulars could not describe each other, but they could be very accurate about dogs. We began to catalogue the witnesses as 'man with white labrador', 'woman with two brown and black terriers'. From those statements we began to hear of a sinister character who appeared occasionally very early in the morning carrying a long metal pole. He turned out to be a slightly eccentric police inspector, whose hobby was 'treasure seeking' and who often went through the park in the early morning with a metal detector.

We also ran an Anacapa on the scene and victim. This is a graphic analysis of time and place to locate each witness's movements in relation to those of the victim. Every relevant time and movement is shown on a large chart. Say one witness speaks of seeing two ladies with dogs and then a boy on a bicycle followed by a man with a briefcase. The Anacapa should eventually show those others, with their statements indicating who they saw at that time. Five minutes later, of course, those four witnesses may have seen other fresh faces, and the chart is taken a step further on. When it works successfully, you could find one unidentified person whom everyone has seen but who has not answered police appeals for witnesses. An Anacapa can also be very useful at court to assist the jury.

An additional problem was a campaign by local activists who were describing the killing as a racial murder. Some of my time had to be devoted to attending protest meetings to explain exactly what we were doing, and what help we needed. Any movement into the political arena would be another step away from the concentration needed to trace the murderer. Rumours that this was a racial murder of an Asian woman by a white man would influence potential witnesses. People who may have seen something significant would be unconsciously influenced to think of only white suspects. Media coverage which could attract more information would be diverted to the supposedly racist aspect of the killing. The investigation had to be combined with a community relations exercise.

Six weeks had gone by without our making any significant progress; any detective leading a murder investigation knows that unless there is a strong lead in the first forty-eight hours, the inquiry gets harder and more morale sapping as it goes on. In addition, there are other demands on manpower. You might start a murder inquiry with forty or more officers. Six weeks in, you're lucky if the squad is still in double figures.

Then, on July 25, in Manor Grounds Cemetery, less than half a mile from the scene of Mrs Bhatti's murder, a 22-year-old woman was savagely raped. There were some similarities to the murder. The girl was walking through open and fairly isolated ground. Her attacker had been hiding in a bush and dragged her back into the bush to complete his attack, and her handbag was stolen. It was almost certainly the same man, and we were faced with another inquiry in the same form. But this one produced a witness almost immediately.

An Asian came to Southall Police Station. In the last ten years he had been to court fifteen times on charges ranging from rape to robbery. He lived in a road which gave direct access on to the cemetery in which the rape had taken place. He must have known that the initial inquiries would soon turn him up as a possible suspect.

'Man you want for this thing,' he told us, 'Ogiste. Michael Ogiste. Lives in Warwick Road.'

The houses in Warwick Road also have direct access to the cemetery. He told us that Ogiste had been boasting to friends that he was the man police were looking for and asking other friends to say he was with them at the time of the murder. It was enough to send two officers looking for Ogiste. He was arrested on August 2 and immediately interviewed by two detectives from the murder squad. He had a solicitor, and made a statement in his presence claiming that he had been asleep at home on the Saturday evening and Sunday morning of the murder. He agreed to provide blood samples; we charged him with the rape in the cemetery, and he was remanded in custody at Ealing Magistrates Court.

The purpose of the blood samples was to obtain a DNA specimen which would be matched with the sample of semen taken from Mrs Bhatti's body. DNA processing, which can link a human with a minute specimen of blood, saliva or sperm was a relatively new process developed by a scientist at Leicester University. The first time it was used, the tests showed that a youth that Leicester police were holding in connection with the murders of two young girls, could not have committed them. The result of the test of Ogiste's blood sample, taken with his permission, would not be known for some time, but now with a suspect for the murder, we could make more specific inquiries about his movements.

We quickly found a minicab driver who knew Ogiste, and remembered picking him up in Southall at about 6.30 a.m. on the morning of the murder. He knew Ogiste because the latter had beaten him up three weeks before. So we had the suspect close to the scene of the murder just after the time of the murder. This was the first gap in his alibi. Next, two friends of Ogiste, the Toussaint brothers, said that Ogiste had been at a Southall nightclub between 3.30 a.m. and 5.00 a.m. on the morning of the murder. Then, another trace from inside Southall police station itself. Ogiste was on bail at the time of the murder for an offence of handling stolen property.

One of the conditions of his bail was that he reported twice a week to Southall Police Station.

The reporting form, form 41, showed that Ogiste had called at the station at 3.40 a.m., claiming that the court had changed the conditions under which he reported. But we now had more material evidence. When he had been arrested, his house was searched, and among the property taken away was a pair of training shoes. The footprints made by the shoes were almost identical with prints found at the point at which Mrs Bhatti's handbag had been recovered. At first we thought that 'almost' was not good enough, until the scientist who had examined the shoes was prepared to give expert evidence that the difference would have been caused by the wear on the shoe between the murder date, and the date of arrest.

Ogiste returned to Ealing Court on September 23, and was remanded for three days to police custody. Remember he was still only being held on the rape charge. (Prisoners remanded in custody are usually held in jail, but occasionally a magistrate will agree to remand a particular prisoner to a police station if he is convinced that it is necessary for further investigation.) We began interviewing him about Mrs Bhatti's murder as soon as he was back at the station and his solicitor had arrived. At first he refused to answer any questions, but eventually named a West Indian as the murderer.

He said that this man had admitted the murder to him four days afterwards, and that he had shown him the gold bracelets stolen from Mrs Bhatti. He also claimed that the Asian (who had first told us about him) had been there when the West Indian admitted the murder. (In fact the Asian had been in prison at that time.) He took us to the Grand Union Canal to the place at which he alleged the West Indian had thrown in bloodstained clothing. The canal was searched without result; the West Indian himself was brought into the station and denied the murder.

Ogiste's mother was seen in an attempt to confirm or

disprove his alibi that he was at home in bed at the time of the murder. Mrs Ogiste was a Seventh Day Adventist, apparently incapable of answering any question without quoting from the Old Testament source that she felt most relevant.

'The sleep of a labouring man is sweet, whether he eat little or much, but the abundance of the rich will not suffer him to sleep,' she said, when I asked her if her son always slept at home, and when I asked if he had ever come in late on a Sunday morning, 'Remember the Sabbath day to keep it holy. Six days shalt thou labour and do all thy work. The seventh day is the Sabbath day of the Lord Thy God.'

Mrs Ogiste might not be able to confirm that her son was away from home on the night of the murder, but I was fairly confident that, called as a defence witness, she would be unlikely to prove that he was at home either.

Just before 7.30 p.m. on Saturday, Ogiste was charged with Mrs Bhatti's murder. He went berserk, trying to force his way out of the charge room, pushing police officers aside, ignoring his solicitor. It took seven police officers to hold him and get him back to his cell. What chance would Mrs Bhatti have had?

What chance would Mrs Bhatti have had when Ogiste's friends, even knowing he was in custody, were unwilling to tell all they knew. Once Ogiste had been charged, and was clearly not going to be free for some months, Jabble, and one of his friends, added to their statements. They claimed that Ogiste had admitted the murder in their presence. But by then we had the best evidence possible, other than that of an eyewitness. The DNA samples matched. Ogiste's defence was broken. There was positive proof that he had been in physical contact with Mrs Bhatti at the time of her death. He pleaded guilty at the Old Bailey, and was sentenced to life imprisonment. That means he will be free to return to Southall in another nine years.

We also had another aid that would have pointed us to

Ogiste had the witnesses not come forward, a psychological profile. This process pioneered by the FBI enabled a trained investigator to produce an assessment of the character of an unidentified suspect. In this case Dr David Cantor of Surrey University, dealing only with the evidence we had gathered, predicted that the suspect would be a young unskilled man with a significant connection with Sundays. He would live within a mile of the murder scene, and would be apparently sexually inexperienced. He had produced a profile without knowing anything about Ogiste. It was later found to be 90 per cent accurate and would have been most helpful had we not solved the matter earlier. I have every confidence in this comparatively new science which will be most beneficial to investigators in years to come. It is widely used and extremely accurate in tracing offenders in the USA where the FBI have used it for many years. More power to our elbows!

No investigation ever explains every detail of a crime; hardly ever do you get the 100 per cent picture. The puzzle that stays in my mind after the Bhatti case, is the evidence of one witness who heard something at the time of the murder. A man sleeping in a room above the Red Lion, about fifty yards from the murder scene, was awakened by screams from the park, he thought at sometime between 5.00 a.m. and 6.00 a.m. He took no notice and went back to sleep. But he was certain of one thing, the screaming woman had shouted, 'Fuck off, bastard!'

No one who knew Mrs Bhatti had ever heard her use the mildest abuse. It was unthinkable that she would ever use obscenities. So was there another woman in the park facing some sort of trouble before Mrs Bhatti was murdered? None of the statements we took gave any indication of this. Or did Mrs Bhatti, scared out of her wits, knowing she was about to be killed, revert to the sort of language she might have heard in the street but would never willingly use?

# Believe It Or Not

When I decided to call this book *Believe No One*, I intended the advice to apply to other police officers, but I did want them to believe me. I'm afraid this is a tale that they all, whatever their experience, will find it hard to swallow. I've told it on those occasions when coppers reminisce over a pint or two, and I've seen my listeners shake their heads. We all have at least one interesting story from our service. We all, without exception, embroider our favourite stories just a little to make them more interesting. When they go too far, our audience at the bar or in the canteen lets us know that we've stretched the facts a little beyond belief.

That's the response I always get when I tell this one.

'Come on, Roy. You're stretching it a bit.' Actually that's a polite version of the way they normally express their doubt. Well, I'm sorry but all of this is true. I can only hope that you ignore my advice this time. Believe me.

I was driving back from court one morning through some Paddington back streets, when I saw a couple of good suspects. I was waiting at a crossroads when I first saw them. Just two men at the door of a house. One was knocking at the front door standing very close to it, and the other with his back to him was looking up and down the road. Now normally if two of you are calling at a house socially, or on business, you both face the door. If the people in the house are friends, or potential customers, you would not want to be rude by having your back to them when the door opens. Policemen don't work these things out step by step. It's a matter of instant recognition based on experience.

So I drove over the crossroads, parked the car, and walked back towards the two men, who had now moved down the road. They were looking casually at the houses as they passed, not walking too slowly, but not hurrying. I wanted to watch them. They were obviously going to screw the first suitable house they came to. But I was too close behind them. They turned round suddenly as if they had made up their minds to go back to one of the houses they had looked at previously, and almost bumped into me. No point now trying to follow them. I reached into my pocket to pull out my warrant card. I did not even get a chance to tell them I was a police officer.

'It's the Law,' said the one nearest to me. They were both young, well built, and as big as me. The second pulled out a knife, a big knife. I needed instant protection, so I grabbed his friend as a shield. As long as I was holding on to him, I reckoned that I stood little chance of being stabbed. Fortunately, the knife man, seeing that he was out of my reach, backed off, and his friend started kicking and punching away to release himself.

Now, I'm sure there are all sorts of wrist holds and martial arts grips to use in fights like this, but however calm and clear thinking you are, when you are being punched and kicked, you forget about wrist holds and just get stuck in. He had the advantage, in that all he wanted was to get away. I just wanted to hold on to him, so if I tried punching, I'd lose my grip. We were soon on our backs on the pavement with the knife man taking kicks at whatever part of me he could see. One of the parts he could see was my nose, so he kicked it. I let go, and a second later I had lost two prisoners, but had gained a nasal fracture.

We can skip the hospital, where the doctor found the episode to be much funnier than I did, and move on about four hours where I had a meet with some other officers at Chelsea Police Station. (There was little point in my circulating the descriptions of the two suspected burglars all over the Metropolitan Police District. I had not seen them commit any crime, and they could easily get round the assault by claiming that they thought they were being attacked by a drunk. The best that could be done was a local message with their descriptions as potential burglars. But at Chelsea my luck was in. In their parade room was the usual board marked 'Target Criminals'. Target criminals are CRO men (men with criminal records) living on the patch who are believed to be actively engaged in crime, but who are not wanted for any particular job.

The two men who had attacked me that morning were Chelsea's Target Criminals of the week with their full names and addresses under their photos. We waited until 6.00 the following morning before calling on them with search warrants. Much better to wait until they were home, rather than call too early and have friends or relatives warn them off.

I picked the knife man, made certain that his flat was surrounded and knocked on the front door. Our information said that he was still living with his mum and dad. Mum answered the door. I was as polite as anyone can be with a broken nose who is looking for the man who broke it, and Mum, sensing a certain impatience, pointed out his bedroom. Two of us went in, and I switched on the light. The knife man, who had been fast asleep, groaned, swore violently, and sat half up, before he saw me.

'Oh no. Tell me it's all a dream.'

'It's no dream, old son,' I answered. 'More like a nightmare. You're nicked.'

We didn't find any property in the flat that looked as if it had been stolen, but we did find a box containing almost thirty pawn tickets. So the next day accompanied by one of my DCs, Sean Gleeson, I went round to the pawn shop which had issued all the tickets. It was a one man business just off Praed Street, and the one man looked rather pale when I introduced myself and told him we wanted the pledge for each ticket.

'Better close the shop for a while,' I advised him. 'This

could take some time, and I'm sure your customers won't
want to come in while the police are talking to you.'

That made sense to him, and, having locked the shop door,
he started sorting out the pledges: some jewellery, a camera,
a set of golf-clubs, hopefully all property that would later be
identified as coming from burglaries in the area.

We were listing the property carefully, when suddenly
there was a violent knocking on the door. Obviously a
customer in need of money, or perhaps someone anxious
to redeem an office clock before the boss noticed it was
missing. We had our backs to the door, and took no notice.
The knocking continued.

'Tell them to come back later,' I said, intent on getting
the description of a gold wristwatch into my notebook. The
pawnbroker was looking straight at the door, and was even
paler than when we had come in. I turned round. There were
two men at the door, each wearing a full face balaclava with
eye holes, and each carrying a sledge-hammer. Even as I was
turning round they had given up hope that the pawnbroker
was going to open the door, and started smashing the shop
window with the pick handles, and passing the few pieces of
jewellery and electrical equipment in the window to a third
man in the car behind them.

'Open the door, quickly,' I yelled at the pawnbroker.

Smash went another piece of the window.

'They'll kill us all,' yelled the pawnbroker.

'Unlock the door,' I shouted.

'We'll be murdered,' shrieked the pawnbroker.

'It's the fucking Law,' screamed one of the robbers, seeing
Sean Gleeson trying to pull open the shop door from the
inside and realising that only a policeman would be silly
enough to try and get at two men with pick handles.

They jumped into the car and drove off. I'm very good at
car numbers. And I'm very good at remembering cars. The
car was one I had seen parked most nights of the week outside
a club in Notting Hill. But it had a different number plate
than that used in the robbery. So we finished our business in

the pawn shop, matched the property to five or six burglaries which the knifeman and his mate admitted, found the car that night in Notting Hill with its correct plates back on, and when a uniform PC had called out the owner on the pretext of a parking offence, we looked in the boot and found the two sledge-hammers and the two balaclavas.

It's all a matter of swings and roundabouts. If I had a broken nose from the swings, I reckon that I had a fair old turn on the roundabouts that day. This is the only time that I've known a criminal use a hammer to knock down a door in order to be arrested.

# The Ealing Vicarage Rape

St Mary's stands in the older part of Ealing. Ealing, for me, is the new shopping centre, the beginning of the Uxbridge Road, the tree-lined common which mocks the traffic jammed on the North Circular Road. The church and its vicarage is cut off from the shopping centre by a handful of eighteenth-century houses, a couple of pubs that look from the outside like archetypical locals that most Englishmen dream of living opposite, and a village green. At the back of the vicarage is a railway line that acts as the geographical and social boundary of a council estate. At 12.45 p.m. on March 6, 1986, three men, from the other side of the tracks, came to the vicarage and rang the front door bell.

Their leader, Robert Horscroft, then aged 34, was a professional burglar. He had a local reputation and a number of previous convictions. His companions, Martin McCall and Christopher Byrne, each aged 21 were both convicted thieves, but were a few steps below Horscroft on the local criminal ladder. The three men were still drunk. They had spent the night before drinking bottles of vodka stolen from an off-licence, and had woken in the morning knowing that they needed more money. Horscroft had led them first to a house near the vicarage, but the lady living there had seen them from her bedroom window when they knocked on her door and shouted at them to go away. For some reason they took notice of her and carried on to their next target, the vicarage. Having rung the bell, they stood close to the door. There was a pause before the door was opened. The vicar, Michael Saward, thought that his daughter would answer the door. Jill Saward, watching a video with her boyfriend, waited for her father to answer. It was obviously parish business.

When the Reverend Saward eventually opened the door, he was not surprised to see three men outside. Vicars are used to strangers at the door. He did not immediately register that each man had his face concealed by a balaclava. A momentary irritation at being disturbed was replaced by alarm as the men pushed into the hall. McCall produced a knife and told him to get back inside. There was an immediate and expected demand for money. Michael Saward pointed to his wallet lying on the desk in his study and to a drawer in which he kept the coppers and small change from the Sunday collections and charity boxes. Horscroft – for all his experience – and his two companions were not sophisticated thieves. They divided the money immediately. The older man then felt a need to mark his role as leader.

'Where's the safe?' There was no safe. There was a pause. Then: 'Anyone else in the house?' It is conceivable that if Michael Saward had said 'No', this trio of petty crooks might have left, making the most of a bad job. But the vicar told them that his daughter and her boyfriend were watching television in another room.

His daughter, Jill Saward, was 21 years old; a virgin; strong-minded; independent; a devout Christian, with a strong sense of humour; and devoid of humbug. She had inherited some of her grandfather's character. He had been the captain of the ship in which Crippen had tried to escape to America.

Jill, at the age of 12, had survived, with much grief, but without trauma, the death of a friend who had drowned at a summer camp they were both attending. She was a prison visitor. She was strong. She needed that strength to survive the brutality she was about to face, and the consequent insensitivity of the judge who in sentencing, I felt demonstrated that he thought theft deserved a more severe penalty than rape.

David, Jill's boyfriend, was the same age, respectful of her chastity, used to Jill's independence of character that a lesser male would have categorised as bossiness. When Christopher Byrne came into the room, they took him for one of the workmen who had been working around the vicarage for the past months. Jill's first feeling was one of annoyance at her father's failure to warn her that there would still be workmen around. Then McCall came in with a knife and the couple realised that these were no workmen, they were facing aggressive burglars. It was frighteningly clear that the two men wanted them out of the room. Jill walked out without protest, and was sickened to see her boyfriend, who was leaving the room with the same willingness, being hit and kicked as they were driven along the passage to the study.

Her father was there. The desk drawers were open, and the collection boxes empty.

'Keep cool,' her father advised her needlessly. He must have known his daughter's power of self control. Byrne pointed a knife at her face and demanded to be taken to search for jewellery. Jill knew the only jewellery in the vicarage would be in her mother's bedroom, and took Byrne there. He clearly knew something about jewellery and picked out the few good pieces, in contrast to the earlier juvenile division of the small change in the study.

'Remember I was kind to you,' he told her before leading her back to the study. He must have suspected what was likely to happen. McCall, also with a knife, was clearly not satisfied with the few rings and brooches that Byrne had taken. With the knife waving at her, Jill was forced to another bedroom. She knew, all the men knew, that McCall's interests were now beyond theft. In the bedroom he forced her to undress. During the next three-quarters of an hour McCall raped Jill, took her into another room where he buggered her. She was so innocent she did not know what was happening to her. Then he forced her into oral sex. At one stage he drove the knife towards her vagina, reversing it at the last second and pushing the handle into her. Horscroft and Byrne wandered in and out of the rooms while she was being abused. Byrne, excited by the degradation, demanded to be fellated. Through real fear, Jill complied. Her father and boyfriend were pushed past the open doors of the room in which she was being raped, in a vain search for more money.

Finally Jill was bound hand and foot. McCall tried to force her to drink from a bottle of vodka. Face down, terrified, and bound, Jill was unable to obey him. She had steeled herself to ignore the continuing foulness, having little doubt that McCall would use the knife at the first sign of resistance. She knew that her father and boyfriend were being beaten in other rooms. At one stage she had seen Byrne carrying a cricket bat, and the part of her mind that had detached itself from her ordeal wondered what value it could have. When she heard the thud and David's howl of pain, she knew what the bat was for. The two men were beaten with it, not tapped, beaten with full blooded strokes. Michael Saward's skull was fractured. He described it as feeling 'his head explode'.

The men left. Jill did not know it, but the three attackers had been joined by Andrew Byrne, Christopher's older brother, who had been too drunk at midday to take part in the expedition to St Mary's Vicarage. Still thinking of the others rather than of herself, Jill struggled free of the washing line tying her wrists and ankles, found a towel to wrap around herself and staggered through the house to look for David and her father, afraid to think what might have happened to them. She found them, bound, beaten, and semi-conscious in the study. She freed them, and, in spite of her own distress and injury, searched through the house to find the only phone that the rapists had not disconnected. She called the police. It was still less than an hour since McCall had rung the front door bell.

Uniformed police arrived quickly in response to the emergency call.

'St Mary's Vicarage. Church Place W5. Female alleging rape and assault. Three male suspects.'

Jill opened the door to them still wrapped in a towel. She was the only one of the three victims able to speak clearly. She took the officers to the two men. The shocked and sympathetic PCs called ambulances. Jill expected to be taken to the police station. Very properly she was taken to hospital.

The investigation started immediately. Jill had been able to provide descriptions of the men concerned. The evening papers, radio and TV broadcasts immediately labelled the crime 'The Ealing Vicarage Rape' and carried out police appeals for witnesses, giving descriptions of the suspects. Rape victims are entitled to anonymity. One tabloid went as far as it could to break the ban by publishing a photo of Jill leaving church with her face blacked out but identifying her as the vicar's daughter. Their concern was with circulation, not with the casualty of crime.

We received over 1,000 calls in three days. That's an unusual number for any police appeal. What was not unusual was the variety of calls. Some, as with all appeals, were abusive. Some were from cranks who bemoaned the current lack of respect for the Royal family, and the failure of bakers to include stone ground flour in all their products, but many, very many were genuine. Every one had to be followed if it seemed in any way likely to produce evidence. Many were well meaning but just not worth following. Typical of these latter calls was one from an old lady who, seeing a photofit of one of the men in her daily paper, rang to say that she had seen him on the Isle of Wight ferry.

'When was this, Madam?

'It must have been, now let me think, I was going over to Emily's. She died about three years ago. It must have been in the summer, about 1982.' But there were calls that provided some essential information. The little details that form a pattern. Three men crossing a path near the railway line. A man staggering up to the vicarage sometime before 2.00 a.m. Something overheard in a pub.

Jill had been gently questioned after being examined at the hospital. She was so sexually inexperienced that the investigating officers (I had not yet joined the team) had to explain the terms for some of the outrages that she had undergone. David Lamper, the Detective Chief Superintendent then at the head of the investigation, knew fairly quickly that three men had been involved. Jill, her boyfriend, and her father had each seen three men. People answering the call for witnesses had seen three or four men approaching the vicarage, and three or more men walking away from it. Witnesses can easily become confused when they have seen more than two suspects. Jill, the best of the three witnesses in the vicarage, was understandably confused about who had done what. There could have been a fourth man in the house without her knowing about it. We were not absolutely certain how many suspects we were looking for.

It is one of the ironies of the investigation that Horscroft was questioned within two hours of the rape. He was drinking in a local pub, and when the first police asked the customers if they had seen anything suspicious, he claimed to know nothing about it. At that stage, of course, there was no reason to suspect him.

I joined the investigation team a few days after the incident itself. Despite the enormous national interest, the intense local sympathy, despite the hundreds of offers of help, the inquiry had hardly moved any further. There were none of the usual leads from local informants. When any major investigation is launched, police expect to pick up relevant and irrelevant scraps of information. Detectives get in touch with their regular informants, with saloon bar acquaintances, with all local major and minor criminals who owe them favours. They hope to hear of people suddenly missing from their usual haunts, anyone looking unusually nervous, anyone who has come into money.

You may think that we would be unlikely to get information from criminals, but men and women who would not usually speak to the Old Bill pass on any news they think might help to bring the investigation to an end. This has nothing to do with sympathy for the victim. The abnormal number of extra police on the manor inhibits the normal daily business of the petty criminal. There are risks in moving stolen property about, in being seen in the company of receivers, even in not following a normal routine. The sooner the big one is out of the way, the sooner can they return to their normal trade in stolen credit cars, scrap metal, TVs, car radios, suits and dresses.

But nothing had been heard in Ealing. The property stolen from the vicarage had included some distinctive jewellery and an antique clock. None of it had been offered to local fences. We had very few clues to follow through. There was little chance of fingerprints being found at the vicarage. Jill remembered that the three men had all worn gloves or mittens. Even had any of the attackers left prints, it would be weeks before they would be found. In a vicarage there would be hundreds of other prints to be eliminated. We needed to find everyone who had visited the vicarage in the last six months, obtain their prints and then check them against those found on the walls, furniture, cutlery. Our best leads were the statements from witnesses which spoke of a number of men, two, three or four, seen near the vicarage using a path across the railway line. This was a path only known to local people. So at least one of the men lived, or had lived in the area. But there was one other detail in the statement from the vicar himself. One of the men had asked, 'Where's the safe?'

Now the average burglar does not concern himself with safes. They're too much bother. They take time to open, even when you've a knife to the throat of the person with the key or combination. Once the safe's open, you may end up with little more than a box of useless documents. Some burglars depend on open or insecure doors. A quick search, anything that can be hidden in a pocket, then a quick exit. Professionals can open doors and perhaps safes without noise. Professionals know where most people keep their money and valuables. Professionals don't expect to spend much time searching. They work alone, choose one or two proven methods, and stick to them. The best burgle houses about which they have detailed information. Some form gangs to turn over expensive flats and country houses. Professionals don't burgle houses which are occupied.

Then there are the cowboys. They chat in pubs, get a little drunk, egg each other on, decide that there must be something worth thieving in a particular house and go there team-handed without any further planning, hoping that at least there'll be a TV and video to sell for £40 or £50. They rarely worry if the drum is occupied. If anyone gets in their way, well, they might get a bit of a whacking. So we were looking for cowboys, but one of these cowboys had ambitions beyond the money box, TV and table ornaments.

'Where's the safe?' he had asked. 'Show me the safe.' Perhaps he had wanted to show his companions that he had a bit more class. If you're good at safes, you're a few steps up the criminal ladder.

So I was interested in a local man with convictions for safebreaking. And I wanted anything that had been thrown away. The cricket bat, for instance. Michael Saward, Jill, and her boyfriend had all seen the men with the cricket bat, but it was no longer in the vicarage. Probably it had been carried away as an additional weapon against anyone who might challenge them, but anyone carrying a cricket bat in March would soon attract attention. My bet was that it had been thrown away near the vicarage, thrown away with some fingerprints on it. I knew roughly the route that the suspects had taken away from the vicarage. They could have thrown other property away. There could be something caught on a bush, on a fence, something that would later connect the suspect to the escape route. So I went looking. I didn't go looking on my own, of course.

Most officers with an investigation like this on their hands, needing a large scale search carried out, would have called out the Territorial Support Group. This is a unit of 240 experienced officers available to any London station which needs urgent assistance. They're very good, very reliable, and very professional. I'd served for four years with their predecessors, the Special Patrol Group, and I'd used the TSG on door to door inquiries in some murder investigations. But I didn't want them on this search. I wanted the nervous, inexperienced naïve cadets from the Training School at Hendon. I wanted them to make a thorough search of the area. I wanted to see everything they discovered, and I've always found them excellent in this type of police work. I'm sure that it helps them in their careers to see this type of work in the raw.

The lads from the TSG would have carried out a very thorough search, but they would have used their experience and their judgement. They would have decided what was important and what to bring to the attention of the officers leading the search. I didn't want that. I wanted to see everything: every cigarette end, every sweet paper, every old newspaper, every discarded contraceptive. I wanted to be the judge of what was important. So I called in the cadets. They found the cricket bat very quickly, as the TSG would have, but they also called me to some discarded newspapers marked with old and muddy footprints. The newspapers, like all other exhibits, went immediately into a plastic bag tagged with a label, the date and my initials. Later on, they were matched to the shoes taken from the three suspects.

While the physical search was going on, a second team was going through collator's records at local police stations. Every station in the Metropolitan Police has its own collator's records. These are informal collections of information about criminals and suspected criminals living in the station area. The information is kept on cards rather than on a computer database, where it would become accessible by law to anyone listed on it. The information comes from the notifications of convictions sent out by the National Intelligence Bureau, messages from other stations: (*PC 123 Jones stopped a Jimmy*

*Smith CRO 1264/78 who gave an address on your ground. He had been visiting a known crack dealer over here*.) and local unverified rumours: (*Mrs Jones, No 26 The Avenue, told 456 Brown that her male lodger invites little boys into his room after school*). The collator at Ealing kept quite extensive records. One of the entries was John Ronald Horscroft.

He had Horscroft listed under safebreakers. There were not many, and Horscroft, whose CRO details were on the card, was the only one that fitted the description given by Jill Saward. He was shown as living five minutes from the vicarage, and his listed convictions included some for burglary, and for burglary with violence. Collator's cards also list the subject's known associates. On Horscroft's card we found Christopher and Andrew Byrne and Martin McCall. Somewhere, among the hundreds of statements already taken, I remembered one from a local thief which mentioned Horscroft with Christopher Byrne and another man being seen near the vicarage around midday on the day of the rape.

Horscroft was certainly worth speaking to. He was a possible suspect, but just one of dozens of people who would be questioned during the investigation. But the first police visit to Horscroft's flat made him a major suspect immediately.

He was seen six days after the rape at 6.30 a.m. That's a good time to find someone at home. A call during the day, or when the suspect is out at the pub in the evening, is as good as a warning. If chummy's facing serious trouble he can go on the run. For a minor matter he can prepare an alibi. But the 6.30 a.m. call is normally a surprise. Two officers knocked on Horscroft's door, one in uniform, one in plain clothes. There were none of the usual protests, none of the exaggerated shouting that some criminals use to distract inexperienced officers, to draw attention to this unwarranted police harassment. Horscroft was not surprised at being pulled out of bed at dawn. It had happened to him before.

'John Horscroft?' asked one of the officers, 'We've come from . . .' Horscroft did not wait for him to finish.

'Suppose you've come about that Paki I did over in Acton.' The officers said nothing. Horscroft got dressed without further question and came with them.

They told me after that they had no idea what Horscroft was talking about, but he was obviously willing to talk about a particular offence so they were justified in bringing him in. And someone who willingly admitted a crime of which he had not been accused must have a good reason; like wanting to hide his involvement in something much more serious.

'A Paki I did over in Acton.' This would not have been some pub fight, Horscroft was a robbery with violence man, so he was talking about a serious crime.

It did not take us too long to decide, after we had made a few phone calls and sorted through local records, that this was a reference to an attack with an iron bar and a knife on an Asian shopkeeper at his home. Horscroft had not been suspected of it, but his implied admission afforded ample grounds for his detention, and relieved us of the need to tell him we were making inquiries connected with the vicarage rape. I began to interview him. Within thirty minutes he had admitted 100 burglaries, and named eighteen accomplices. But the vicarage rape? A nasty business that. Not his style at all.

'Nothing to do with me, Mr Herridge.'

But while I was speaking to Horscroft, other officers looking for Christopher Byrne, found his brother Andrew. We were looking for the Byrnes because of their listed connection with Horscroft. Andrew was at Christopher's flat. He didn't know where his brother was, and significantly, didn't ask why police were looking for him. But Andrew was in a bit of a state. He had been quite badly beaten up. He was seen by a police surgeon soon after he arrived at the station, and very soon began talking about the day of the rape. He gave me three different versions of what he had been doing that day, but twelve hours on, at 7.00 p.m., admitted that he had taken part in planning the raid on the vicarage, and that he had gone later to help them to take property away. He agreed that the rape had been planned beforehand. He told me who had taken part.

I expected him to name Horscroft and his brother, and he did. But he also gave us the name of the third man, Martin McCall. After the raid on the vicarage, McCall had called at the Byrnes' flat, and, in a fury, had attacked the two Byrnes and their mother, warning them to say nothing about what had happened. Christopher's nose had been broken, their mother's collar bone had been fractured; Andrew had some injuries to his head. I'd had him seen three or four times by the police surgeon while he was making his statement. Five days later, on remand in Wormwood Scrubs, he fell into a coma. He was admitted to hospital, never recovered, never faced trial, and died on December 20, 1990. McCall never faced any charges in connection with his death, and Andrew had never put his allegations in a statement which could be used in evidence.

But at this stage Andrew told us that Horscroft's common-law wife, Jacqueline Defelice, was the person who had disposed of the knives and clothing used during the attack. The credit cards which had been stolen, most of the jewellery and the antique clock, had been passed on to a local receiver, who was later charged, but acquitted at court. When I passed this information on to the investigation team, one detective beat his head against his desk in mock despair. He had stopped and questioned this man soon after the rape, but had not searched his van which probably had most of the stolen property on board. I said nothing to him. No one makes a mistake like that twice. I'm sure this officer will be a much better detective because of this incident. We can all be great detectives in hindsight.

The receiver and Jacqueline were quickly traced and brought into the station at West Drayton from which the investigation was being run. Jacqueline was an alcoholic, totally dependent on Horscroft. She told us everything she knew about the robbery and drove round with us pointing out the locations at which she had thrown away the knives and the clothing. The men still had the credit cards.

McCall and Christopher Byrne were arrested at a flat belonging to another of the Byrnes. They were brought to West Drayton police station and McCall asked to see the officers in charge of the case.

Dave Lamper and I saw him at 1.30 a.m.

'So what's this all about?'

'It's the vicarage rape,' I told him.

'I've been worried sick about it,' he said without hesitation. 'I'm glad you caught me.' He admitted the burglary immediately but blamed the rape on Horscroft. He put all his admissions into a statement which he signed at 3.30 a.m. We then saw Christopher Byrne. He also admitted his part in forcing Jill Saward to have oral sex, but named McCall as the rapist. They repeated the admissions later in the day when their solicitors were present.

Horscroft, however, despite continuous questioning, denied everything, other than taking part in the planning. I decided against putting any of the men on identity parades. Each man had changed his appearance considerably, shaving off moustaches and drastically altering hairstyles. They could perhaps have been identified by voice, but why should Jill have to go through the ordeal of being in the same room as the men who had abused her so wickedly. The three men had all gone to the same hairdresser at the same time. And I had a statement from the hairdresser describing how they looked before she cut their hair. There was enough evidence to charge them.

Horscroft, McCall and Christopher Byrne were charged with rape. The three of them, with Andrew Byrne and Defelice, were charged with other offences in connection with the various thefts as well as causing grievous bodily harm to the two male victims. Horscroft was charged with two violent burglaries at Asian newsagents. (For some reason, which I have never fully understood, the Crown Prosecution

Service did not proceed with the 100 burglaries which he had admitted when he was first came into police custody.)

They all, except for Andrew Byrne, appeared at the Old Bailey on February 2 in the following year, 1987. We had prepared for a long trial with the prospect of Jill Saward facing days of cross-examination in the witness box. Anything could have been alleged against her, that she dressed provocatively, that she had consented to sex, that she had a local reputation for being promiscuous, even that she had not been raped by the three burglars, and that her injuries had been inflicted by an angry boyfriend. An unscrupulous defence is allowed to advance all these possibilities, without giving any advance notice of the line they intend to take. When we arrived at the Old Bailey, with Jill, there was not even a court ready for the trial, and we had to find a room in which Jill could wait, away from the press which had attended in force. Two hours later, the trial started and we found that the defendants were pleading guilty to the major offences.

McCall, Horscroft and Byrne pleaded guilty to aggravated burglary, the technical term for stealing from a house and using violence at the same time. McCall and Byrne pleaded guilty to the rape. (All the sexual offences against Jill had been included in the single charge of rape.) McCall admitted being the principal rapist, and counsel for Byrne, who had never before admitted his part in the rape, told the court that he was pleading only as one who had 'aided and abetted' the rape, but who had taken no active part in it. Then came the stunning sentences.

McCall received five years for the burglary and five years for the rape. That is, the same sentence for stealing a video recorder, some jewellery and credit cards valued together at £2,000, as for raping and buggering a woman, forcing her to take part in oral sex, and pushing a knife into her vagina. Byrne was given five years for the burglary, and only three years for the rape. Horscroft, who had taken no part at all in the attacks on Jill, and at one point had said to McCall, 'This is not what we came for,' was sentenced to fourteen years.

Mr Justice Leonard commented that the trauma suffered by Jill 'was not so great' and that McCall, who was then 22 years old, should not spend a disproportionate amount of time in prison. The sentences for rape were later condemned by Lord Chief Justice Lane as too low; he pointed out that existing guidelines for sentencing recommended a minimum of eight years with increased sentences where more than one man was involved, if the rape was repeated, and if there were other sexual indignities. Jill, who was in court to hear the judge's remarks, felt that his Lordship gave more emphasis to praising the hairdresser for volunteering evidence than to commenting on her own ordeal.

Every time I think about this case, I feel angry. It does take a lot to make me upset, even though I have always had a sympathy for the victims in all my cases. Some officers still see the victim as of secondary importance, a witness to be pushed out of the way before getting on with the main business of the investigation. So I have never been able to understand the judge's attitude. It seems as if Jill's rape was of less importance than the thefts and the assaults on the two men. The only good thing that came out of the affair was Jill's public appreciation of the manner in which she had been treated by police, and her encouragement to other rape victims to go to the police for help. The only reminder I want to keep about the Ealing Vicarage Rape is a picture given me by Jill inscribed, 'With thanks to Roy Herridge and his private army'.

# Shaggy Dog Stories

Never quite made up my mind about police dogs. Some, of course, are very good, some never seem to trace anything, but I've never heard of a police dog being sacked. All dogs are, of course, only as good as their handlers, and dog handlers are not universally respected among the rest of the force. They work an hour less than anyone else on the grounds that they need an extra hour to groom the hound.

Two dogs stay in my memory, one good, and one . . . Well, you'll have to judge for yourself when you read it.

The first dog came to my help one night at King's Cross. It was a quiet hot July night, nothing happening, and I was walking through Chapel Market. A white Ford van drove past me at the wrong speed. That is to say, it wasn't going too fast, nor was it going too slow. But it was certainly not a van that was being driven home. Just something about it that made me remember the number. When I came back to Chapel Market about an hour later, there was a white Ford van at the far end. Two men were loading something into the back. I called up on the personal radio but the van drove off almost immediately, and it was three or four minutes before anyone reached me. By then I'd reached the shop at which the van had been parked. The front door had been forced, and it looked as if a number of the clothes racks and shelves inside the shop had been emptied.

I circulated the number of the van I had seen earlier, as I was convinced it was the van that had been outside the clothes shop, and about 2.00 a.m. a car patrol found it parked outside a block of flats in Caledonian Road. Of course, it was empty.

So I had a message sent to the Yard to trace the registered owner, and I called for a dog van in the hopes that the dog could track from the van. Luckily, we got a good dog.

After sniffing around the floor of the van, the dog started determinedly off on a track leading to the flats. Without hesitation it led us up four flights of stairs and stopped beneath a trapdoor in a ceiling. We found a ladder, and a PC went into the loft. Suits, shirts, and shoes, had been stacked just inside.

The thieves were obviously in one of the nearby flats. I was all for knocking on every door until we came across someone who would not answer, but the Duty Inspector thought this was a bit over the top.

'Can't go waking up people at this time of the morning,' he said. 'Just have to give it up as a bad job.' And off he went with the half-dozen PCs who had been helping out. As I said, it was a hot July night and despite the hour, the police activity had brought a few people out onto the balconies to see what was going on. I was left with the two constables who had come with me from the canteen when we had first heard that the van had been found. While we had been at the flats the owner of the van had been traced, a David O'Sullivan with an address in Holloway. A quick check had shown that he had left there a week ago.

'Let's hang around a while,' I told the PCs. 'Chummy and his mates will have heard us going into the loft. Sooner or later they're going to pop out and have a shufti to see if we've really gone. Keep in the shadows here, pick a floor each and just keep your eyes open for anyone moving.'

It only took ten minutes. The PC beside me nudged me and nodded towards the fourth floor. There were two heads poking over the balcony looking around the courtyard. We stayed perfectly still. The heads disappeared, and within seconds we heard a door close. We knew what floor they were on but not which flat they were hiding in. So up to the fourth floor, check on the doors nearest the spot where we saw the heads looking out, and there's a choice of three.

We took one each. I got an answer, the PC on the left got an answer, but the PC to my right drew a blank. The woman who opened the door to me was still wide awake. She must have been one of those who came out when we first arrived.

'Sorry to disturb you, Madam. We believe that a number of smash and grab thieves are in one of the flats on this landing. Do you mind if I take a quick look round?'

'No robbers here, darlin'. But you're welcome to take a quick butcher's. The old man's gone back to bed, but there ain't no one else here.'

It might have been worth looking, but the PC from the next flat came in.

'Can't get an answer from mine, Skip. Funny, 'cos there's a window open.'

'Who lives next door, love?' I asked the old lady.

Bingo!

'Just moved in this week. Come from somewhere over Holloway, Irish name, something like O'Sullivan.'

It didn't take long after that. One of the PCs wriggled into the flat through the open window and unlocked the front door. We went through each room, finding odd shirts and suits draped over the backs of chairs. We went into the main bedroom last and switched on the light. I don't think I'll ever forget the scene; it was the clearest possible example of the ostrich syndrome.

There was a double bed in the centre of the room with three people in. They had pulled up the coverlet over their faces, leaving their feet sticking out at the end. Each pair of feet was clad in brand new shoes with unmarked soles. Two shoes still had labels on the soles. I pulled gently at the coverlet. Three faces blinked in the light, the man in the centre looked at me and at the two PCs. For the first and last time in my career I heard the immortal words.

'It's a fair cop, Guv.'

\*   \*   \*

The next dog was a little different. The same circumstances. One o'clock in the morning. A shop broken into, a van number noted, the van found in the courtyard of a block of flats. Call for a dog. The nearest dog van was about ten miles away, so by the time it arrived there was a substantial audience of police officers, residents leaning over balconies, and two or three drunks on their way home.

The dog van arrived with some drama. Headlights full on, blue light flashing, and the driver pounding away on his horn. (Dog vans don't have sirens.) The driver leapt out.

'Stand back!' he shouted, running round to the rear of the van. 'She's vicious when she's on a track.' He flung the doors open.

He had forgotten to bring the dog.

# Death Of An Accountant

Accountancy is not the most glamorous of jobs. You spend most of your time checking the work of other people who mostly do not want their work to be checked. Hayes is not the most glamorous of places. Most of it lies outside the reach of the *London A-Z*, unnoticed between the M4 and the Asian centre of Southall. Nothing special about Hayes at all. So a trainee accountant living and working in Hayes is unlikely to command much public attention, unless, of course, he is murdered. Then, for a very short time, he is considered important enough to merit a place on the front page of the local paper. Local murders, unless they involve sex or children, rarely make more in the nationals than a few lines on an inside page. Only the relatives left to grieve, the police left to investigate, and the murderer left to hide, remain interested.

On the evening of December 2, 1985, Peter Avery was not expecting to be front page news. Christmas was near at hand with the office party arranged. He had one more evening left at night-school, before the Christmas break. He was getting on well. Peter Avery had a future. He had just left his office in Station Road in Hayes where he worked as a trainee accountant. Peter was 19 years old and had been given the job when he had successfully completed an accountancy course. One of his fellow students, with whom he still attended night-class, had been given a job at the same firm after completing the same course. She was Jean Rushton. (This is not her real name. The young lady will now have embarked on a new life and should not be embarrassed by the recital of events over which she had no control.)

She was an outstandingly beautiful girl, about to become engaged to another local man, Larry Jones. There had been a close friendship between Jean and Peter, but she had brought it to an end when friends suggested that she really had to make up her mind about who was her regular boyfriend. Peter also had a girlfriend. But he had been more reluctant to end the relationship with Jean. The break up had been amicable and, as they worked together, they remained good friends, but to someone who might have been watching them together, perhaps as they left work, or attended evening-classes, it might have seemed that their good-humoured friendship concealed something deeper; that perhaps there was still a more significant relationship which both were hiding from their friends.

And there was someone watching them, or rather watching Peter. Since the beginning of the year, he had been aware that he was being followed, that someone was watching the family home, that, occasionally, there was someone waiting near the office when he left it. This was not the paranoia of an overly sensitive youth, his brother and father also suspected that the house was being watched, and two or three family friends confirmed that a young man 'was hanging around' when they called. There'd been a late night caller at the front door claiming to be lost. But it's not really a matter that you can report to the police.

'I think I'm being followed.' How do you go into a police station and expect the officer behind the counter to take the slightest notice of such a claim? Especially when you're a 19-year-old trainee accountant with no apparent enemies, no connection with crime, nothing at all about you to attract attention.

But police became interested when there was a more serious development. In September someone poured petrol through the Averys' front letter box late at night. Peter's brother, sleeping downstairs heard the noise at the letter box, and ran to the front door. There was someone running in the

distance, too far away to describe. There were no witnesses,
no suspects, no indication that there had been an intention to
set the petrol alight. Who would want to do a thing like that?
Never had trouble with the neighbours. Some of them didn't
get on that well with each other. Perhaps the Averys' house
had been mistaken for someone else's.

'But we haven't upset anyone that we know of.' They opened
the doors and windows, put the rug out in the garden, and
hoped the smell would go away, claiming for the damaged
carpet off the insurance.

But there was a suspect. Peter Avery thought he knew who
might have been involved, and told his girlfriend. Why not tell
the police?

'Nothing concrete to go on. I thought it could be that Larry
Jones, the fellow that Jean's going out with. You know I've
mentioned about someone following me. Well, I think it's him.
Jean says he used to get funny when he heard that we'd been out
a few times. She told him straight out once that she quite liked
me. He started to cry. I thought he'd got over all that. I bought
him a drink about a month ago at a disco. Didn't seem upset at
me then. Didn't say much, but you'd think if he had a grudge,
that was a good time to tell me about it.'

So at 5.00 p.m. on December 2, Peter Avery left work and
walked to the car-park at Hayes and Harlington Station, a
car-park used by hundreds of commuters and many of the
local business community. Crowded, not very well lit. Two
or three dozen other drivers were returning to their cars, as
Peter opened the driver's door of his own. That was almost
his last conscious action on this earth. A man, in a balaclava
and motorcycle helmet, came from behind him as the door
was being opened and stabbed him savagely and repeatedly in
the back and the stomach. The attacker's rage was such that one
of his blows missed his victim and cut open his own thigh. Peter
Avery, with at least four potentially fatal wounds, staggered a
few yards before falling to the ground and his attacker ran off
to the car-park entrance.

Other motorists who had seen the sudden and brief attack,

thinking that Peter had been merely punched by another motorist, ran to help him. His lungs, liver and kidneys had been cut into by the knife. He lost blood rapidly. By the time the first person there had lifted his head – 'I heard a sort of gurgle in his throat' – Peter Avery, 19 years old, trainee accountant, was dead.

The call to the police came very quickly. Because the station was so near, I, amongst other officers, was at the scene before the ambulance arrived. It was absolutely clear that the attacked man was beyond any assistance. A great pool of blood surrounded his body, so much that there was hardly any now flowing from the wounds. The eventual autopsy established that Peter Avery had less blood left in his body than had soaked into the ground on which he had died.

An investigation into a murder like this begins with no preconceptions. There is a menu of options, and every opportunity for any of the team to advance his or her own theory if there are facts to back it. There are two parts to it which have to be conducted at the same time. In the first part the scene must be preserved and photographed, the body and its clothing must be examined meticulously, and the weapon must be found.

There is no pattern in murders which indicate what will happen to the weapon. If it's a gun, it will almost certainly be retained. A knife is more likely to be thrown away. The post-mortem would eventually tell us what sort of knife we should be looking for, but until then we had to search for any knife. There was the railway embankment, the whole of the car-park, a nearby canal, all the little bins in the area; thankless boring necessary drudgery. The officers just know that they're looking for a knife, and also know there is no guarantee that there is a knife to be found. And have you thought what it means to search through a row of litter bins, search the entire contents? Collect each and every car number in the car-park, trace and speak to each car driver and passenger who had been there that day. Try and trace every visitor to the station during the crucial hours. A mammoth task. But this is undertaken in most murder investigations.

In the second part of the investigation, it is important to establish a motive, then you can limit the suspects by asking: who had the motive? It might be a motiveless murder, but those are comparatively rare in this country, so that option is · usually put to the bottom of the list.

Was it a car thief killing? Did Avery surprise someone breaking into his own car? The time made it unlikely. Thefts in car-parks normally take place when the commuters have parked and are unlikely to return for eight hours. British Transport Police confirmed that reports of thefts from cars in that car-park were very rare. Might it even be another motorist mistakenly attacking Peter because he thought that Peter was a car thief? The descriptions of the attacker, which we had very quickly, ruled that possibility out.

Was it connected with Avery's work? Had he found something out during an audit; something that gave him the power to blackmail a person of some consequence. Had he stumbled, or was he about to stumble, across a fraud; something so serious that a person would kill rather than risk being found out? Some small businessman making regular payments to a mistress? A VAT fiddle? No. His employer looked at the work he had been doing. Routine checking, small firms with regular audits. No one in trouble. No one trying to hide anything. Everything with which Peter was involved looked completely honest.

Or was it old-fashioned sexual jealousy? Something that we think is confined to the Continent, but which is a more common feature of English murders than is realised. When you consider that the majority of murders in this country are domestic murders in which killer and victim are related; when you consider that a high proportion of domestic murders involve some form of jealousy, *crime passionnel* is not confined to the Continent. It is common enough to form a routine part of police investigations when other motives are not immediately apparent. So one team questioned all Avery's friends and workmates, and their friends to see if there were any unknown sexual relationships. The office meetings held during the investigation made certain that every member of the team knew what was going on. Everyone's ideas were listened to and discussed. Everyone knew which way the inquiry was leading and that we were now looking for a jealous rival.

DS Tom Hoey was in charge of this part of the investigation. An old, experienced detective, Tom, was an expert at spotting witnesses who were lying, who were holding something back. He had a more important skill. He could work out when a witness was lying, for some innocent reason, when an attempt was being made to hide knowledge about the matter under investigation. He spoke to all the people with whom Peter Avery had worked and came across Jean Rushton. She would be getting engaged to her boyfriend, Larry Jones, on her 21st birthday. She had been friendly with Avery, knew his feeling that he was being followed, but had no interest in him beyond work. Yes, she'd been out with Peter two or three times, perhaps more. But it had upset Larry so she stopped. Tom spoke to Avery's girlfriend. Between her tears she told Tom about Larry Jones.

'Peter had this feeling that he had been followed. He did tell me that it could be Jean's boyfriend. Jean had hinted that he was jealous. Peter never saw him. There was never enough evidence to speak to anyone about it. It was just a feeling.'

This was the first sign of anyone with a possible motive. Jean was an exceptionally attractive girl with a career ahead of her. Her boyfriend was in something of a dead-end job. The murdered youth had been followed. Yes, there was just the shadow of a motive.

Other of their friends knew, or suspected, that Larry was unusually jealous of Peter. 'You know, spent quite a bit of time talking about it. Nothing violent, more sad than anything. Just sort of took it as something that had happened. Wasn't mad or anything.'

Tom Hoey interviewed Jones at the double-glazing factory where he worked.

Remember the old black and white films, the detectives

would talk to the boss, who called in the employee. 'These two police officers. They want to have a word with you.' All clean and straightforward.

The real thing can be quite tricky. All the exits to the office or factory have to be covered discreetly. A suspect with murder on his mind, however well he thinks he may have covered his tracks, can panic and try to run off at the sight of police. Even worse, he might attempt suicide. The arresting officers must be able to get to him without any workmate warning him. There is also the matter of timing.

Other officers had gone to question a friend of Larry's who worked in the same factory as him. Tom's previous inquiries had established that Jones had a close friend, Kevin Thatcher, and close friends can often back up or destroy a suspect's alibi. So the interviews had to be synchronised. Tom didn't know if they had confided in anyone else, so he could not risk a phone call warning one of the other's arrest. The interviews were not just a matter of two men in long macs asking a few questions. There had to be careful planning. Nothing like that in the black and white movies.

So at first it was a routine interview.

'Mr Jones. Sorry to disturb you at work. We're inquiring into the murder of a 19-year-old man in the car-park at Hayes. We believe you might have known him?'

'Yes. He worked with my girlfriend. We're going to be engaged soon. The murder was just terrible. Jean, that's my girlfriend, we're getting engaged soon, she's been very upset.' *But*, thought Tom Hoey to himself. *You're not upset. Your girlfriend's upset. But you're not.*

Did Jones know Avery? Avery? Was that his name? No he didn't know him. He would remember someone with a name like that. Jane had known him, of course. *Not quite the casual answer expected from someone with no connection with the incident. He could have just said he didn't know him. He was trying to appear unconcerned.*

'Killed in the car-park, just after work, wasn't he? I wasn't anywhere near the car-park. Know where it is, of course.' *Who suggested that he was near the car-park?* Did Jean Rushton ever tell him about Jones' theory that he was being followed?

'Yes, she mentioned it a couple of times. I don't know where Jones lived. Wouldn't know him if he passed me in the street. Jean's spoken about him, of course, but I didn't take much notice. Bit fanciful, young bloke like that thinking he was being followed.' *Just a little too much emphasis on his attitude towards someone that he allegedly did not know.*

Did Jones ever go to the car-park at Hayes station? Never. No reason to do so. The evening of the murder, it just happened that he knew what he was doing from the time he left work. His car had broken down in Slough, some ten miles away. A friend had picked him up to take him to the car, and the AA had towed the car back to his home. Someone was with him almost all the time that evening.

Tom Hoey wondered why someone with nothing to fear was so ready to advance an alibi for the evening of the murder. This wasn't a witness answering routine questions, this was someone who wanted to create an impression about himself. For what reason? He had not been a strong suspect until then. His answers put him in the frame, and Tom brought him back to the station so that I could have a word with him.

In the car on the way to the station, after he had been cautioned, Jones denied he even knew Avery. He told Tom that he could provide a complete account of what he had done on the day of the murder, a very detailed account. He went into some of the details. The time he left work, his car breaking down, the phone call to a friend to take him to the car. A much more detailed and spontaneous account than you or I could produce on the spur of the moment if we were asked to list our movements of forty-eight hours previously.

As soon as Jones had been brought in, he was put in the detention room, and Tom came to see me with his reasons for believing that the suspect knew more than he was saying. I went down to the detention room and found Jones washing his hands in the lavatory in the corner. He denied he was washing his hands. To me it looked like some feeble and mistaken attempt to remove forensic evidence.

'No honest. I was just having a piss.'

Jones had a long cut across the palm of his right hand. We called in a doctor to examine it straight away. The doctor found another cut on Jones's left thigh, a deep cut which had been sewn together with ordinary cotton. How had he done that?

'Bit of do it yourself. Knife slipped. Couldn't be bothered going off and waiting for hours round the hospital.'

Jones and Thatcher were interviewed at the same time, but separately. Thatcher also provided a surprisingly detailed account of what he had been doing over the last two days.

Jones, in his role as a man with nothing to hide, made no objection when we asked his permission to search his flat. The officers carrying out the search took Thatcher with them. They took possession of all the property they thought might connect Jones with the murder, but the most relevant items were a pair of gauntlets, and a pair of Adidas trainers. Thatcher suddenly cracked. He admitted that Jones had given him a knife to hide on the evening of the murder. He, Thatcher had taken it to a friend's asking him to put it away as he had bought it for a relative as a Christmas present.

We had found an unusual number of witnesses to the actual murder. They were able to give a detailed description of the man who ran away. We knew he was wearing a balaclava, training shoes and gauntlets.

When the officers had returned with Thatcher, he was ready to tell us where he had hidden a balaclava that Jones had given him, and who was looking after the knife for him. Jones, faced with these admissions, decided to tell us the truth. This was not a killing carried out on the spur of the moment, an attack motivated by sudden jealousy and hatred. Leslie Jones had not come home from work on December 2nd, decided that he could no longer bear the jealousy he felt at knowing that his girlfriend was so often in the company of another man. No, this was not impulsive. The killing of Peter Avery had been planned three months earlier.

Jones and Thatcher lived together with Jones' brother in a maisonette which Jones was buying. It was Jones who had been following Avery for the past year, driven by an unreasoning jealousy which convinced him that his girlfriend, Jean Rushton, was in love with Peter Avery. As early as September he had brought the knife he used in the killing, telling Thatcher, 'This is for my friend'.

Even when Jean agreed to become formally engaged to him in October, Jones' jealousy continued. More significantly he continued to plot with Thatcher. In November they bought a balaclava helmet from a motor-cycle shop to ensure that Jones' face was covered at the time of the attack. Two days before the murder, Jones carefully arranged that his car would break down about ten miles away from his house so that he could set up an alibi for the evening that Peter Avery was to be stabbed to death.

On December 2, Jones and Thatcher finished work together at 4.30 p.m. Jones cycled home, and Thatcher, with a motor-bike, arrived before him. At about 4.30 p.m. Jones phoned a girl friend, told her that his car had broken down in Slough, and asked that she give him a lift there that evening. Between then and 5.00 p.m., Jones changed, collected the knife, balaclava helmet, and a pair of motorcycle gauntlets and went to the car-park at Hayes railway station, knowing that Avery would leave work around five and collect his car.

Thatcher went to a local supermarket during the same half hour, and made certain that his visit would be remembered by not having enough money to pay his bill, and returning with the extra 30p a few minutes later. That still gave him time to take Jones on his motorcycle to the car-park to be there when Avery came out of work.

Jones knew Avery's car and was waiting near it. As the latter opened the driver's door, Jones, wearing gauntlets, his face hidden by the balaclava, ran at him and stabbed him savagely and repeatedly in the stomach and sides. His attack was so savage that he cut his own right hand as it slipped from the hilt and ran along the blade as the knife entered Avery's body and hit a bone. At another point he stabbed at his victim so wildly that he missed and cut into his own thigh. Avery clearly had no time to defend himself. Normally a person attacked with a knife has cuts to one or both hands, sustained in attempts to grab at or ward off the weapon. Peter Avery's hands were unmarked.

His attacker ran off. Peter staggered away from his own car, made one weak cry for help and fell down between two cars to watch his very life oozing from his many wounds. In seconds, he was dead in a pool of his own blood. Jones ran quickly away, and was taken back home by Thatcher on his motorbike. Some half-dozen witnesses who thought they had seen one man punch another several times, went to Avery, now lying on his back, his face already growing pale through the massive loss of blood.

Back at their flat, Jones and Thatcher continued with a well-arranged plan. There was one hitch. Up to that point, Thatcher sincerely believed that his friend was living in a fantasy, that he had followed Avery about, and plotted to kill him without any intention of following it through. But now Thatcher had to face reality. His friend had killed the man he saw as his rival. Thatcher, instead of humouring an obsession, was now a party to murder. He had no choice but to continue with what up to then had been an elaborate charade.

The knife was washed clean, replaced in the plastic presentation pack in which it had been bought, and later taken to a friend's house by Thatcher. The friend was told it was a Christmas present that had to be kept out of sight of the person for whom it was intended. Jones was picked up by a girl friend who knew nothing about the conspiracy at 5.55 p.m. and driven to Slough where he had left his car. He arrived there at 7.10 p.m. and immediately phoned the AA. Twenty minutes later, a patrol attended, and, being unable to fix the fault, towed Jones' car back to his flat. Jones gave the patrolman the impression that the car had been driven to Slough that day; the AA man, who made a statement later, was also puzzled by Jones' apparent indifference to the time it took to tow the car back. Jones, unlike the average motorist calling on the AA's services, appeared to be in no hurry at all.

The only real divergence between the two statements lay in their account of Thatcher's actions at the time of the murder itself. Jones claimed that he had returned to the car-park on his pedal cycle, but was unable to remember where he had left it during the attack on Avery. Thatcher, however, knew the location of most of the wounds inflicted. He may even have watched the killing. He admitted that he had helped to sew up the wound on Jones' leg with domestic needle and cotton.

There was little more to do. Jones pleaded guilty to murder and was sentenced to life imprisonment. Thatcher pleaded guilty to being an 'accessory before and after the fact' and was given a suspended sentence. Incidentally, the accessory charge, like the charge of murder itself, has never been made an offence by statute. When they are put to the prisoner at the police station, and at Crown Court, the charge reads simply, 'that you did murder . . . contrary to the Common Law'.

There was a sad postscript to this murder which had itself caused so much unhappiness for so many people whose lives would never normally be touched by crime.

Larry Jones' father came into Hayes Police Station after the trial to speak to the CID officers who had investigated the murder.

'I just wanted to say,' he told them, 'there's no hard feelings. You had a job to do, and you did it properly.' They nodded silently. They all knew about Mr Jones. In fact some of them had worked with him. He had been a PC at Hayes until he retired five years earlier. Shortly after his son had been sentenced, ex-PC Jones died.

# A Night At The Opera

It was not strictly a night at the opera, it was more of an evening. The night, and its events, came later. The Royal Opera House at Covent Garden is not, I understand, a recognised place to pick up a sexual partner, whatever your sexual preference may be, and whether your intentions be temporary or long-term. For one thing all the seats are very expensive. For another you have to book months in advance. With those two restrictions, it is understandable that any customer's first priority is to get full value from *The Flying Dutchman* rather some temporary titillation from flirting. I spend very little time at Covent Garden. To be truthful, I've never been there, so I can not explain the circumstances in which Laura, an American tourist, met Mike, a music teacher at a large public school. They certainly met at the Royal Opera House. They were certainly on their own, and possibly pushed against each other in one of the bars at the interval. Nothing historic or unusual, such encounters happen hundreds of times every day.

'So sorry about that. I seem to have spilled most of your drink. Let me get you another one. It's the least I can do.'

'Why, that's real kind of you. I had a sort of tough fight to get this one, and I reckon that I need a stiff drink to see me through the second act. Never knew that a few hours of Wagner required so much stamina.'

So Mike pushed his way through the crowd at the bar, had one of those lucky breaks in which the barman is looking in your direction at the moment you want to order and was back to Laura with two dry white wines in less than a minute.

'Possibly a Covent Garden record,' he told her. At their age, 20, they had few problems in communicating. They quickly found that they were sitting near each other, decided just as quickly that they would like to know each other better, and had no trouble in persuading two groups of four opera lovers to move one to the left to enable them to sit together.

After the opera, luck was still with them. They found a table for two in one of the nearby restaurants, and, over two Dover soles and a bottle of Australian Chardonnay, discovered tastes, experiences, and places in common. At the end of the meal it was clear that they had started on some sort of relationship. Whatever the nature of the relationship, it was able to survive the next awkward moment.

'It's late. We better think of moving.'

'Mike. This has been great. Now this sounds corny. Ordinarily I'd have been out of the opera, into a cab, and straight home. What with the meal and all, I don't fancy getting back to Notting Hill at this time of night on my own. You think you could be sort of white knightish and see me back there? That's if it's not taking you out of your way.'

No, it was not out of Mike's way. He lived a little further on in Fulham, and he had budgeted for a taxi back there. They talked non-stop in the taxi, and it seemed silly to stop talking just because the taxi had arrived at Laura's flat.

'Look, why not come in for coffee? I'm not going to get to sleep until I know just what tune it is we keep on humming. There's a whole heap of tapes in the flat. If we're both convinced it's Mozart, we should be able to nail the mother. I swear I just won't be able to sleep until I can give it a name.'

Again Mike had no objections. It was a very warm July night, not at all the night to spend alone in Fulham. Especially when there was a very attractive girl who was clearly interested in getting to know him better. Especially when, on the way back from the restaurant, she had unfastened two buttons of the silk shirt she was wearing. Mike was very careful not to make any chauvinist assumptions. It was a very warm evening, and her shirt might have felt a little too heavy after the Opera House and the restaurant. But, well it might have been an indication that she was interested in a little more than identifying an aria.

They went into her flat. She made coffee. He started to sort through the tape collection.

'I'll make a pile of all those with vocals on,' he called to her in the kitchen. 'Then we can eliminate the obvious non-runners, and sort through the possibles.'

He was kneeling on the floor when she came in with the coffees.

'Look,' she said. 'Don't take this the wrong way. But nights like this, when it's so warm, and there's no air conditioning, I like to be naked. Would that upset you?'

No, it certainly would not upset Mike. Laura was perhaps a little too broad, not quite tall enough to be a model, but there was nothing disturbing about the thought of seeing her without clothes on.

'If it makes you feel awkward, why not take your clothes off too?'

Mike thought that this type of dialogue was confined to soft porn films, and Soho bookshops. There was now a slight suspicion in his mind.

'No problem. Mind if I use your bathroom first though?' Laura was already taking off her shirt before he had left the room.

'This is just too good to be true,' Mike told himself. 'There has to be a catch.' On his way to the bathroom, he checked the other two rooms in the flat. Was there someone there with a camera, a boyfriend perhaps, ready to spring some blackmail scam? But no. The only people in the flat were Mike and Laura, and when he came back, Laura was completely naked.

'I'm not a committed nudist,' she said, with her back to him, crouching over the tapes he had already sorted out. 'Just sometimes it seems silly to be wearing clothes. Come on. Take yours off. Makes me feel a bit silly if you stay dressed.'

It took Mike less than a minute to strip completely. Laura seemingly took little notice of him, and concentrated on the tapes on the floor. Mike had a second suspicion. He had not yet seen Laura naked from the front. She certainly had breasts, but supposing they were just large male pectorals. Say Laura was really a man? He knew Notting Hill had its fair share of sexual deviants. He knelt cautiously beside her, and just as cautiously looked at Laura's pubic area. He gave an unconscious sigh of relief as he saw her pubic hair and the front of her vagina. The sigh of relief was replaced by a sigh of pleasure as he felt Laura's thigh touch his, without any sense of her flinching.

'I'm into touching,' she told him, picking up and putting down the tapes on the floor in front of her. 'Bodies are real fun.' She ran her hand round Mike's back before sliding it down over his buttocks. She seemed to touch him half-consciously, as if her real attention was still focused on the tapes.

Still slightly uneasy, he put his own arm round her, moving so that they were kneeling face to face from their original side by side position. She put her other arm round his neck, and as he felt her breasts against his chest he bent forward slightly to kiss her.

'Just touching, remember. Nothing heavy.' She responded to his kiss by holding him closer to her. With their mouths open and together, he put his tongue between her teeth, and his right hand between her legs.

Then he screamed in sheer agony as she bit hard and deliberately through his tongue. There was a slight tug of her clenched teeth, before she spat the tip of his tongue onto the floor.

I was the night duty Detective Sergeant at Notting Hill when the call came through.

'Male – seriously assaulted – Cornwall Crescent.'

The ambulance had already picked him up by the time

I arrived with two DCs, but there was still a group of passers-by telling each other excitedly what they had seen. I picked out the calmest of them, and asked him just what he had seen.

'This bloke, stark bollock naked, blood pouring out his mouth, and screaming, comes running out. Couldn't tell us what had happened. Poor bugger couldn't talk. His mouth was just full of blood pouring out. Lucky thing for him, there was this ambulance coming past. I waved it down. They took him into the back. Lady that's standing in the door of that house, she said something to them. One of them went in, and came running out quick. Then they were off. Sirens, lights, the lot. She knows all about it, but I reckon she's a bit shaken up. Someone should have a word with her. See if she's all right.'

So we went over to see what the lady in the doorway knew. It was Laura, of course. She was white and shaking. She looked as if she had just pulled a dress on.

'I had to do it.' She was holding her arms round her body in some sort of protective panic. 'He tried to rape me. I told him not to, but he just kept on.'

I found out, as tactfully as I could, that she was on her own in the flat, and that she had no close friends or relatives we could contact. I had a WPC called quickly from the station. The WPC talked gently with Laura, helped her to put a coat and some shoes on, and took her down to the station to be examined by a police doctor.

While that was going on, I went to the hospital. Mike was already in the operating theatre. One of the ambulance crew had recovered the half-inch of tongue, and the surgeon was hopeful that it could be stitched back on if they worked quickly enough. Mike would obviously not be talking to anyone that night.

Back to the station where the woman police surgeon had finished her examination.

'Ah, Sergeant Herridge. Shouldn't think you'll get far with this one. No injuries, bruises, scratches. No penetration. No signs even of an ejaculation. She's not a virgin. Most you'll get is an attempted. But I wouldn't even bet on that. Asked her about her knickers. Wasn't wearing any. Fact, wasn't wearing anything. Nor was he. They were sorting music tapes out when he made his move.'

'Sorting tapes out in the nude?'

'This is Notting Hill, Sergeant Herridge, not Surbiton. Very free thinking, the music lovers of Notting Hill.'

Laura was still white when I saw her.

I had a quick word with the WPC who had been looking after her. 'She's no little innocent, Sarge. Knows the words for all the parts and how they work. But she is frightened and shocked. I don't think she's putting it on.'

'Did she say anything about the man?'

'Nothing at all. Just that he went too far.'

'Went too far?'

'That's all she'll say. She's too shocked to say anything else.'

'She asked how he was?'

'No. No sign of interest.'

It's not a cast iron rule, but I've found it's usually a good indication, that if a supposed attacker, other than a murderer, doesn't ask about the victim, then they've committed the assault deliberately. They don't want to know the consequences of their action. It was too early to take a statement from Laura, so I just asked her to tell me briefly what had happened. She told me what she had told the doctor. Neither of them had any clothes on. He had kissed her. That was OK. But when he tried to enter her . . .

'Excuse me asking this, but I have to. Was he erect?'

'He might have been, or it might have been his finger. I was just scared. But he just wouldn't stop. I'd told him that I didn't want to go any further. I bit him instinctively. It was self-defence.'

She stuck with this story later in the day when she made a full statement, making no attempt to hide the facts that she and Mike had been naked, that they had only met five hours or so earlier, and that he was in her flat at her invitation.

Mike, when he could eventually speak, agreed with everything she said.

'I honestly can't remember if I was erect. I certainly expected that we were going to have sex. I wasn't rushing things, and she was certainly cooperating. You could say she was enthusiastic. Then, just like that, she bit through my tongue. Not just a warning nip. A deliberate bite. You can imagine the strength it took. She meant to go right through all right. It was no accident. She knew what she was doing.'

Well, we either had a GBH on Mike, or an attempted rape on Laura, but no one could expect a jury to decide what had really happened. I'm certain that Mike had no intention of rape. He struck me as very sensitive. If Laura had said that they would just stick to touching, he wasn't the type to assume that she really wanted the whole thing. But nor can I accept that Laura was some sort of vampire who deliberately lured Mike to her flat in order to bite off his tongue. But her attack, or her panic, had gone on a little longer, and was a little more deliberate than some unconscious reaction.

We had to mark it up as no further action. Neither of them wanted to press charges.

Some months later I was discussing the case with a more cultured colleague. His first question was, 'Any idea what the opera was?'

I'd found the programme when I had gone back to Laura's flat to collect Mike's clothes.

'Something about Valkyrie,' I told him. 'What are they?'

'Group of very fierce women,' he told me. 'Think nothing of biting off a chap's tongue. He was lucky really. There were nine of them all together. Had this Laura bird had eight mates with her, they'd have bitten off a lot more than his tongue.'

# Far From Professional

There were three of them. Jimmy Ryan was 16, Amit Patel, 15, and Bobby Thompson, 14. They could see Riordans office block from Jimmy's house just off the Harrow Road, and it gave them an ambition beyond their routine nicking from shop counters and unattended cars. Offices, they reasoned, were bound to have money. Offices would have things that could be sold easily. Offices closed at 5.00 or 6.00 p.m., and had no one around until the next day.

So one late February evening, the three Paddington boys decided to become burglars and chose Riordans as their target. There was one little difficulty. To get to the back of Riordans, you had to go through an old graveyard, and an old graveyard on a winter's night takes a bit of courage even for the average adult burglar. The three youngsters, having never carried out a burglary before, had enough to be nervous about. Naturally none of them was going to admit to any unease and there was a certain comfort in numbers. So, having assured themselves that Harrow Road was free of patrolling policemen, they climbed over the graveyard gate and stumbled through the tombstones to the back wall of the office block. Even the sound of the traffic in the Harrow Road, fifty yards away, could not completely remove the niggling feeling that there just might be something behind one of the headstones. They fought the temptation to keep looking behind them, fixing their eyes determinedly on the tree that Jimmy had picked out as the easiest way in earlier in the day.

'This one,' he hissed, and within a minute they were up

and onto a flat roof. There were no giggles or nervous jokes.
This was serious thieving. Jimmy had already looked at the
window they wanted to open and knew it was protected
by iron bars. They had brought a hacksaw, but with a few
tugs the rust and old concrete gave way without too much
noise, the sash window was opened and they were in. But
what was there to steal? They had a vague idea that there
would be money lying around. They had brought nothing
with them to open locked drawers, and they were still too
inexperienced to put aside the natural fear that any moment
all the lights would come on and they would find themselves
surrounded by policemen. Almost desperately they grabbed
at what was on the desk tops, a few calculators, pens, paper
knives, and a leather briefcase with a combination lock. Back
through the window. This time the graveyard didn't look
so threatening. They were coming out of it, not going in.
They split the meagre haul with Jimmy keeping the locked
briefcase and promising to share whatever he found in it and
went quickly back to their different homes.

Jimmy's older brother, Rory, woke up as he got into
the other single bed in the house they occupied with their
parents.

'Where you been, Jim?'

'Broke into that office place round the corner.'

'Did you so? And what did you get?'

'No money. Few bits of machines, might get a few quid
from Greasy Annie for them.'

'Well then. I've got me eyes on a better place. Give it a
few nights and we'll try that one. Night, now Jimmy.'

So a few nights later, Jimmy, Rory, and 15-year-old
Nicky O'Brien broke into the Kigu warehouse through
a rear window. Nicky was unable to read or write. His
mother took little notice of him and his friends sometimes
gave him food when his mother had not left a meal for him.
He was there as more out of pity then for the practical help
he might be.

Now this was better. This was what burglary was all

about. Plenty of stuff here. Pens, tie pins, cuff links, penknives, a calculator, someone's electric razor, and a brand new anorak. They stuffed everything into their pockets and plastic carrier bags, went back through the window, a quick look and down the road and then home. Nicky had a bag of pens and cuff links with him and was quite happy with his share. Back at the Ryan house they looked through the haul.

'Nice lot of gear, Jimmy.'

'Not bad for a night's work then. What you reckon it's worth?'

'Must be, easily . . .' and then the doubts set in. All those tie pins. Who wears tie pins? Ball points? In the market you could buy them for a few pence each. The calculator? Greasy Annie had bought the last lot. Would she want any more? Fifteen rolls of Sellotape. Not such a good night after all. Almost a waste of time. The gear was put away in different cupboards and lockers. Jimmy saw Greasy Annie about the pens and tie pins. Greasy Annie was Greek and her only adjective was 'fucking'.

'Must be fucking joking. Fucking tie pins. Fucking pens. Why you no steal something worthwhile? I can't sell no fucking tie pins. Come back when you got something fucking decent to sell.'

It was May before Jimmy felt confident or desperate enough to try Riordans again. He went with 14-year-old Bobby Thompson. The night was not at all as dark as it had been in February. And they were luckier. This time there was a cash box with £60 in it. They took that and a calculator.

Jimmy went back the next night with Bobby, Nicky O'Brien, and Amit Patel.

'Bound to be a lot of stuff that we missed,' Jimmy told them. 'This'll be a good one.' There was only £1 in cash this time, and the usual assortment of calculators, dictating machines, pens, and a watch. They broke open the doors of other offices, ran up to other floors and forced doors and desks. No cash. Just the usual machines.

'Greasy Annie won't buy this lot,' a despondent Jimmy told them. 'She's got too many already. "Can't fucking sell this," she'll say. "Why you no steal something I can fucking sell?"' The rest of them laughed half-heartedly, split the takings and went back to their homes in the side streets off the Harrow Road.

Jimmy's mother, by this time, knew what he was doing. There was so much office equipment, so many pens, so many useless bits and pieces around the house that she had to hide some in her bedroom.

'Be careful son,' she would tell him. 'Don't let your father know. It would kill the poor man.' Two weeks later the two brothers went back to Riordans with Bobby Thompson. It was for them an all-time low; reduced to stealing a coffee mug, a hammer, some pens, and a calculator, they took their frustration out in forcing open drawers, smashing windows, breaking down doors. They caused twice as much damage to the offices as the value of the equipment stolen. But Amit Patel and Nicky O'Brien, seeing no profit in the pointless thieving of the Ryans, had decided on a separate enterprise.

'That Greasy Annie. She's a Greek. Them Greek blokes are keen on shotguns. We could nick a few of those. Make a bit more money than those pisspoor calculator things.'

A little more sophisticated, this project. There was a gunsmiths on the Harrow Road, Holland and Holland. The factory backed onto the railway line, and the two boys had to walk through a tunnel to reach the embankment at the back of the gunsmiths. There was a burglar alarm, nothing very elaborate. It took the boys a few seconds to disconnect it, and remove the iron bars from a first floor window and scramble through. Amit stayed at the window, and Nicky went down to the workshop. He picked out four shotguns from the rack on the wall and went back to the window. Amit looked at them quickly.

'This one ain't no good. The barrel's bent.' Nicky left it on the floor and went obediently back down to the workshop to find a replacement. They had not planned on the number that would be stolen, but as Nicky had taken four, it seemed logical that they should come away with four. The two boys took the shotguns to a derelict house a few hundred yards away and hid them in the loft. They were home before midnight.

Jimmy Ryan had decided to go solo. Walking through the streets near his home, he noticed one house in which the back window had been broken. There was a wooden board nailed insecurely to the frame. Late in the evening, there were no lights on in the house. Jimmy pulled the board away, climbed through the window over the kitchen sink, pulled out drawers and opened cupboards without finding anything that Greasy Annie might want, and decided on the television set. He picked up the set, opened the kitchen door and walked the half-mile back to his own house. If anyone thought it strange that a 16-year-old boy should be walking through the streets carrying a television set at midnight, they didn't communicate their curiosity to the police.

Back at the Ryans', Mrs Ryan shook her head.

'I don't know what will become of you son at all. Better be putting it in the bathroom until we think what to do with it.' Rory was more enthusiastic.

'Should get a few bob for that. We'll ask around, see who's interested.'

There was no one interested for the next few days until 7.30 a.m. on Wednesday, when Jimmy and Rory were woken by their mother.

'The police is here. Some nonsense about stolen property.'

I looked at them. They looked at me. It was hard to stop them talking.

I'd been called in to form a small burglary squad after the shotguns were stolen. The previous burglaries at Riordans and Kigu were recognisably the work of kids. Many easily

opened drawers and cupboards had not been forced. Others
had just been pulled out and tipped on the floor. Professional
burglars search systematically opening bottom drawers first
and working their way upwards without closing anything.
If you do it the other way round, you have to close each
drawer to look in the next. But the shotguns were a serious
change. It might have been kids, it might have been kids
stealing on behalf of older criminals. It might have been a
professional stealing to order, the guns were worth perhaps
£15,000 each at today's prices.

So we started by looking through the collator's records.
Who were the local burglars? The receivers who would be
willing to name petty thieves, the kids with a reputation
for staying away from school. Had the Juvenile Bureau any
ideas? More importantly, did the local shopkeepers have any
suspicions? It's getting to be almost an old-fashioned idea
now, but I've always believed in speaking to newsagents,
greengrocers, people who deal every day with the local
residents, who hear the local rumours.

The police records were not much help, but the shopkeepers did the trick.

'That Ryan lad lives round the corner. I've been coming
back late from the pub some nights, and he's always around
with one or two of his mates.'

'Bit of a simple lad, Nicky. He was in here the other day
trying to sell a handful of pens. Poor lad. Don't think his
mum's much help to him. Wouldn't want to get him into
trouble. He knocks around with those Ryan boys. Don't
think their father is too bright either. It's always Mrs Ryan
that pays the bills.'

There were several bits of gossip like this. Nothing
definite, a lot of suspicion about the Ryans, and then . . .

'He was playing about with one of those little tape-
recorder things. You know, speaking into it, and then
listening to himself. Him and a couple of other lads.'

So I applied for a search warrant. That's not as informal
a procedure as is sometimes imagined. You have to list the

reasons for wanting the warrant on a form known as an 'information'. You also have to show some factual grounds for your suspicions, and you have to swear to it on oath.

'I swear, that the contents of this, my information, are true and correct to the best of my knowledge and belief.'

So, with the three PCs who had worked on the squad, I knocked at Mrs Ryan's door the next morning at 7.30 a.m. (One of the three had gone round to the back of the house, just in case anyone should throw anything stolen out of the back window.) I produced the search warrant, showed her my warrant card, and told her why we were there.

'God bless you, Sergeant. You won't find a stick of anything stolen in this house.' Mrs Ryan in her curlers and dressing-gown.

'May we speak to the two boys?'

'Well, they're both fast asleep. But they'd never do anything wrong at all. Now you're sure you've got the right house?' Yes, I was sure. So upstairs we went to the back bedroom. Jimmy was asleep in the bed on the right, Rory on the left. They both woke quickly. I told them who I was, and what I was doing there. I hardly had time to get through the official caution before Jimmy told me that he'd done the office block opposite him three times. Rory joined in. 'I helped him once.'

I looked at Mrs Ryan. She looked at me.

'I just can't understand why you do things like this. You know what your father will do. He'll kill you both, that's what he'll do.'

'And what about the warehouse?'

'Yes, that's down to us.' Rory got out of bed. 'We've still got most of the stuff.' He took PC Dick Quinn to the landing. They came back with a calculator and a few pens.

Frankly it was boring and routine. These were no professionals who would deny everything, try to put the blame on other people, and finally insist on having a solicitor. They were just unemployed kids who had failed to make any money out of crime. We went through the house collecting calculators, pens, paper knives, even the TV set that had been left under a towel in the bathroom. The boys admitted everything. Mrs Ryan dropped her pretence of not knowing anything.

'They're my sons,' she said with a shrug. 'I couldn't stop them, and you wouldn't expect me to give them away now, would you?' Not only did the three of them talk quite freely, but they also told us who else had been involved with them. We took out more search warrants and went first to find Amit Patel. He had a stolen bicycle in his hall that we knew nothing about, but he admitted breaking into Riordans. And he told us about Bobby Thompson. Bobby had joined in some of the burglaries and had carried one out on his own. Next was Nicky O'Brien. The others had not been too bright, but poor Nicky, unable to read or write, just about able to steal, his only pastime, his only means of forming friendships.

'I took this thing you talk in and gave it to Greasy Annie. She only gave me two quid for it that I spent on food. She said there was cracks in it and it wasn't worth much.'

Nicky was the first to tell us about the shotguns. 'Amit wanted a gun, and said that he knew where there was some. We took four guns and hid them in a dump house. Greasy Annie took us to some Greek women who said they would buy two of them for their husbands if they weren't stolen. We're supposed to go back tomorrow and get the money.'

What about the other two guns?

'I think Amit wanted to get bullets for them so I hid them again. I think he was being stupid.'

Next came Greasy Annie. She had a shop on the Harrow Road and deserved her local nickname. She was overweight and underwashed, and had no respect for anyone. She had some dictation machines hidden in her shop and one or two calculators. She was abusive from the moment she was arrested to the moment she was bailed.

'Fucking kids, always fucking pestering me. Must have

left their fucking things in my shop. I never fucking bought any fucking thing from them.'

Even Annie, in the end, admitted taking Nicky and Amit to friends who thought that their husbands might like 'the fucking little nuisances. Wouldn't leave me in fucking peace.'

'Look,' she said, as she left the station after being bailed. 'I tell you what I do. You forget about all this and you can come round and fuck me.'

No one took her offer up.

So that was about the end of it. Rory went off to Borstal. The rest were put on probation apart from Nicky. His mother was too busy to attend court. He went off to a home in the country. I hope he was happier there.

There are only two things that stick in my mind about this team of amateur burglars. The first is a conversation I had with a young DC just before I retired.

'Kids,' he was saying. 'You've got no chance. Nick a 15-year-old, he goes shtum and demands a solicitor even when we have him bang to rights.'

Perhaps he had never tried talking patiently to a suspect. Perhaps I've got a kind face. Perhaps I was just lucky in the people I arrested. I think if I arrested the Ryans today, the results would be the same. A lot of people who have committed crimes genuinely want to get it off their chests. It's usually solicitors who want them to keep quiet.

And the other thing, the other two shotguns. I'll never forget the look of despair on the face of the Holland and Holland manager when I called him in to identify the guns. They had been a matched pair made to order for a very wealthy sportsman. Amit had seen *The Sweeney* too often. He knew what you did with shotguns. You sawed off the stocks and the barrels. In ten minutes he had reduced £40,000 worth of the gunmaker's craft to a couple of hundred quids' worth of an armed robber's close friend. One of the other guns had gold emblems embedded in the butt. The gold had been taken out and was later recovered from under the floorboards of another derelict house. The duke for whom the gun was being repaired was not at all amused.

# The Old Lady Who Lived Down The Road

There's one in every town, every village, nearly every road – an old lady who lives on her own. Some of them have plenty of friends, relatives who call on them frequently, a strong network built through a local church or pensioners' association. Some are lonely, unknown, out of touch with living relatives, ignored by neighbours. Some, like Rosa Keen, live alone, and live happily without the contacts that most of us think are essential for a normal life.

Rosa Keen was 72 years old; a spinster, who had lived in the same house for over fifty years. Her parents had died in the early '70s. She had no brothers or sisters, and one regular visitor, Arthur Purser, aged 68 years, who called on her every other Sunday. But Rosa was not a complete recluse. She had an old bicycle on which she could be seen almost every day riding to the local shops. Almost every day, she could be found sitting on a bench outside the local Sainsbury's talking to other shoppers. She certainly did not shun company, but her real concerns were with the birds and hedgehogs which thrived in her wildly overgrown garden. Her house in West End Road, Ruislip, a typical '30s semi-detached, could hardly be seen for the overgrown bushes in the front. The path to the front door was almost invisible under unmown grass and weeds.

Inside, the house had hardly changed since her family moved in in 1934. Electricity was available but Rosa never used it, relying on candles for light if she had to move about in the dark. She used the front ground-floor room as her bedroom, and left the upstairs almost unused. In the sideboard she had a nest of mice, not an accidental nest, a nest cherished for the little lives that brightened her own days. She was healthy, in full control of her life, and could be there to this day, standing in her garden throwing crumbs to the birds, leaving out saucers of milk for the hedgehogs at night, cycling to Sainsbury's, perhaps adding something to the lives of those to whom she chatted.

'If she's happy, living alone, no holidays, no telly,' they may have asked themselves, 'what have I got to be miserable about?' Perhaps they left the bench outside Sainsbury's feeling a bit better for having talked to that old lady who lives down the road. Probably they didn't even know Rosa's name. It could all have gone on, quietly, suburbanly, but on April 8, 1988, about 3.00 p.m. on a Friday afternoon, a man knocked on Rosa's door, and when she answered it, hit her so hard with a hammer that she was knocked out of her slippers. Imagine that. The old lady opens her front door, and a stranger hits her so hard with a hammer that for a half-second, her body is airborne, before it falls lifeless to the floor. Then the man with a hammer bends over her and hits her so hard on the head again that her blood splashes the faded paper in the dark hall.. Then he hits her twice again with the hammer. Once on each side of the face. Imagine that. Imagine hitting the face of an old lady already dead. You would have to be mad, or drunk or heartless.

On the afternoon of Rosa Keen's murder, David and Karen Taylor were drinking heavily in the Bell pub, about half a mile from her house. David, 36 years old, unemployed (jobs were not as hard to come by in 1988 as they are now), a petty criminal on bail for theft, a man with a history of violence, had married Karen three months earlier. Both of them had been married before, with the three children of their previous unions being cared for by their discarded spouses. Their income was £95 a fortnight from the DSS. The money they needed for their heavy drinking came from borrowings and from petty thefts. David Taylor's lifestyle can be epitomised by a futile attempt to persuade a local off-licence owner to let him have a crate of lager on credit, and by the theft for which he was on bail, stealing £700 from Karen's grandmother.

So, on that Friday afternoon, they were in the Bell public house at midday, drinking continually, talking to bar friends, hoping someone would lend them money or at least buy a round, keeping their ears open for an opportunity without risk. They left the Bell at 3.15 p.m.

When they were later questioned by police, both claimed that they had walked down West End Road in Ruislip. They had certainly passed Rosa Keen's house at number 156.

'Place I told you about,' David said to Karen. 'Called there few days ago. Bank Holiday must have been. Thought the old lady might have a few jobs she needed doing. Earn meself a few quid. Showed me all round. Right old ruin. Nothing been touched for years.'

David, if the conversation with Karen ever took place, did not enlarge on the work that he hoped he would be paid to carry out. They were at Ruislip just after 5.00 p.m. and spent most of the evening in another public house in Pinner.

It was, unsurprisingly, the milkman who called police to Rosa Keen's house. When he called on Monday morning at 7.00 a.m., he found the pint of milk that he had left the previous Saturday still on the step. The milkman called a neighbour and the neighbour called the police. Two uniformed constables arrived, listened to the milkman's fears for Miss Keen's welfare, and kicked open the front door. There was Miss Keen just inside the door, her head bloodied, and her skirts pulled up obscenely revealing her underclothes and her partially opened corsets. She had been first robbed of life and then robbed of the dignity that the dead deserve. Had this been done to check for and steal cash from her underclothes? We never found out. We did learn during the investigation that it was common in Victorian times for women to store money and valuables in their underclothes and corsets.

Poor Rosa Keen had to stay there dead and undignified while the necessary bureaucracy of an investigation slowly unwound. The two uniform officers, satisfying themselves quickly that there was no one else in the house, called their Duty Officer, a uniformed Inspector. He collected a Detective Sergeant who had come in early to deal with the crime book entries that had accumulated over the weekend. They satisfied themselves that the two PCs had not exaggerated the circumstances of the death (young inexperienced officers often imagine that every dead person they are called to has been murdered), touched nothing and called AMIP, the Area Major Investigation Pool, at Kensington. I took two Detective Sergeants and went to 156 West End Road.

The body was inside the hall a few feet from the front door. One of Rosa's slippers was still in the position in which she had been standing when she had been hit. It seemed clear that she had been hit with such force that she had been lifted out of her slippers. There were clear blood splashes on the wall, indicating that she had been struck on the head while she was lying on the ground. The blood had spurted upwards. Had the blood hit the wall while she was falling down, it would have had a similar falling pattern. Significantly, there were no obvious blood stains on the disturbed skirt and underclothing. Whoever had struck Rosa Keen would have been spattered with wet blood, but whoever had opened her corsets had not transferred any blood to them. If only one person was involved that meant that he, or she, had washed very thoroughly after killing her; much more likely then that there were two people.

It was difficult to tell from the state of Rosa's house if anything had been stolen. There were no close friends or relatives who could say what, if anything, was missing. But as it seemed clear that whoever had killed Rosa had also some part in pulling up her skirt to see if she had money tucked in her corsets, it appeared we were looking at a murder that had occurred in the course of a robbery. We were probably also looking for someone who was a stranger to Rosa, otherwise the murder would have been carried out further inside the house.

We left a policewoman on the door of the house after it had been searched, and went back to the station to set up an incident room and assemble an inquiry team. We leave police officers at murder scenes for a number of reasons. The most obvious is to keep the property secure until we find someone to take it over. But the officer can also record the names and addresses of relatives, or friends who might call, not knowing about the murder, and from whom we may later want statements.

At the end of the day, the policewoman had an interesting tale to tell us. A young woman had come up to the house three times during the day. On the third occasion she had started speaking to the policewoman.

What had happened to the old lady? Did police know who had done it? Had anyone seen them? Was there more than one? Was it someone local? Was she really dead? Would they be going round local pubs asking for witnesses?

The policewoman recognised that these were more than spontaneous questions put by a simple-minded girl. It was almost as if she had been given a list of them to ask. The policewoman decided that the girl was local and easily traceable, and so did not alarm her by asking her name and address. But she gave us a very detailed description.

But another thing was happening. All the little local criminals were genuinely horrified by this senseless murder, and very quickly information was filtering back to the team, through the usual half-pint with informants, and even the direct telephone call.

'That David Taylor, guv. Drinks in the Bell. He's been talking about the old girl for weeks. They was in the Bell just before it happened. Him and his bird. Must have been walking down the road at the time.'

We checked on the collator's records, found out where he

lived, and put a surveillance van outside so that we would know his movements. David and Karen Taylor came home late at night. Karen's description matched that of the woman who had spoken to the WPC earlier that day.

The four officers who were to carry out the arrests had no problems at David Taylor's house when they called on Wednesday morning. He answered the door, half-dressed, unshaven, but not obviously alarmed even having been shown the search warrant, and told that it had been issued in connection with a murder investigation. Karen Taylor, still in bed, confronted by a WPC, appeared equally unconcerned. David was quick to tell police that he had been round Rosa Keen's house. He had been there on Easter Monday hoping to get work. The old lady had shown him all round the house, every room in the house, even inviting him to look inside cupboards. The listening detectives recognised the caution of a man uncertain as to where he may have left his fingerprints.

David and Karen were both willing to talk about how and where they had spent the weekend. They had spent it together. Unfortunately, David, in the kitchen, gave a different sequence of events to those supplied by Karen in the bedroom. They were arrested, cautioned, allowed to dress, and taken to Uxbridge Police Station. There they were shown the notes that had been made so far about their conversations with the officers who had arrested them. Karen willingly signed the police notebook in which her replies had been recorded, David refused to sign those relating to him.

At the Taylors' house, and at that of Rosa Keen, teams of SOCOs (Scenes of Crime Officers) were searching for links, evidence that would prove that David and/or Karen Taylor had been in physical contact with Rosa Keen. They would be looking for clothes that either of them had worn, tickets for bloodstained garments taken to the cleaners, ashes of a garden bonfire in which such clothes may have been burnt, shoes which had been recently brushed, seeds, dead leaves, grass which might have been picked up from Rosa's over-grown garden. At Rosa's house, in addition to the samples of blood taken from the walls, they would look for marks on doors, skirtings, or window-sills, marks which could not have been made by a frail old lady; marks which would have transferred paint or wood chippings to the clothes or shoes of an intruder. And of course, they would be looking for fingerprints.

At the station both David and Karen, still maintaining their 'this is nothing to do with us' attitude, allowed us to take samples of their blood, their hair, their saliva, their nails. Their solicitor came to the station, and was present while they were separately interviewed. Three times they gave the same version of that Friday afternoon's walk. They passed Rosa Keen's house. David pointed it out as a place he had looked over with the old woman who had lived there. Neither of them went in the house on the Friday that Rosa was killed.

But the neighbours were now talking.

One of the checks that police always make in a major inquiry is with anyone who might have been able to confirm or disprove anything said by the suspect. So the Taylors' neighbours were asked if they saw them on the Friday of the murder. Well, no, they hadn't seen the Taylors on the Friday, but the Taylors had dropped in on the Monday evening. Lynn Bevans, aged 30, knew the Taylors only as neighbours; her common-law husband, Ian Burgess, sometimes had a drink with them. Their lodger Deborah Steers knew the Taylors by sight. But in the flat on that Monday evening, David Taylor told Ian Burgess that he had hit Rosa Keen with a hammer. He found he had some blood on his sheepskin coat. Could Ian get rid of the coat for him? A remarkable conversation you might think to be held in a council flat in West London.

'It's all true,' Karen told the two women, 'Dave hit her with a hammer.'

Dave also told Ian that he was worried because one of

the gloves that he had worn had a split in one of the fingers. It was just possible that he had left a fingerprint at the old lady's house. Later that Monday evening, the five neighbours watched *News at Ten*. The presenter gave details of Rosa Keen's murder.

'That's the one I was talking about,' Dave said. 'Did her with a hammer. Fuck all in the house worth nicking.'

A very remarkable conversation for a West London council flat.

'Don't think much of the weather. Wish the council would get its act together over the rubbish collection. See Wogan on telly last night? By the way I've killed an old lady. Can you give me a bit of a hand in case the police come round.' It must have been that casual, it must have been that unthinking.

I can never really understand why people do this. If a killer was so haunted by his conscience I could see why he would have to tell a close friend or relative. If it was a cold-blooded gang killing, taking out a rival drugs dealer for instance, there's a commercial necessity that certain friends and enemies should know that you were responsible. But a mindless murder like that of Rosa Keen, a killing that appeared to cause so little concern to the Taylors who were able to go to a Wimpy Bar while poor Rosa's body was still warm, who spent the evening drinking without showing any signs of distress, why should anyone tell the next door neighbours about it?

With the neighbours' statements there was now enough evidence to justify charging the Taylors with murder. They were charged at 4.00 p.m. but made no answers. About three hours later, Karen asked to see her solicitor, and then asked to see me.

'I want to change my statement, Mr Herridge. I want to tell you all the truth.' This was 'Yes', she had been drinking with David in the Bell until after 3.00 p.m.; 'yes' she had walked down West End Road with him. But he had gone into number 156, the old lady's house, while she had walked on to the Wimpy in Ruislip. When he came in later, he told

Roy after receiving his Queen's Police Medal from Lord Bramall of Bushfield, the Lord Lieutenant of Greater London.

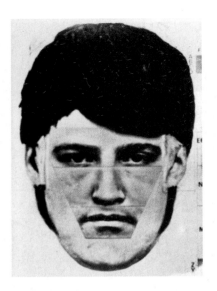

Photofits of two of the three men who attacked Jill Sawar at Ealing Vicarage.
(© Press Association Photos)

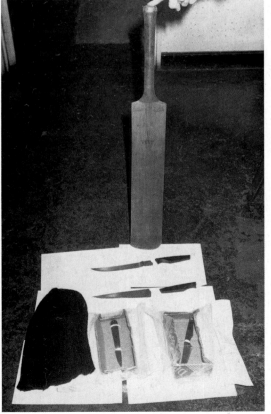

The weapons used against Jill, her boyfriend and father at Ealing Vicarage.
(© Press Association Photos)

Rev. Michael Saward, Jill's father, who was beaten around the head with a cricket bat. (© Press Association/Topham)

Health visitor Julie Iddles, whom Nicholas Price prevented seeing his stepdaughter Heidi. (© Press Association Photos)

Nicholas Price and his stepdaughter Heidi, whom he allowed to starve to death.
(© Press Association Photos)

Ian Erskine, the wealthy Bank of England official, who was killed during a sado-masochistic beating session.
(© Press Association/Topham)

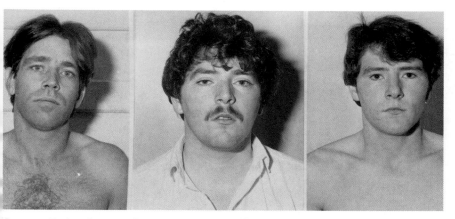

George Daly, George Stephenson, John Daly (l to r) who murdered four people during a burglary to obtain shotguns to carry out a wages robbery. (© Press Association Photos)

Joseph Cleaver and his invalid wife Hilda who were burned to death by Stephenson and the Daly brothers at their home in Fordingbridge. (© Press Association Photos)

Rosa Keen, the Old Lady
Who Lived Down the Road,
and the sitting room of
her house which had not
changed since the 1930s.
(© Press Association Photos)

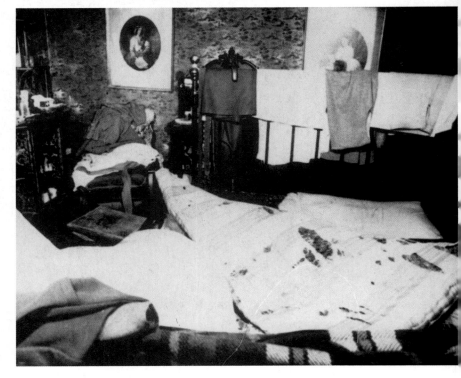

Muriel McKay. Two men were convicted of her murder, but her body was never found. (© Popperfoto)

The billhook found at Mrs McKay's house in Wimbledon after her disappearance. It was later found to belong to a neighbour of the Hoseins'. (© Topham)

Police searching Rook's Farm to find some trace of the missing Mrs McKay. The search lasted for over a month without finding any sign of her. (© Press Association Photos)

her that he had hit the old lady. He had some blood on his coat. When they heard the old lady was dead, they knew they would have to get rid of the coat. When the statement had been taken, I gave a copy to David Taylor sitting alone in his cell in another part of the station.

In the morning, just a week after Rosa Keen's life had been ended, I went with the two Taylors to Uxbridge Magistrates Court where their names appeared on the list posted outside the court. The list just shows the defendant's name and the charge; so you get a mixture of the most trivial and the most serious crimes in the country:

J Smith. Theft.
W Brown. Drunk.
S Williams. Drink/drive.
D and K Taylor. Murder.

Before we went into court, David Taylor told me that he also wanted to change his statement. He admitted going into 156 and hitting the old lady. He told us approximately where he had thrown away all the clothes he had worn at the time of the murder, and the hammer which he had used as a weapon. Karen had said in her statement that David had been carrying a hammer on the day of the murder, he admitted using a hammer, and the injuries to Rosa Keen were consistent with hammer blows.

It might not seem very urgent then that we recovered the hammer, but this would not be the first time that defendants had admitted a crime, and had then pleaded not guilty when the case came to trial. So there was a thorough search of the area between Rosa's house and the Wimpy Bar at Ruislip. This included seeing the bin men who had emptied street receptacles, the foremen of the depot at which they had been unloaded, and even an inspection of the site at which waste was dumped or incinerated. A number of hammers were recovered and tested forensically. Even the brightly polished surface of a new hammer can retain sufficient samples of blood, hair, or bone to enable a connection to be proved, and the scratches and grooves in older tools could hold a wealth of evidence; but none of the recovered hammers carried any indication that they had been used by Taylor.

But one other puzzle we had to solve was the extent of Karen's part in the murder. She said she had left David outside the old lady's house, and that he had joined her later. He confirmed this in his own statement. But I was not happy that we had the real story. Right at the front of my mind was the fact that whoever had interfered with Rosa's clothing, obviously to see if she had money hidden on her, whoever had done that, was not bloodstained. David Taylor must have been heavily splashed with blood. The house had been ransacked after Rosa had been killed, perhaps even while she was dying, and there were bloodstains in a number of the rooms. The two sinks had not been used, so the murderer had not tried to wash any blood away. It seems certain that there was someone with him. Neither of the Taylors would admit that Karen had gone into the house. So what other ways were there to connect her to the killing?

The fact that she was with David all day and was not seen on her own at any time was strong evidence, but not strong enough. But a conversation in the Bell pub before the murder indicates that not only was the murder planned, but that Karen knew what was going to happen. During the conversation one of the other people in the bar remembered David saying, 'I've got a job to do later over the weekend and I'll have some money then.' He also remembered that Karen seemed disturbed by this and told David that he should not be talking about it.

In another conversation after the murder, when the Taylors were talking to their neighbours, David was heard saying to Karen, 'If I get done for it, tell them that she tried to shut the door on me.'

This seems to be a clear indication that Karen was at least present when David knocked on the door of his victim's house. But we were never able to prove that Karen went into the house. The statements that both of them made were sufficient to convict David of murder, for which he was given a life sentence. Karen pleaded guilty to being an accessory before and after. She received a suspended sentence.

As far as the law is concerned, Karen took no part in the murder. She admitted staying outside the house, and David Taylor supported her in this. David Taylor was certainly callous enough to have searched the old lady's body as she lay dying behind her own front door, but he never admitted it. Not the first murder that has been solved without everything being accounted for.

If you should think that this murder was a one-off, a temporary error by a man with no money and too much to drink, think about Sally Monks. Sally Monks was an old lady who lived on her own in Ruislip. When neighbours had not seen her for three days, they broke in and found her lying bloody and unconscious in a back room. She had been hit round the head several times with a hammer. David Taylor did that as well, about four weeks before he killed Rosa Keen.

# A Touch Of Sideways Thinking

Investigation, 90 per cent of the time, is just hard work: reading statements, interviewing witnesses, trying to find out who is lying and why. But now and again you get a flash of inspiration that, when it works, cuts out all that hard work.

Jennie and Margie had opened a dress shop in a new shopping centre at Staines. It was small enough for the two of them to keep an eye out for amateur and professional shoplifters, so when their stock-taking began to show shortages, they became concerned about security. They introduced alarm tags. No one tried to steal anything but they continued to lose dresses, shirts, blouses. Some of them were worth £40, some £400. Had someone got a duplicate key? They changed keys, but continued to lose stock, nothing dramatic, one or two garments per week.

Eventually they called in the police. The DC dealing with it was baffled. He had narrowed the times down. A single dress, sometimes two, would disappear overnight. The owners were certainly not stealing and claiming the loss on insurance. There were no signs of break-ins, no rear entrance. The only way into the shop was through the front door, and as Margie said, 'Unless there's a midget wriggling through the letter box, there's no other way anyone can get in.'

The DC came to ask my advice about it. So I went back to the shop with him. He was right. There was no way into the shop other than by the front door. The rear wall, the roof and the floor were sound. The side walls were covered with store cupboards which had never shown any signs of being disturbed. As Margie had said, the only way in was through the letter box.

But suppose it was not someone coming through the letter box, but something. Who was working in the shopping centre when all the shops were closed? The DC had found out that there were visits by a security firm, but that most nights there were three cleaners working for four or five hours. We got the key of the cleaners' room from the precinct manager, went to their room, and found what I hoped we would. There were two broom handles in a corner, with a roll of industrial masking tape on the floor beside them. One of the broom handles had a large hook screwed into the end. We taped the two broom handles together and went back to the dress shop. With the front door closed it was quite possible to push the handles through the letter box and manoeuvre them to use the hook to lift a dress from a rack and pull it towards the letter box until it was near enough to reach a hand through and pull the dress and its coat-hanger through.

Three search warrants for the three cleaners' houses, half a dozen dresses and shirts recovered, and three pleas of guilty. Not one of the great cases in the history of 20th century crime, but satisfying enough to stay in my mind.

It was still in my mind six or seven years later when I was asked for help by a former police officer who was now acting as head of security for a large wholesale warehouse. They were losing video recorders, not just the one or two that the owners would expect and accept as a normal business risk, but dozens. Bob had carried out all the usual checks, impromptu searches of staff vehicles, increased patrols at night and weekends, a few security officers in plain clothes posing as customers, all to no result.

'How many regular customers do you have, Bob?' I asked him.

'Hundreds, easily. Small shopkeepers who stock up every

week, can't take the risk of stocking more than they are likely to sell.'

'Anyone using more than one trolley?' The store trollies looked big enough to carry enough stock for a small shop for a week.

'No, just the teacup man. Stuff he buys is disposable, takes up a lot of room.'

'Teacup man?'

'Yes, he sells disposable cups and beakers to canteens and places like that. Fills up every week. Buys so much that he brings a mate with him to load the trollies.'

'Let's have a look at what he takes.'

The cartons that the teacup man took were eighteen inches wide by fifteen inches deep by twelve inches high. The tops were not sealed. (Who was going to steal a handful of disposable plastic cups?) There were about 2,000 to a carton.

'What else does the teacup man buy?'

'Just these. Nothing else. Must do well out of it. Got a smart new van.'

I made a quick calculation. The teacup man might be making money elsewhere, but if he was living off disposable cups, his profits were low. He was buying something like 100,000 cups a week. Even at a 200 per cent mark up, he could not make more than £100 a week. I opened one of the cartons. The foam and plastic cups were just stacked inside. There was a warning on the top of each carton that the contents could be easily crushed. I looked at Bob, and Bob looked at me. If they were easily crushed, it would be possible to open the carton, put a video recorder in the top, crush the cups underneath, and close the carton again.

And that's just what he was doing. They caught him the following week. He had been taking out half a dozen video recorders a week for the past six months. He got two years. His assistant, who kept a look out at the end of the stack, and who carried all the cartons, so that staff would not be suspicious over the weight, got two years suspended.

I can't claim any originality in my way of thinking. It was based on that old story of the factory worker who was stopped every week taking out a wheelbarrow filled with odds and ends of discarded factory rubbish. The security guards searched through the rubbish every time, never finding anything that the worker should not have had. On his last day at the factory, the guards asked him to tell them, for the record only, what he had been stealing.

'Wheelbarrows.'

# A Love Of Country Houses

Estate agents are very good judges of character. They need to be able to distinguish the optimists from the realists among prospective purchasers. They need an ambassador's tact to persuade vendors that their properties are not worth £100,000 more than the price for which they can be sold. We are talking of course of experienced estate agents, not the fly-by-nights who saw no reason why their lack of expertise and professional knowledge should debar them from the quick profits that were made at the end of the 1980s. We are talking of agents who have been in business for forty or fifty years, agents whose clients want their houses listed in *Country Life*. Barshaw's is such a firm (not its real name of course), Barshaw's of Kensington. So when their Mr Benson saw the Rolls Royce stop outside the office, and the well-dressed Mr Mason step out, Mr Benson was not immediately impressed.

He had seen clients before who had hired Rollers simply to create an impression, time-wasters who had enough money to indulge in the bourgeois vice of wanting to look round stately homes, but not enough money to buy that sort of property; con men who used a Rolls and expensive estate agents to fool prospective victims. Part of Mr Benson's expertise lay in sorting out the curious from the committed. Mr Mason was given a seat in Mr Benson's office. Mr Benson noticed with approval the elegance of Mr Mason's suit, the absence of the school or regimental tie favoured by those too anxious to make an impression, the apparently genuine Rolex Oyster.

So how could we help Mr Mason? Mr Mason was looking for a country house. His voice was not out of the top drawer, but that's not where the money is nowadays is it? He had seen photos of two such houses in Surrey in a recent issue of *Country Life*, placed there by Mr Benson's own firm. The interior photographs had been particularly appealing; he had, in the past, seen both houses from a distance when driving past. Without undue haste or discourtesy, Mr Benson was able to establish that Mr Mason had a large house in Wimbledon and a large apartment in Madrid. It was clear that the price sought for the *Country Life* properties did not present a problem. Mr Mason would find no difficulty in paying cash. He did not of course make such a vulgar claim. He merely indicated that there would be no delays while banks or building societies made their various inquiries. Mr Mason would be very willing to give a reference at Coutt's Bank when and if he found a suitable property. Without Mr Benson having to ask, Mr Mason also made it clear that if it was required he would be very willing to give some proof of identity.

Mr Mason was leaving for France later that day; he spent more time out of the country than in it, and while not wanting to make a too hasty decision, he would appreciate being able to make arrangements today to view at some convenient future date. He had a rather full diary, but if Mr Benson was able to propose dates now, he would willingly rearrange his own schedule. He handed Mr Benson a typed list of his engagements, with those that could be rearranged, circled in red.

Mr Benson would be happy to see what could be done immediately. Perhaps Mr Mason would like coffee while he made his phone calls? During the next twenty minutes, Mr Benson found two mutually convenient dates for Mr Mason to view the houses, allowing him about two hours for each visit. Two hours is a reasonable time to look over houses with six bedrooms, servants' quarters, a tennis court, and fourteen surrounding acres.

'Who are the present owners?'

'Publishers, Mr Mason. Ditchling. They do these rather grand books on capital cities.' Mr Mason knew of the firm, and showed that he was impressed but not overwhelmed. He made a firm appointment for three weeks hence at one house, and decided that the other, when he had seen the sizes of the rooms, was not quite what he had in mind.

He called at Ditchling Manor, and was shown round by the owners. Yes, this appeared to be what he was looking for, but of course, the final decision depended on his wife. When would it be convenient for both of them to return, preferably in a fortnight's time?

The owners consulted their diaries. They would be away for the two days at the beginning of the month. Then they were up in London, for two nights the next week. Would the 10th be convenient.? Mr Mason consulted his diary. No problem. He and his wife would return on the 10th. He was certain she would like it.

They came back on the 10th. Mrs Mason did not like the house. It may be that the owners were a little too preoccupied with their recent misfortunes. They'd had the burglars in. Some quite good paintings, and a few antiques had been taken. Mr and Mrs Mason expressed their sympathy, thanked the owners for their time, and drove away.

'I thought they had a Rolls when he came last time,' said the lady of the house as she closed the front door.

'They did, dear. They did,' agreed her husband. 'Jaguar now I see. Pity she didn't like the place.'

Mr Mason made many similar visits to country houses, arriving in an expensive car, and charming the owners with his appreciation of the particular qualities of their house, the fine staircase, the fireplaces by a contemporary of Adams, the 'rather fun' chimney pot on the west side. Mr Mason paid little apparent attention to the paintings and furnishing other than, when necessary, to congratulate the owners on a particularly fine piece. Invariably, he made an appointment to come back with his wife at a convenient date. Invariably they had to tell the owners that it was not quite what they wanted.

You will have recognised by now that Mr Mason was a very sophisticated burglar specialising in paintings and silver, with a fairly simple technique. He kept his eye on the pages of the fashionable magazines, and checked the photographs of fashionable houses to see what was on display and easily removable. He used his visits to estate agents to discover when a house would be empty. He could use the same technique at a local country pub. Mr Mason had the charm that made conversation with him easy.

'Who lives in that big house up the road?' And in five minutes Mr Mason would know if the owners were home or away. Sometimes, acting on a hunch, he would drive straight into the grounds of a house, go to the front door, and look expectant if it was opened to his knock.

'Mrs Porson? Mr Mason, we have an appointment at midday.' When Mrs Porson professed ignorance of the appointment, Mr Mason became enormously embarrassed, consulted his copy of *Country Life*, and apologised profusely for mistaking the house. If no one answered the door, he made a careful survey of the outside, and once convinced that the house was closed for a period would break in and help himself. His good car (with false number plates), and his willingness to provide a card with his address were strong insurances against his being suspected of common theft.

Had Marcantonio Cohen, Mr Mason's real name, spent all his time burgling country houses, he might still be free today, although by now his *modus operandi* would have been on the computer at the National Identification Bureau at Scotland Yard. He had carried out something like twenty country house burglaries, netting him several hundred thousand pounds, and in hindsight appeared to have established a pattern which would have merited a dedicated police squad to track him. But the burglaries were spread over about eight police forces, and four different regional crime squad areas and criminal intelligence areas. So no really strong pattern would ever be logged.

One station might deal with the theft of paintings and silver from Abercorn House, but there would be no reason for the detective investigating the crime to see it as anything other than an enterprising burglary, without any other connection. If he had the time, or there was a Detective Inspector supervising him who realised that this was something more than a local burglary, a description of the property might be circulated a little more widely. It might even rate an entry in the *Police Gazette*, the twice weekly confidential publication that lists escaped prisoners, major wanted criminals, and expensive, identifiable property. If the owners knew enough, if they had been sufficiently farsighted to have their valuables photographed, and if the property had been properly insured, the theft might figure in one of the many magazines for antiques collectors. So Marcantonio Cohen went on being lucky, or went on cunningly dodging detection through avoiding repeating burglaries in the same area, or visiting the same estate agents.

He stole what he knew he could sell. Pictures that were valuable but not sufficiently well-known to attract attention when they appeared in a dealer's gallery; silver that was too good to melt down, but again not so old that it would be out of place when used for fairly grand dinners. He made one or two mistakes, but, as I said, had he stuck to country houses he might still be free. But Marcantonio was an almost obsessive burglar, and he had another speciality. He stole milkmen's round books. They were of no apparent value to anyone. The milkmen who had them stolen did not even think they had been stolen. The loss put them to a good deal of work, and they spent a lot of time checking details with their customers. One or two dairies may have suspected very honest milkmen of deliberately losing their books to hide their own fiddles. But the thefts were never reported to police.

And why was Marcantonio so interested in these books? Well, think of the information they contained. Names and addresses for a start, always useful for a burglar who likes to knock at a door first to ensure that a house is empty. And, of course, the dates when people were away. When Marcantonio was not screwing country houses, he was breaking into modest suburban semi-detacheds, and stealing property lower down the scale: videos, jewellery, trinkets, one list of property stolen even showed a child's Swatch watch. He liked to keep busy, and keeping busy meant selling antiques to shops that asked few questions, or at auctions at which there was little time for anyone to check the provenance of the items offered. He was using stolen cheques and cheque cards to buy more antiques to sell at auction. He bought or rented three houses to store property that he could not quickly dispose of. He changed cars frequently using names from stolen credit cards, and he nearly always carried £2,000 in cash. The lady who passed as his wife at country houses, Pat Gentry, also helped in his more routine thieving. He was with Pat when his luck ran out.

They were driving round Paddington with a stolen cheque book. Pat was following their usual practice of buying small antiques with stolen cheques to sell later, when one of the dealers from whom she had bought two small figurines became suspicious.

'Something wrong there,' thought the dealer. 'Anyone buying that way must be trade, and anyone buying trade would have asked for a discount.' The dealer rang the police station, gave details of the cheque used and the index number of the car in which she had seen Pat drive away. It was one of those days when everything in the police system worked. The cheque had already been reported stolen and was logged on a computer; the index number of the car was passed to Information Room and circulated, and three officers in plain clothes in Chelsea saw the car and stopped it.

They explained courteously to the well-dressed Miss

Gentry that they were inquiring into the theft of some cheques, that someone of her description had passed one of the cheques to a shopkeeper. Might they look at the cheques she had in her handbag?

'Certainly,' she said, handing them her cheque book, and the cheque card identifying her as Mrs Pethick, the real owner of the cheque book. At this stage, there was still a slight chance that she, with the help of the very plausible Marcantonio, might have bluffed her way out. Once away from the police, they would be untraceable. The car was not in their name, they lived nowhere near this part of London. They could conceivably have just talked their way out. But Marcantonio took on the aggressive role of a man whose wife is being unjustly accused.

'What's going on?' he demanded. 'Why are you annoying my wife?' Two of the officers took Gentry to the back of the car, while the other stayed at the front to prevent Marcantonio interfering.

'Look,' she said, 'there's a grand in it if you let us go.' When the officers looked puzzled, she mistook their bewilderment for greed. 'All right. Two grand then. Just take it and pretend you haven't seen us.'

The officers recovered from the surprise of being offered an enormous bribe by someone who appeared to be a routine kite artist. They arrested her and Marcantonio immediately and had Marcantonio open the car boot. In the boot were the two ornaments bought at the antique shop and a British Airways bag.

'Take the bag,' she urged them, 'There's about seven grand in it. Use your sense. Take it and forget about us.'

The bag was crammed full of bank notes. The officers took them to Notting Hill Police Station. When the cash was counted it came to £7,200.

To be fair to Gentry, we discovered later that she was not so much interested in saving her own skin as that of Marcantonio who was wanted on a three-year-old warrant on twenty-three charges of burglary. At Notting Hill Police Station Marcantonio denied that he knew Gentry, claiming that he had only met her that morning. He gave his own name as John Collins and stuck to it. He refused to supply any details about himself, and officers from the Cheque Squad were called in to interview them. They weren't getting very far and decided to check the address that the couple gave. They took Gentry to Portland Road in Ashford, opened the front door and then called me. I had a quick look at the house, ordered it to be secured and then went to see Marcantonio.

'Aladdin's Cave' has become a bit of a cliché for stores of stolen property, but that's the only adequate description I can give for Marcantonio's house. There were boxes of ornaments and antiques in the hall. One back room was full of cassette and video tapes, radios and TV sets. A bedroom had a number of mink coats and new suits. Another room had pictures lying against the wall, small statues and ornaments. You may get an idea of the amount of property when I tell you it took two officers four days to list and label it all. Then there were the cheque books, building society deposit books, cheque cards and credit cards. It was time to speak to Marcantonio Cohen.

I've mentioned before, I always believe in being pleasant to prisoners, whatever they've done. Perhaps there have been one or two exceptions to that, but generally I try to convince prisoners that their best chance is to tell everything and cooperate with me. I'm not knocking the other officers who had been dealing with Marcantonio, but it was almost as if he was waiting for me to interview him.

'It's all been thirty miles per hour up to now,' he told me at the outset. 'But I can see you're a hundred mile per hour man. What can I tell you?'

Well, he told me a lot. I had a succession of interviews with him, took him to court, had him remanded in police

custody, had more interviews, and in the end he had
admitted burglaries totalling in today's figures almost £1
million.

I took him to his house at Ashford first and went through
all the property there. It was here that he first showed signs
of the 'no honour among thieves syndrome', blaming many
of the thefts on other named and unnamed accomplices, but
trying to keep Gentry out of as much trouble as possible.
(Two of the burglars he named I found, after a lot of
inquiries, just did not exist, but we did arrest another
man who had carried out many of the minor burglaries
with him.)

'So Marc, where did this lamp come from?'

'That was from the house in Wimbledon, Mr Herridge.
The one I got those vases from.' A note in my pocket book,
and his initial to agree that was what he said.

'These candlesticks?'

'Same place, Mr Herridge.' Another note, another initial.

'This inkwell? Looks like silver to me.'

'Silver, all right, Mr Herridge. I think it's Georgian.
Dealer wouldn't have it. Said it was a reproduction, so I
wasn't going to let it go cheap.'

'But where did it come from?'

'Got me there, Mr Herridge. Had it for a year. Might
have been from that big place in Surrey. Just can't be
certain.'

So when I had taken Marcantonio through every item
in the house, and identified a number of burglaries, we
had to go on a second stage, taking him around in a
car so that he could point out the houses that he had
broken into. That led onto a third exercise which one
unfortunate DS of mine had to undertake. Making a list
of the house he had pointed out, searching the crime
books at the local stations, listing the property stolen,
and then checking it against the property unidentified in
his house.

There could not be a 100 per cent tally because of his practice of selling at auctions and to antique dealers. There was
little prospect of recovering anything that had been sold this
way with one very notable exception. One of his burglaries
had been at the house of an art collector. Marcantonio had
taken about twelve pictures whose value then was around
£100,000. Some of them were too well known to sell to
dealers, but one minor work found its way to the United
States. I found myself in the unusual position of having to
send a detective to New York's Christie's to recover one of
the stolen paintings that had been put up for auction, not by
Marcantonio but by someone well down the line of dealers
from the one to whom it was first sold. Christie's, the US
Customs, and the US Embassy were most cooperative, and
what might have been a bureaucratic nightmare turned out
to be a pleasant cultural experience for a DC, who, when he
saw the picture, wondered what the fuss was all about. (Art
lovers might care to know that it was Lucien Freud's *Unripe
Tangerine* painted in 1946.)

Well, that was the story of Marcantonio Cohen except for
two other features, and it's those by which I still remember
him. He was clearly distressed when he found that we were
going to proceed against Gentry for a number of offences
including attempting to bribe a police officer, handling stolen
property (she had helped him to dispose of and store much of
the property he had stolen in the six months they had been
together) and passing stolen cheques. He was even more
distressed when I told him that we would be applying for
her to be kept in custody until he had been tried. However
she was granted bail. He then said, 'Could you put a good
word in for her at her trial? She has always been under my
influence.'

I told him, 'I'll tell the truth at the trial. She is under your
influence. Without that she would hardly be in this position
and I'm sure not involved in crime.'

'Can I see her before she leaves court?'

I told him that it was the prerogative of the jailer at the court, but that I had no objection to it. A quick meeting took place under the supervision of the uniformed jailer, and they parted with a farewell kiss. As she walked up the stairs and left the court she turned to me and a colleague and said, 'Give me your personal office number.'

'Why?' I asked.

'I might ring you about 8.00 tonight. Stay by the phone after 8.00 tonight.'

Again I asked, 'Why?'

'Marc asked me to try to find something out that may help you.'

So three of us sat by the phone in my office until 10.00 p.m. We were almost giving up, when a young officer came up from the reserve room with a message for me. It read:

> *Go to the post-box at the corner of Pope's Lane, Acton, outside a firm called AM Roy's. It's in the box.*

The reserve officer said that the message had come from a woman who refused to identify herself.

We went to Pope's Lane and easily found the post-box. It was much harder to persuade the post-office authorities to open a letter-box before collection time. Eventually a controller at Mount Pleasant came out about 2.00 in the morning and opened it up. Besides the letters, there were three drawings rolled up carefully. They looked like squiggles to me, but I knew that Marcantonio could tell one squiggle from another, so these must be important squiggles. They turned out to be drawings by Matisse, valued at £50,000 each which had been stolen from a director of the National Gallery. Marcantonio would never admit that he knew anything about them, so they did not feature in any charge.

He and Gentry pleaded guilty to a number of charges at the Old Bailey. Marcantonio went off for seven years, Gentry was put on probation. When Marcantonio came out of prison, he made a very cheeky request. A lot of the property that had been recovered was restored to the people from whom it had been stolen, but a substantial part of it was never claimed; it had seemingly never been reported stolen. So in police records it was listed and stored as Marcantonio's personal property, just as his watch and three cars had been stored.

'Well,' he said, 'You haven't been able to prove that the rest of that property was stolen so it has to be restored to me.' And he was right. It was property which he had been unable to link to any particular burglary, which had never been claimed, and which was therefore legally his. He got it back.

About three years after he had been released, I had a call from a Detective Sergeant in south London.

'Got a bloke in at the nick, Guv,' he said. 'Turned his drum over, and he's got a load of boxes with your name and an old property number on them.' Yes, it was Marcantonio. He'd been caught thieving again, and he had been so busy that he had not even had time to unload the property that had been returned to him. He's inside again. That property is back in the prisoners' property store, and I haven't the slightest doubt that when he's free again, it will be returned to him for the second time, probably with a few more boxes of untraceables from this second arrest.

I had one more surprise from the Marcantonio case. He had a number of mink coats and could not remember where or when they had been stolen. When we eventually put them on display – you know the sort of thing where police put together a whole range of stolen property and then ask people who have reported crimes which might relate to the thefts to see if they can identify any of their own goods – when we put the minks on display, we had about four positive claimants for each coat. Do you really blame me for the title of this book?

# Keystone Robbers

I've come across a lot of very clever villains. But I've also known some masters in the art of cocking things up. There was the man who took his dog with him to hold up a local garage. He ran off with the money and left his dog behind. All the police had to do was let the dog loose and follow it home. I've heard of a burglar who tried to get into a house through a bathroom window and became wedged there until the owner came home, and I've been told about (and don't know whether to believe it or not) the two armed robbers who parked their car with the engine running, ran into a supermarket, took the contents of the till, and then leapt back into the wrong car. But the most inept were the three lads who robbed the coal-yard.

They told the whole story afterwards so there's no reason to doubt them. It began after the pub turned out on a Friday night. Now this was in the days before central heating was common and coal lorries were a common sight. Our three heroes were passing the local coal-yard when one of them pointed out that as it was Friday night, the safe in the coal-yard should be full, the coalmen having paid in their round monies. In seconds they were over the gate, across the yard and had broken into the office. And there was the safe. Not a monster safe, a fairly reasonably-sized safe which three strong young men could easily move onto the back of a lorry.

Mind you, it had not been planned exactly like that. There was some vague idea that once they had found the safe they would be able to force it open on the spot. As they had no tools, they were naturally frustrated in their first objective, but they were men of vision, men of action, and all around them were coal lorries. What could be more simple than to heave the safe onto the back of one of the lorries and drive off to some secluded spot where they could obtain the necessary tools and open the safe without alarming anyone.

So up on the lorry it went.

'Who can drive one of these then? They've left the keys in.' (I told you it was a few years ago.)

'I'll have a go. Can't be much different from a car.' And off they went. They did not stop to open the gate, but just drove through it, before noticing the other phenomenon which must have been present when they left the pub but which drink had perhaps caused them to ignore: there was a very thick fog about. (When I started thinking about this story it suddenly struck me that a lot of things had changed in thirty years. There are no thick fogs now, because there's very little coal used. And the policemen are all looking younger.)

So the Coal-Yard Conspirators turned left slowly and began to drive down the road. Most other drivers had given up their journeys, so our three heroes were in little danger of colliding with anyone. What they needed now was a quiet place to stop and discover how rich they were. But, as one of them said later on, 'Every bleeding time we thought we'd stop, there was a copper standing in a doorway.' (See, I told you it was a long time ago.) So they drove on and on through the streets of south London, looking vainly for a quiet place in which they could open the safe. But all they could see was street lamps and this wall of fog. Give it another few miles.

And about 4.00 in the morning, they were clear of London and in the green deserted countryside. Just what they wanted, a field. So into the middle of the field they drove into almost complete blackness. They stopped and felt their way to the back of the lorry. What about tools? I told you they were men of enterprise and initiative.

'Bleeding coal lorry in'it? Bound to have a hammer, stuff like that.'

Sure enough, in a tool box they found a sledge-hammer, a large chisel, and a shovel. They first tried prising the door open with the shovel, and the blade snapped off. They took a few half-hearted swings at the lock. The hammer skidded off and almost removed a kneecap. It was time for the thinker of the group to take over.

'These safes,' he declared. 'These safes made to stand against a wall. Weakest point is the back. Stands to reason.'

They turned the safe over. The fog was lifting slightly, and dawn was breaking, so there was now enough light to see a slight seam at the back. They would attack the seam with the chisel and hammer, taking it in turns. Half an hour should do it.

They made a considerable noise. Not the sort of noise that would disturb anyone out in the country in the middle of a field. Unfortunately, as the light grew stronger, and the fog grew thinner, they realised they were not in the middle of a field in the country. They were in the middle of a rather select estate in Orpington, and the good citizens of Orpington had been ringing the police in their dozens.

And police in their dozens had responded. There's not a lot doing on the edges of London at 4.00 in the morning, and wireless cars from miles around had come to investigate the disturbance. The Coal-Yard Conspirators were completely surrounded. They surrendered peacefully.

That's the story, except for the last irony. When the coal-yard manager attended the station to open the safe, it contained a load of invoices and 55p. To be fair to the robbers, they laughed as loudly as the police.

# Knuckleduster

That winter (1990) there were a handful of schoolgirls – 12 year olds, 14 year olds, 15 year olds – hanging around together. Some of the 14 year olds had much older boy-friends. Lee Taylor, aged 21, was said to be 'knocking off' 14-year-old Dinah. Dinah was tanned, with her nose and ears pierced. Her hair was drawn back into a pony tail. She wore lots of eyeliner and many gold necklaces. When she went into a pub with Lee, the licensee could not be blamed for thinking she was 20 or over. Lee's friend, Lee Bowdrey, on the run from prison, had a 20-year-old girlfriend – Karen Bailey, a short fat girl who wore leather jackets and went to Weight-Watchers. Bowdrey had been known to beat her up. He had also been known to beat up his friends. The six foot skinhead saw himself as a hard man. He had a Red Devil tattoo on his forearm with F U beneath. His friends described him as overweight with a fat face.

The girls drove round in the boys' cars smoking pot, drinking beer, just driving around. No destination most of the time. Just driving around because they could not think of anything else to do.

'See if Jimmy's in.'

'Let's go round your place.'

'Anything good on telly?'

The girls skipped school to watch television at each other's houses. No one had any ambitions beyond a little petty thieving. In the evenings the girls often went into pubs with the boys. The boys got drunk. One night Lee Bowdrey smashed up a car at the side of the road while he was driving Lee Taylor's car.

'We didn't stop. We just drove off. Some man came out and took our number. Never heard no more about it.'

Heidi Jayne Cable and her boyfriend Billy McCreath were part of the group. Heidi was 15, and fat; at least her friends described her as fat. The girls might hang around together. That did not make them any kinder when it came to describing each other. Billy was 21. Heidi had known Lee Bowdrey for two years.

'He used to write me letters from prison. I know that sometimes he goes a bit nutty and hits people for no reason.'

One afternoon in February 1991, while they were all 'hanging around', Bowdrey and Taylor told Heidi that they wanted to 'do' her neighbours' house. Not very professional. No 'spur of the minute' enterprise. The two Lees went in and out of Heidi's house, standing outside and talking; coming back in and talking; going back out again and talking. After two hours they conquered their indecision.

'Get us a pair of gloves and a screwdriver.' The two professionals lacked even the basic tools of their trade. Heidi got the gloves and the screwdriver from her kitchen.

'I want them back,' she told them, 'or Mum'll see that they're missing.' The Lees broke into her neighbours' house, and took the video, a cassette-player and some jewellery. Heidi heard her neighbours telling her mother about it later. She kept quiet. Nothing to do with her. Didn't get the gloves and the screwdriver back afterwards.

'Had to throw them away,' Bowdrey told her. 'Don't want the evidence lying around, do we?' Very professional.

The very professional Lee Bowdrey, six foot tall, jeans, trainers, black leather jacket, skinhead, always carried a knuckleduster with him.

'It was all silver,' recalled one of his young admirers. 'It wasn't for show, like a toy,' said another. "It had points sticking out.'

Lee Bowdrey, six foot tall, hard man and local hero, decided, after thinking about it, talking about it for three or four days, on another burglary. He decided to rob Daisy Gilbert. Daisy was 83 years old, five foot tall and five stone in weight. She was recovering from a broken arm and a broken pelvis. Bowdrey hit her repeatedly with his silver knuckleduster. She died. This is how it happened.

Daisy Gilbert lived alone in a retired person's bungalow in Moorfield Road, Hayes. She had refused to go into a nursing home, or sheltered housing. She was a semi-invalid who spent most of her day sitting by a coal fire in her lounge watching television. Her health visitor described her as independent and aggressive. She lived off custard cream tarts, crisps, and cream crackers. The meals on wheels delivered to her daily were never touched. Daisy washed very rarely and told the health visitor to mind her own business when she offered to wash her. She was not lonely or neglected. A son and daughter visited her frequently to see that she was coping properly. Local tradesmen, the postman, her newsboy, all knew her and chatted to her. And there were the girls. Half a dozen or more schoolgirls knew Daisy. They called at her house singly or in pairs. Talked to her, ran messages for her, occasionally made tea. Daisy gave them sweets and sometimes a pound coin.

Daisy was frightened of some of them, and hid when she heard them ring at the door. She found two of them helping themselves to money one day from the shelf beside her chair when she had been to the toilet. There were often pound coins lying loose on that shelf, and the wooden chair that she always sat in was tight against the door of a wooden cabinet behind her. There were rumours that Daisy had a lot of money lying around, a suitcase full of it. That's what the girls told each other. But you must not think they were all greedy. Most of Daisy's callers came out of curiosity, and stayed out of kindness. There were no signs that they called on her in the hope that she would give them money. But a suitcase full of money? No schoolgirl could be blamed for being curious about that, for feeling that it was some sort of secret.

Lyndsey Johnson certainly thought it was a secret worth sharing. She lived near Daisy, and told the secret to her friend Rebecca Le Surf who was staying with her for the weekend, just before the summer holidays in 1990. Rebecca lived five miles away in Hillingdon.

'You keep a secret?' Lyndsey asked Rebecca.

'What you mean?'

'See down there,' said Lyndsey, pointing out of her bedroom window. 'See that bungalow. Well, there's this old lady living there, and she's got money all over the place. There's coins and old pound notes just lying around. A lot of people have told me about it.'

Rebecca didn't think that was much of a secret, but Lyndsey said that she had been told not to tell anyone. The next day they walked past the house on the way to look at horses in a field. Lyndsey told her that the house belonged to Granny Gilbert. It became clear that she had never been inside. Friends had told her about the money.

The next time that Rebecca stayed with Lyndsey she learned that her friend had been into Granny Gilbert's house with a girl who already knew the old lady. That weekend both girls went to visit her. They stayed talking with her for half an hour. Daisy Gilbert gave Rebecca some sweets and gave Lyndsey a bag of crisps and a pound coin. Rebecca said later that she didn't see any money lying around other than a few coins on the shelf by Granny Gilbert's chair. They visited Daisy twice again before Christmas. Then Lyndsey went to stay with Rebecca for a weekend.

Rebecca's sister Sarah had a boyfriend, Ray McGinnis. Sarah was 17 and Ray about 20. Lyndsey and Rebecca went round to Ray's house one evening. There were one or two of Ray's mates there. There was cannabis about, or 'puff' as this group called it, a few cans of lager. Lyndsey felt she should make some sort of impression on the others who were all older than her.

'I know an old lady who has a lot of money,' Lyndsey told them, putting the first stitch into what became Daisy Gilbert's shroud.

'How much?' asked Ray.

'Quite a lot,' Lyndsey told him. 'I don't know exactly, but she lives near me.'

In the middle of January, just as Rebecca came home from school, Ray McGinnis turned up in a car. He had Lee Taylor, and Dinah, Lee's girlfriend, with him.

'Show us where this old lady lives.'

So they all went in the car to Moorfield Road, and Rebecca pointed out Granny Gilbert's bungalow. There was a crate of beer in the back of the car. Dinah opened the bottles by pulling the tops off with her teeth. The group drove on to Uxbridge, where they picked up Lee Bowdrey and Karen. There were now six in the car. They bought some more 'puff'. They stopped in a pub car-park. A man came out and paid Lee Bowdrey £60 for some undisclosed debt. They drove around again. There was more talk about how much the old lady had. They returned to Moorfield Road. Rebecca might have been 14 years old but she knew why Ray and Lee Bowdrey were so interested in the house.

Lee Bowdrey wanted a screwdriver 'to do it now'. Lee Taylor did not have a screwdriver in his car, but 14-year-old Dinah volunteered to get one from her house. Rebecca did not want to be with them when they 'did' it. Lee Taylor thought they should wait. A screwdriver seemed to have a disproportionate importance. It was almost a symbol. It was as if rules were laid down that you were not allowed to break in unless you had a screwdriver. So Daisy's death was postponed. Bowdrey had made no secret of how he intended to treat Mrs Gilbert.

'I don't care if she dies as long as I get the money . . . She'll probably have a heart attack, then it ain't my fault . . . She tries to phone the law or anything, I'll have to smack her . . . Best way is to Sellotape a back window and then smash it with a hammer. I could do it in a balaclava.' A balaclava was another symbol.

Ray and Rebecca were dropped off. The two Lees, Karen and Dinah went on a pub crawl. The conversation centred on the old lady and how much she had.

'Could be enough to buy a few smart motors. Go on a holiday. Four of us off to Florida or Spain. How you fancy that then? She wakes up while I'm in there, I'll stick a pillow case over her head to shut her up.'

When the foursome split up, there was an understanding that the old lady's house was to be 'done' on a Friday. Which Friday, however, had not been decided.

By Friday February 1, the talking had finished. Lee Taylor and Lee Bowdrey has steeled themselves to break into Granny Gilbert's house and help themselves to the suitcase full of money. They knew from the girls who had visited Daisy that she was normally asleep by 7.00 p.m. So they broke in at the rear of the bungalow, opening a bedroom window with a screwdriver. They climbed over the sill and found their way to the kitchen. Daisy had not gone to bed, but was in the next room, sound asleep in her chair near the fire. They started looking for money. And there was money there. £50 notes in an envelope stuffed down the side of the chair. A bundle of £10 notes under a cushion. Another bundle of £5 notes in an open handbag. The two Lees stuffed the money into their pockets looking round all the time for the suitcase with the fortune in it.

Daisy woke up. Taylor moved behind her. Bowdrey told her, 'Don't worry. We're detectives. We think there's a burglar upstairs.'

Daisy started to protest, and they quickly tied her to her chair with a belt. Bowdrey had found a suitcase when Daisy started screaming. He dropped it hurriedly and they left with the money they had already taken. They had about £800 and Bowdrey had taken some jewellery. But as they drove away, there was a sense of failure. They hadn't taken the suitcase. They would need to pay Daisy a second visit.

Two days after the robbery, Daisy had a visitor: Kelly Fiddes, a 12-year-old girl who had been a regular caller at the bungalow. She did not notice anything different about the house, or about Granny Gilbert.

'Can I get you anything from the shops?' Daisy looked in her cupboard and decided she needed some custard creams, and then had trouble finding money to pay for them. She went down on her hands and knees looking and eventually found a 50p piece in a jug which she gave to Kelly.

'My arms don't half hurt,' she told her. 'I opened the door last night and this man came in, put me on the floor and tied my hands behind my back and took everything.'

Kelly made sympathetic noises, but took little notice. 'Everyone said she was a nutter.'

She went to the shop, brought the biscuits, and had to pay 4p extra out of her own money. She took the biscuits back and then went home to dinner. Granny Gilbert had somehow freed herself from the strap binding her, found that much of her savings had been stolen, and just got on with her life. No calling the police, asking a neighbour to contact her relatives, just got on with life.

But other people knew about the robbery. Lee Taylor and Lee Bowdrey, two professionals, could not keep it a secret. Lee Taylor told Dinah and showed her the £200 that he had taken. The two Lees treated Dinah and Karen to a slap-up meal at a Berni Inn. There was no doubt that they were going back to the house to get the rest of the money.

Dinah told Heidi Cable about the robbery. Lee Taylor told 18-year-old Marisa Mills about it. She was a friend of Karen's. Everyone in the group knew that the robbery had taken place. Everyone knew that the old lady had been tied to a chair. Everyone knew that that the two men were going back again.

On Monday, February 4, Lee Bowdrey decided it was time to go back for the suitcase. Lee Taylor was not about, and Bowdrey was impatient. This time he took Billy McCreath with him. It was about 7.00 p.m.

Bowdrey gave McCreath a briefing on the burglary.

'It's this old bird that Lee Taylor and me did last week. Piece of piss. She's almost blind, can't hear a thing. Got this suitcase full of money. All we got to do is nip in quickly, get the suitcase and get out.'

So they went down the alleyway behind Daisy's house, found the window that had been opened on Friday and which had not been closed and were quickly in the kitchen. Once again, Daisy was asleep in front of the fire in the lounge.

But not deeply asleep. She may have been half-watching Wogan on the television. The two men paused before going into the lounge, waiting behind a door which they had pushed slightly open. Daisy got up slowly out of her chair, walked across the lounge to another door and went out of the room. McCreath looked at Bowdrey, raised his eyebrows signalling, 'What do we do now?'

'Stay put,' whispered Bowdrey. 'Few minutes she'll be kipping again. We can do it easy then.'

They heard a lavatory flush and saw Daisy come back into the room. The old lady walked back to her chair. The voices on the television giggled on. Then suddenly Daisy stopped and looked directly at the door behind which the two men were standing. At the same time, the door moved slightly. McCreath involuntarily reached out to stop it opening further. Bowdrey was out like an animal, grabbing Daisy and pulling her to the floor.

Most old ladies, surprised and pulled down by a stranger in their own house would be literally half-dead with fright. The shock would be too much for their hearts to handle. At five feet tall and five stone in weight, recovering from two serious fractures, Daisy should have at least collapsed unconscious. But Daisy screamed. On her back with Bowdrey's sixteen stone on top of her, she struggled and punched with her fist. The lounge, in which the only sound had been from the television set, was suddenly full of fear and noise.

'Shut it, you stupid old bitch!' from Bowdrey.

'Stick a pillow over her mouth!' from McCreath.

'Get off. Get away. Get away!' from Daisy.

'Where's the money, you stupid fucking old whore?' Then Bowdrey lifted his fist, and McCreath saw the knuckleduster for the first time, the silver knuckleduster 'with points sticking out'. The first blow was against the back of Daisy's skull. The second against the side of her head. So hard that the blood spurted out in a fountain. McCreath tried to pull Bowdrey off.

'For fuck's sake, Lee, lay off, you'll kill her!'

Bowdrey pushed Billy away, and again hit Daisy on the side of his head. Daisy's face was now covered in blood. Bowdrey was soaked in it. He lifted his hand again.

'Where's the fucking money, you old slag?' McCreath ran from the house and stood weak with fear in the garden. He could still hear Terry Wogan's voice. Inside the house Bowdrey was frantically trying to find the suitcase. He hurled over chairs, pulled out drawers, ran into the bedroom and heaved the mattress onto the floor. Nothing. There was a groan from the lounge where Daisy lay bleeding. Bowdrey ran out of the house, almost knocking down McCreath standing shocked near the back door.

'Better clear off. Come back later for the money.' McCreath shook his head.

Bowdrey walked quickly away out of the alleyway turning in the other direction. It was still early evening. The roads were still busy. Billy ran, walked, stood at bus stops, went into a phone box, ran again, and found himself back at the house. It was as he had left it. No neighbours clustered round the door. No Old Bill. No ambulance. Perhaps she had already been taken to the hospital. He walked, still frightened, down the alley, waited, then into Daisy's garden, and looked in through the lounge window. A studio audience laughed on television. Daisy was still there. Lying with her head in a pool of blood. Not moving. Billy ran off again. He found a phone box, rang his girlfriend, told her he was in trouble, and asked her to meet him at a bus stop. She went to the bus stop and met him. Almost as soon as he had stepped off the bus, the full story came rushing out. He told her exactly what had happened. They argued fiercely over what he should do. Should he get away from the area? Should he phone for an ambulance for the old lady? He did nothing. That night he stayed at his brother's house. Lesley told a friend, Michele, all about the robbery.

Lee Bowdrey went to Lee Taylor's grandmother where Lee was staying. He told him exactly what had happened, and asked the grandmother to wash his T-shirt and jumper. She agreed to that but asked them to stop bothering her as she wanted to get back to watching television. As they left she put the clothes in the bottom of a cupboard and never got round to washing them. Bowdrey then went back to his own parents. He explained the bloodstains on his jeans and trainers by saying that he had been attacked by three men, and rescued by Billy McCreath who had used a jack handle to fight off his attackers. He left the house about 11.30 p.m. and returned about two days later, coming in long after midnight and looking very upset.

'What's the matter, Son?'

'That fight I was in. Think one of the blokes might have died. Lee Taylor's brother's putting it about that I might have killed him.' He had a sandwich and went out again. His parents' attention returned to the television.

Daisy Gilbert had not yet died. Just before midday on the Tuesday following the attack, a neighbour noticed the curtains were still closed. She phoned the local council's Careline. In turn, Careline phoned Ian Burford, Daisy's grandson.

When Ian arrived, he let himself into the house through the front door, checking the bedroom and kitchen to make sure his Nan was not there, and then tried to push open the door of the lounge. There was a pressure against it. He moved the door with some difficulty and found Daisy lying face down against it. He could see blood on the bottom of the door and on his grandmother's hands. He phoned for an ambulance and the police. His grandmother could not talk, but she was moving her arms and legs.

The ambulance arrived, and the two-man crew went to put Daisy onto a stretcher. Daisy, 83 years old, five feet high, five stone in weight, with a fractured skull, a broken nose, most of her ribs fractured; Daisy, who had been lying partially conscious for sixteen hours, fought them. She hit them in the chest. She held onto the edge of the carpet. Even when she was put into a carrying chair, wrapped in blankets and strapped in, she continued to struggle. She struggled all the way to casualty. And then police arrived at the house, and the investigation started.

Constable Andrew Hutchinson listened to Ian Burford's account of what he had found, and quickly realised from the way that the furniture and bedding had been disturbed that this was not a case of an old woman living in squalor who had fallen over. Investigations can often be delayed by the inexperience or incompetence of the first officer at the scene, but Andrew Hutchinson did everything right. He took an exact note of everything that the ambulance men and Mr Burford had moved after coming into the bungalow, phoned the station to inform the CID, and then went with Mr Burford to the hospital where he arranged for all Daisy's clothes to be kept in a plastic bag for forensic examination. In itself, this is a necessary and time-consuming process. He had to take the names of the ambulance crew, the casualty nurse, sister and doctor, in order that statements could later be taken from them confirming the state of Daisy's clothing when each of them first saw her, and the fact that none of them allowed the clothes to come into contact with any other blood or material that might have destroyed the forensic link. He also arranged that when Daisy was being treated in casualty, a sample of her blood be obtained for later forensic comparison.

PC Hutchinson also recorded the names of the three doctors who first examined Daisy. Again, statements would have to be taken later from them. There was little prospect of Daisy surviving, so you may be surprised to hear that two weeks after the attack she had recovered enough to provide a short statement describing how she had been robbed twice by the 'same two young fellows' and all her money taken.

Within hours of the attack, the news had been passed around the group of people who knew Bowdrey. Lee Taylor knew all about it and told Dinah. Dinah told Heidi Cable, Billy McCreath told Lesley Colin, and then told her sister Joan. Lesley Colin told Michelle Fulbrooke. Michelle also heard about the robbery from Tracey Stevens who had seen an item about it on Thames News. Michelle told her parents, and at last, at long last, someone decided to tell the police.

I can't pretend that this was one of the most difficult investigations I've ever been involved in. If there were problems, the problems were those of having too many witnesses, and too many people whose roles in knowing of the robbery before or after it had happened had to be carefully studied. There's a fine line between knowing a little about a crime and doing nothing, and knowing so much about it that by failing to tell police you become an accessory.

At first it just appeared to be a serious burglary, and it was a matter of finding out what had been stolen and who had still got the property. But it never seemed likely that Daisy would survive, so the investigation was conducted as if this was a murder.

There was a time when a Detective Superintendent running an investigation into an attempted murder could have counted on having forty officers in his team with no restrictions on the hours they worked. Nowadays, the officer in charge has to justify the services of every single officer on the inquiry, and is allocated an overtime budget. After a week if there is no definite suspect, there is a bureaucratic battle to keep even ten officers on the investigation.

So with Peter Meikle, my Detective Inspector and Graham Barker, the Detective Sergeant, we had to first sift through all the names that Michelle Fulbrooke had provided, girls who had spoken to girls, boyfriends who went around with them. And we had to decide on the best way of arresting the three suspects. Call at their usual addresses too early, and they would be warned and might leave the area. Keep observation outside their houses, and they could also be frightened off. By now they would be expecting police interest.

But the investigation had scarcely begun when the two Lees were arrested.

After Michelle had made her statement, a team of CID and uniform officers were assembled, given the names of the suspects and the numbers of the cars they had been known to use and were then allocated to the tracing of the two dozen or more people who might have known about the attacks. Stephen Hughson, a Detective Constable, and Edward Collins, a uniform PC, were on their way to trace one of the girls when they saw one of the cars that were known to be used by Lee Taylor. It was parked in a side road with two men in the back seat. As the officers radioed for assistance, they saw Lee Bowdrey come to the car which was driven away. The officers followed it, using their radio to keep other police units informed.

The car stopped in a cul-de-sac. Other police cars arrived, quietly; this was not an incident which required them to attend at speed with their sirens screaming. Bowdrey left the car, and DC Hughson went to him. There was the routine production of the warrant card, 'You are wanted for failing to return to prison, and for a serious assault in Cowley a couple of days ago,' followed by the routine caution.

'I ain't talking to you.'

Not only was Lee Bowdrey not talking to policemen, he wasn't standing around to be questioned further. He pushed his way past DC Hughson who grabbed hold of his arm.

'Take your fucking hands off me.' Bowdrey was obviously

going to have a go for it. No copper was going to take this
hard man in. A police Land-rover turned into the cul-de-sac.
Two uniform officers joined DC Hughson, and the hard man
came quietly. He was put into the back of a police car. Lee
Taylor, still sitting in the back of the car, was arrested by PC
Collins.

'What fucking assault?' he asked. When he was told about
the attempted murder of Daisy Gilbert he replied, 'You're
taking the piss, you really are.'

The third man in the car was Adam Henderson who was
arrested because he was in the company of two suspected
murderers. He was released later when it was clear that he
was not involved.

We were told about McCreath's likely movements. There
was no drama about his arrest. Two uniformed PCs were
watching a bus stop that he was known to use. He arrived
at the stop at 7.20 p.m.

'You Billy McCreath?' The PC had his photograph in his
hand, so Billy could hardly deny it.

'Yes. That's me.'

'We're arresting you in connection with a serious assault
two days ago in Cowley.' The officer scarcely had time to
formally caution him.

'Yes. I been expecting this.'

When we searched Bowdrey's own house we found his
knuckleduster with spikes about half an inch long. It was
still bloodstained. We also found his bloodstained jeans and
trainers. At Lee Taylor's grandmother's house, we found the
bloodstained T-shirt and sweater that he had asked her to
wash and which she had left untouched in the bottom of the
cupboard.

McCreath admitted taking part in the burglary, but
denied that he had taken any part in the attack on Granny
Gilbert. Lee Taylor admitted that he had taken part in the
first burglary. The hard man, in spite of their statements,
denied that he had taken any part in anything.

*    *    *

Granny Gilbert unfortunately died in due course. About two weeks after Bowdrey had hit her three times round the head with his spiked knuckleduster she passed away. So the charges were now murder and burglary. In spite of his protestations we charged McCreath as well as Bowdrey with murder. Billy might be telling the truth now, but what would happen when he got into the witness box and changed his story? But at the Old Bailey, Bowdrey insisted on pleading not guilty to everything. McCreath pleaded not guilty to the murder, but admitted the burglary, and described how Bowdrey had attacked the old lady. Bowdrey was sentenced to life, and two years for the burglaries, McCreath received a twelve months' sentence, and Taylor thirty months.

As the hard man was taken out of the dock, described by his counsel as 'stupid and immature', he waved to friends in the gallery, many of them the girls who used to hang around, and shouted, 'Give Mum my love.'

# What Happened To The Body?

She was 55 years old and she had been lying tied and gagged with sticking plaster in a cabin trunk in a cold shed. She had no idea any longer how many days it had been since her kidnappers took her from her kitchen where she had been preparing her husband's dinner. It could have been last week. It might have been a month ago. Most of the time she was also blindfolded. She had been put into a cabin trunk and taken in a car, across London? . . . To the coast? . . . Or had the car just gone round and round? Perhaps she was still near her home in Wimbledon.

Sometimes the two men left her in the trunk. Sometimes she was left lying on the floor of the shed. Twice she had been untied and told to write to her husband to persuade him to pay money to the men.

For the last days the only sounds she could hear were those made by two part-wild Alsatians chained outside. One of the men came in each day to feed her. He carried a machete, threatening to use it if she tried to cry out for help.

'We are a long way from anywhere. No one will hear you. You must hope that your husband hurries up with the money.'

Sometimes, after being fed, she was put back in the trunk. Some instinct told her that this was a precaution against being discovered by people who were visiting the two men. This time, she heard someone come into the shed. She recognised the footsteps of the one she only knew as man two, she had never seen either of their faces properly and took some comfort from that. She had remembered reading somewhere that kidnappers who intended to kill their victim were unconcerned about being seen.

Man two opened the trunk and pulled her out. She was not going to be fed then. When she was fed, and when she was in the trunk, she could hear the pause as the kidnapper put the plate on the floor before opening the trunk. Perhaps they wanted her to write another letter. Perhaps this was the day they were going to let her go.

This was the day they were going to make her disappear forever. She was hit savagely on the head and dragged unconscious from the hut into the muddy field outside. The two men treated her body like that of one of the many unwanted calves they had disposed of in the same place and in the same way. They hacked her to pieces and threw the pieces around the field. Then one of them opened the gate to let back in the normal occupants of the field who had been left without food for two days. The pigs scrambled and grunted. Within a few days there was no trace left of Mrs McKay.

No one really knows if this is what happened. The two killers have never admitted the murder or given any hint as to where the body was left. One has been deported, and the other is still in prison. I made a mistake early in the investigation which may have lengthened the time spent by police in tracing the kidnappers. In my very worst moments I wonder if Mrs McKay was still alive when I came across her kidnappers. I am never likely to know if, by following my normal routine, I might have saved her.

At the end of 1969, Rupert Murdoch owned the *Sun* and the *News of the World*. He was already an international figure. If he needed more publicity he achieved it when he quarrelled with David Frost during an evening TV programme. The audience learned that Mr Murdoch was already a millionaire and had a beautiful young wife. It would have been easy for anyone interested in Mr Murdoch's movements to follow his distinctive gold Rolls-Royce from his office to his home.

It would have easy for anyone interested in Mr Murdoch's

movements to assume that he had sole use of the car. But in December 1969, he was abroad and the car was being used by a colleague, Alick McKay. Mr McKay lived in Wimbledon, and on December 29 drove home in the gold Rolls-Royce for dinner with his wife. But Mrs McKay was missing. The phone in the hall had been pulled out, and the disc with its number had been taken. Muriel's shoes were lying at the foot of the stairs. There was baling twine lying on the floor in the lounge and sticking plaster on a table. There was also a billhook, a hedging tool that looks like a very broad machete on an antique table. Mrs McKay's handbag had been emptied, and much of her jewellery had been taken from a bedroom drawer. After a quick search of the house, Mr McKay called the police.

DC Wilfred Smith and DS Graham Birch from Wimbledon were at the house within thirty minutes. The signs of the burglary meant that this was not a normal missing person inquiry that would normally have been left to a uniform sergeant. Mr McKay was a rich man, but, whatever his status, he had to be asked a number of questions that are routine at the beginning of an investigation into a missing person.

'Was there anyone else in Mrs McKay's life?'

'Certainly not.'

'Any relationship of yours that might have caused her to leave home?'

'No. We got on very well together. There's absolutely no reason for her to leave suddenly. There's a couple of steaks in the kitchen. She was obviously going to cook them for dinner.'

'Any relatives that she might have been called to suddenly?' Two married daughters in Sussex. They were phoned. (The damaged phone in the hall had not affected others in the house.) Mrs McKay was not there, but both daughters were concerned enough to come immediately to Wimbledon with their husbands.

The usual search started for fingerprints inside and foot-prints outside. At 1.00 a.m. BBC radio broadcast the news of Mrs McKay's disappearance. At 1.15 a.m. the phone rang.

'This is Mafia Group Three,' said a voice. 'We have your wife. You will need a million pounds by Wednesday.'

'That's ridiculous. You know I haven't got that sort of money.'

'You've got friends. We meant to take Rupert Murdoch's wife. Get the money or you won't have a wife. We'll speak to you again.'

The phone was put down. But the caller had given the investigators two clues. Mrs McKay had not been identified on the radio broadcast, but the caller had known the right name to call. So it was not one of those cruel pointless hoaxes that often follow the publication of a victim's name. And the operator had heard the demand for a million pounds. He had heard it under circumstances which ruled out any Mafia connection. The caller had been unable to dial the McKays' number and had dialled the operator asking him to call it. The operator had put the call through, and had then heard Mr McKay's angry voice on his discarded headphones. He picked them up and heard the ransom demand. Clue two. The Mafia would be unlikely to ask an operator to dial a number for them.

The family remained uneasily round the house. A police search party gathered at the house the next day. After a search of the ground they went into Wimbledon Park which faced the McKays' house. Officers from the River Police were called to drag the large lake.

At 5.00 p.m. there was another call from Mafia Group Three (M3). There was a letter on its way from Mrs McKay. The following day, a letter, postmarked in Tottenham, arrived at the Wimbledon house. It was in Mrs McKay's handwriting, 'I am blindfolded and cold. Please do something to get me home. Please co-operate or I can't keep going.'

There was an immediate family conference. Alick McKay with his knowledge of the press, and son-in-law David Dyer decided that publication of the letter would frighten the kidnappers. The police agreed. They had very little experience of the kidnapping of public figures. (The modern practice of keeping secret, with media cooperation, every fact about a kidnapping had not yet been adopted – the logic of that procedure being that the only news that kidnappers can gain of the success of their plot comes through the media. Deprive them of that news and they become uncertain and more likely to make mistakes.)

The newspaper copies of the letter were accompanied by a request for the kidnappers to provide details of how the ransom money was to be paid over. There were also details describing Muriel's need for regular injections and tablets. This was not true, but was added to make the kidnappers' work less easy. The newspaper articles were followed on the same day by another phone call from M3 repeating a demand for £1 million.

The investigation slowed down. Other than knowing they were dealing with amateurs who had kidnapped the wrong victim, the investigators had nothing to go on. None of the vast network of police informers, or crime reporter contacts, could provide any information about criminals who had suddenly changed their habits, had spoken about pulling such a kidnap, or were no longer seen in the usual pubs and clubs. Every call from the public claiming to have seen Mrs McKay had to be followed up.

On January 10, the *News of The World* received a letter from M3 threatening that Mrs McKay would be 'disposed of' if the £1 million was not paid. The writer also complained that he had been unable to phone the McKay house because the line was constantly engaged. Alick McKay acted quickly to stop the constant stream of inquiries from friends and relatives that was keeping the line blocked. There was a call to the editor of the *News of the World*. 'Tell McKay we want a million.'

Then, the line at the McKay house having been kept clear, the calls to the house from M3 resumed. Now there was an amused, a taunting tone to them.

'The medicine for your lovely wife is costing a lot of

money.' There was a change, a request for a down payment of £500,000, but still no directions on how it was to be handed over.

On January 22, almost four weeks after she had been kidnapped, Alick received another letter from Muriel. 'Keep the police out of this.' There was also a reference to a television appearance by her daughter, but that appearance had been two weeks earlier.

But the letter was the first to contain any details about a possible handover. It was set ten days ahead for February 1. The day after the letter had been delivered, there were three calls from M3 threatening to kill Mrs McKay if their demands were not met. Three days later there were two more letters from Muriel. One accused Alick of betraying her by going to the police, the second included small strips cut from her jacket and shoes. There was also a note from M3.

'She will be executed on February 2 unless you keep our business date on February 1. We demand the full million pounds.'

On February 1, a Sunday, police prepared themselves for some closer contact with the kidnappers. The Bank of England had been persuaded to print £1 million in forged money on the understanding that it would be destroyed as soon as the operation had been completed. M3 had demanded that Ian McKay, the couple's son, should take the money in a suitcase to a phone box in Tottenham. They had reluctantly agreed that he should be driven by the family chauffeur. At 9.00 p.m. the gold Rolls-Royce was driven from the McKay house across London to Tottenham.

Ian McKay and his chauffeur were not in it. A Detective Sergeant, Roger Street, was acting as Ian McKay and John Minors, a Detective Inspector, the part of the chauffeur. Roger waited in the phone box at Tottenham for five minutes. The phone rang. He was told to drive to the Cambridge Road and wait by another phone box. The phone rang again.

'On the floor of the phone box, in the corner, there is an empty packet of Piccadilly. Do what it says on the back.'

The packet was there. On the back were printed instruction to drive along the A10 to Dane End in Hertfordshire where they would find two paper flowers under a signpost. The suitcase was to be left there. McKay (Roger Street) was to go back to the first phone box in Tottenham and wait there for instructions. The two detectives left the suitcase and drove back to Tottenham, 200 other officers waited for the kidnappers' next move.

The Rolls-Royce had been shadowed for every mile of its journey by a combination of twenty police cars none of which had stayed long enough behind or in front of the Rolls to make an unknown observer suspicious.

The nearest police car found the forecourt of a transport café from which the crew could see the suitcase and the signpost. Just before midnight a Volvo car came from the direction of London, drove onto the forecourt and turned back to London. The two officers took little note of it other than to notice there were two Asian men in the car and that one of its rear lights was not working. By 4.00 a.m. no one had come near the suitcase. The surveillance was abandoned and the money taken back to Wimbledon.

The family kept its vigil by the phone. It was thirty-six hours before M3 contacted them. The caller sounded amused. They had seen cars waiting at the pick-up point and the boss was at a meeting of 'the intellectuals, the semi-intellectuals, and the ruffians'. The meeting was to decide on the date for Mrs McKay's execution. But the caller was 'going to plead for your mum. I'm fond of her. She's like my own mum.'

Within hours there was another call saying that a decision had been taken to postpone the execution. One of the daughters started to sob. They were being played with. All their lives were controlled by the faceless kidnappers. Ian McKay held his hand up to silence the others. The officers listening on an extension checked their two tape recorders. The money was to be handed over in two days' time, on Friday February 6. M3 wanted the handover to be made by Ian McKay and his sister Diane. The money was to be put in two suitcases.

This time there could be no risk of a following police car being seen by the kidnappers. This time everything had to appear to be done as the kidnappers required. This time could be the last chance to save Mrs McKay's life. John Minors took the part of Ian McKay. A woman detective, Joyce Armitage, posed as Diane, wearing her clothes and a long dark wig.

There was a third detective in the boot. DI John Bland had a pistol, bottles of water and a supply of oxygen. At 4.00 p.m. the Rolls left Wimbledon. At 5.00 p.m. it was at another north London phone box in Church Street in Edmonton. M3 instructed them to double back to another phone in Bethnal Green.

'If we see any police cars, we will execute Mrs McKay.'

At Bethnal Green they were told to drive to Theydon Bois on the eastern outskirts of London. There they were to leave the car and take an underground train to Epping. John Bland was able to leave the car after them and travel on the same train. Another phone call at Epping told them to take a taxi almost forty miles across country to Bishop's Stortford. They were to find a used car lot, where there was a mini-van parked. M3 gave them the number of the van. The money was to be placed on either side of the mini-van.

They called a hire car, and John Bland was able to roll into the back hopefully out of sight of anyone who might be watching the bogus McKays. At the same time John Minors was able to broadcast their next rendezvous over his personal radio. By the time they arrived at Bishop's Stortford, two armed detectives were already lying in wait under the mini-van. John Bland rolled out of the hire car and through a gap in a fence. There he lay also waiting for the pick up. John Minors and Joyce Armitage had, reluctantly, to take the hire car back to Epping, not knowing at what stage the kidnappers' observation on them, if there was an observation, would be withdrawn. At 9.00 p.m. a Volvo car with two Asian men drove onto the lot and halted by the suitcases. The driver leaned out, looked at the suitcase, and then drove off. This happened three times. Each time the detectives beneath the car tensed, John Bland literally held his breath. Each time the driver looked out and then drove off. On the fourth occasion, the Volvo returned in a more determined manner, but a passer-by had seen the suitcases, sent his wife to call the police and stood guard over them. The Volvo drove away. But John Bland had checked its index number, and had noted that one of its rear lights was not working.

The car was registered in the name of Arthur Hosein who owned Rooks Farm just outside Bishop's Stortford. Early in the morning the farm was surrounded by police, and Wilf Smith came face to face with the man he hoped would turn out to be M3.

Arthur Hosein had come to England from Trinidad and until he was called up for National Service was making a great deal of money as a tailor. He liked to be seen with a wad of banknotes. National Service did not suit him, and he spent six months in a military prison for desertion. After that, using the money that he had saved from tailoring, he married a German woman ten years older than him and bought Rooks Farm. He continued his trade as a tailor but bought some pigs, cattle and chickens to fit in with his own image of himself as a landowner. He became well known in the local pubs for his willingness to buy drinks for everyone. In August 1969, his younger brother Nizam left Trinidad and joined him. His family, two of whom he had attacked with a knife, were pleased to be rid of him, hoping that he would settle down on what Arthur called 'his country estate'.

'I have no idea what you are talking about,' Arthur told Wilf Smith. 'I've heard of Mrs McKay of course. She's in the paper all the time. But that's all. You have a job to do. Search the farm by all means. You won't find anything.'

They found some paper flowers of the same make as those left at the signpost. They found an exercise book with paper similar to that used for the notes to Mrs McKay. They found a piece of paper with the number of the mini-van left at the final pickup point. They found sticking plaster of the same type as that left in Mrs McKay's house. They found, a tenuous link, loose Piccadilly cigarettes, and remembered the empty packet in the phone box. And they had the billhook, or rather two billhooks. One was found at the farm. Nizam said it had been borrowed from a neighbouring farmer to cut up a calf.

'What happened to the calf?'

Nizam's voice was so low they had to ask him to repeat what he had said.

'We fed it to the dogs.'

The neighbouring farmer had been told that the billhook was lost. The second billhook left at the McKays' house in Wimbledon was later positively identified by another neighbour as his, lost on his own land.

There was enough to arrest both men. John Bland recognised Arthur as the passenger in the Volvo at the pick-up point in Bishop's Stortford. One of the detectives beneath the mini-van identified Nizam as the driver. They were taken back to London in separate cars, quickly establishing their character differences. Arthur talked continuously of his own standing in the local community. He was well respected, came of a wealthy family in Trinidad, was considering a request that he become a local councillor. Nizam became withdrawn and nervous. Where was he on December 29?

'Ask Arthur. He knows where I was.'

Arthur was being linked more closely to the kidnapping. His fingerprints were on the kidnap notes, the cigarette packet giving directions, and on a copy of the *People* left at Mrs McKay's house. But despite each of these facts being put one by one to Arthur, and then put together in sequence, he made no reference to them, just repeating his wish to help the police 'with this very difficult case'.

Nizam always appeared on the point of confessing, and then withdrew muttering that it was all Arthur's fault. They should ask Arthur about these things.

There was now enough evidence to charge both men with murder, kidnapping, and demanding money with menaces. But there was not the slightest sign of Mrs McKay. Hundreds of officers from the Met and Hertfordshire conducted a foot by foot search of the farm land around the Hosein house. Many of the officers who took part in that search remember Arthur's wife moving about the farm on routine daily tasks, hardly taking any notice of them some days, on others watching with a sardonic amusement. Most of those who saw her at close range were convinced that she knew they would never find anything there.

The architect's plans of the farmhouse were examined to see if any hidden rooms or spaces had been added. The RAF was asked to use heatseeking equipment to detect a buried body. The searches continued into summer watched by Mrs Hosein.

'No. The brothers had not tried to hide anything from her. She could go anywhere she wanted on the farm. This was a silly mistake. When would her husband be free to come back home?'

In a local pub one of the investigating detectives overheard a conversation between locals. The theme apparently was the likelihood of Mrs McKay being eaten by the Hoseins' pigs. It sound far-fetched. But he reported it back to his seniors. They checked with several local farmers. Yes. It was quite possible. Pigs had an unrecognised capacity for biting and grinding. It was not unknown for local farmers to feed them the carcasses of other livestock.

'Give them buggers a few days and there's nothing left. Not even teeth.'

There was certainly nothing left of Mrs McKay.

★      ★      ★

When the trial began in September the prosecution warned that the evidence of murder would be purely circumstantial. It was significant that since the arrest of the Hoseins there had been no calls to the McKays from M3. The defence conceded that Nizam had made inquiries about the Rolls-Royce, had placed the paper flowers at the signpost, had written down the number of the mini-van, and had driven the Volvo to the used-car lot. Nizam's girlfriend gave evidence that she had spoken to Arthur at the farm late in the evening of December 29. She had stayed at the farm over New Year and had seen nothing suspicious. She could go anywhere on the farm she wanted, but she had not gone into the shed in which the two Alsatians were kept. Nizam had to kill a calf and had been very upset.

A neighbouring farmer gave evidence that the billhook found at Mrs McKay's house belonged to him. He had lent it to Arthur to chop up a calf, and when he had asked for its return, he had been told it could not be found.

When Arthur gave evidence his self-possessed manner revealed an increasing instability. He accused Mr Smith of beating him up. He denied that he ever made business telephone calls. His wife did that sort of thing.

Did he boss his younger brother about?

'I try to be lenient and semi-lenient.' The prosecution immediately noticed the similarity of phrase to M3's intellectuals and semi-intellectuals.

'These are the hands of an artist,' he said at a later stage, 'not the hands of a killer.'

His counsel asked him about four men that Nizam had brought to the house before and after Christmas. One of the men may have been Robert Maxwell, who was then an MP.

Was he implying that these men had involved Nizam in the kidnapping?

'I am not making any suggestion.'

What about his fingerprints on the letters to Mrs McKay. How did he explain having a writing pad of the type from which the kidnap letters were taken?

'These four men had access to my home.'

Some of the words in the kidnap letters were misspelt in the same way that he had misspelt them under dictation.

'Mr Smith told me to spell them in that way, after he had beaten me.'

Nizam, when he came to give evidence, had to be warned constantly to keep his voice up. He claimed that he had made inquiries about the Rolls-Royce on his brother's instructions, but had not asked Arthur the reason for wanting to know. He knew nothing about the murder or kidnapping. The notes had all been written on Arthur's orders. He did not know what they were to be used for.

'Is it true that many times while you were in custody, you spoke about killing yourself? Was that because you had done something dreadful?'

'I would rather die than be charged with murder,' Nazim answered, as quietly as always.

His counsel pointed out to the jury that they could be completely satisfied that Mrs McKay had been murdered without being satisfied that Nazim had anything to do with her death. It took the jury four hours to find them both guilty of every charge against them.

Arthur, asked if he had anything to say before sentence was passed, made a long rambling speech in which he accused the judge and jury of being prejudiced against him. He shouted out that injustice had been done.

'The public gallery has seen the provocation of your Lordship. They have seen your immense partiality.'

He referred to his own claim that he had seen Robert Maxwell at the house, and inferred that the judge, being a Jew, had become more prejudiced when he introduced Maxwell's name.

'You must not think that I am anti-semitic,' he told the jury.

★        ★        ★

They were both given life for the murder, fourteen years for blackmail, and ten years for sending threatening letters. Arthur was given twenty-five years for the kidnapping, and Nazim, for whom the jury had recommended some leniency, was sentenced to ten years.

There was an appeal against conviction. Arthur had lost all of his brashness and self-possession and appeared in the dock trembling and nervous. Nazim's attitude appeared the same. Their appeals were dismissed.

Nazim was released and deported in 1990. The Sunday papers reported that a wealthy widow who had formed a 'Release the Hoseins' committee was about to fly to the West Indies to marry him. Arthur has become increasingly unstable and is in a high security prison.

My part in this case was very small. In January 1970, I was working in uniform in the Special Patrol Group. We stopped a Volvo in Stamford Hill. It was being driven by Arthur Hosein with his wife as a passenger. At that time of course, we knew about Mrs McKay's disappearance, but the Hoseins were a long way from being suspects.

I don't think I have ever been abused so violently as I was on that night. Hosein, standing outside the car and within sight and hearing of a long bus queue, accused me of racism, of rudeness, of insulting his wife, of being a stupid bureaucrat. He was a landowner, a local politician, he was well known in his locality. He deserved respect. He maintained the abuse at the top of his voice, obviously putting on an act for the benefit of the watching queue.

Now, very few people react like this when being stopped by police. I've often found that this over the top response is a strategy to stop police searching them or their car. Usually when I'm shouted at, I carry out a more careful search than usual. But sometimes the reaction just indicates a very nervous unstable personality. Well, now that I know Arthur Hosein is an unstable personality, I suppose I should be satisfied that I made the right choice and let him go. But I wish every day that I had followed my instincts and searched the car thoroughly, instead of having the normal policeman's reaction to someone who appears slightly disturbed, which is to break off the encounter as quickly as possible. The Volvo, of course, had a faulty rear light, and the car was the same vehicle used a few weeks later at Bishop's Stortford. What I did not do was to make Hosein show me what was in the large cabin trunk in the boot of the car. It was a mistake that has stayed with me all my life.

He had already made me suspicious by claiming that he had picked his wife up at Heathrow and was on his way back to Rooks Farm with her; Stamford Hill is a long way off the most direct route between the two places. We found later on, of course, the Hoseins knew the Stamford Hill area very well. But I let him go without looking in the trunk. Was Mrs McKay in the trunk, still alive? Was her body in the trunk? Would the trunk have shown signs that it had been used as a prison or a coffin?

There has certainly been no further trace of Mrs McKay. Nor in the many months of searching Rooks Farm was there any trace of the trunk.

After the trial the farm was sold to an East End publican. During a Christmas party at the farm a man was stabbed to death, not just a single wound, but a determined killing in which the victim was stabbed in the body seven or eight times. His body was found in the East End fully dressed in fresh clothes which hid all signs of the stabbing. No one has ever been convicted of the murder.

# Helping With Inquiries

What they really wanted to do was to steal the wages being delivered to the factory in Nuneaton. Two of them, George Stephenson and George Daly, had been in prison together. John Daly, George's brother, the youngest at 21, had also been in prison, and was quite willing to join in any plan put forward by his elders. But the factory was well protected with security guards at the entrance and others patrolling inside. The wages would also be delivered in an armoured van crewed by more security men.

'Need some guns, or something,' said George Daly, after they had driven past the factory. 'Need to frighten the buggers.'

'That's no problem,' answered Stephenson. 'I know a place down south, got plenty of guns. We can get in easy as piss.'

They went south in a hired Rover. Stephenson produced his driving licence at the car hire office, and George Daly paid with one of his own cheques. They were either very stupid, or had no real plans for this particular expedition.

'Nip in quietly. Get the guns. Get back here and sort out this wages job.' That was probably the plan, if there was a plan.

'These people who've got these guns, they always got quite a bit of money round the house. We might have to deal with 'em.'

Stephenson's requirements for 'dealing with 'em' included three baseball bats and two cans of petrol. He told the brothers that he knew about the house because he had worked there once as a handyman. He didn't tell them that he had been sacked only three weeks before. His wife had left him after being beaten by him once too often. She had run for help to the Cleavers, their employers and owners of the house. She was 'a mass of bruises' as one witness later said. Stephenson was dismissed immediately. He thought he had been treated unfairly. No one had wanted to hear his side. They did not know what his wife was like. He had a few scores to pay off.

The three men arrived at Fordingbridge just before 8.00 p.m. on a September evening in 1986. Burgate House lay back from the road down its own drive and secluded from its neighbours. At 8.00 p.m. anglers were taking their last casts on the nearby Avon, the country pubs were beginning to fill, and the Cleavers were sitting down to dinner. Joseph Cleaver, in his 70s, was a retired publisher. His wife, Hilda, also in her 70s, was confined to a wheelchair. At dinner with them was their son, Thomas, crippled, with an artificial leg, Wendy, his wife, and 70-year-old Margaret Murphy, a nurse/companion for Mrs Cleaver. The dining-table had been set with some elegance, and the five companions were finishing the main course when they heard noises in the hall outside. As Joseph Cleaver was getting to his feet, the door was pushed open. Stephenson and the two Dalys rushed in armed with shotguns they had taken from a case in the hall and with the baseball bats they had brought with them.

'It's you, George.' Mr Cleaver recognised Stephenson instantly. 'What are you doing here?'

'Upstairs. Get upstairs. The lot of you.' Five terrified people were prodded with shotguns and driven at gunpoint up the main staircase. The two Cleavers nervously helped Hilda in her wheelchair. In the bedroom, the five prisoners were quickly bound and gagged with torn up sheets, their pockets searched and their wallets taken. There was not a lot of money. Stephenson took hold of Wendy Cleaver by the arm and dragged her with her wrists and ankles bound into another smaller bedroom. There he pulled and tore all her clothing from her body, and, when she was naked, threw her onto the bed where he quickly and brutally raped her. When he had finished, he called in the two brothers.

'If one's done it, we've all got to do it,' he told them. And obediently they also raped the bound and gagged woman. John cried. George, the last to rape her, strangled her with a piece of black ribbon. They then ran through the house looking for money and anything else worth stealing. Stephenson, out of sight of the others, ran to one of the downstairs rooms and took a painting from the wall. He had been told, when he worked at the house, that it was valuable. The three men made a series of visits to the car, packing the boot with anything they thought could be sold, and with all the bottles of drink they could find.

Their last acts in the house were to pour the two cans of petrol over their four victims, throw a blazing firelighter into the room and run from the house. Joseph Cleaver, his wife in her wheelchair, Margaret Murphy, and crippled Thomas Cleaver were burned alive. Thomas was able to free himself from the rags binding his legs and staggered in flames from the bedroom, before dying outside.

John Daly was drunk. Stephenson, his wish for revenge satisfied, filled the car boot with a television and video and other items taken from the house. George Daly sat tense at the wheel expecting to see the house burst fully into flame before they were able to drive away. But Burgate House, in which all the timber had been replaced by concrete during the war, did not burn. When the housekeeper arrived the next morning she saw the smoke and called the fire brigade. The fire officers found the bodies of the five victims still smouldering.

★　　★　　★

DCI Denis Luty from Hampshire was in charge of the investigation. At the top of his list of possible suspects was George Stephenson, sacked a short time earlier, and known to be angry at his treatment. An address book which had escaped the fire gave the names of a local couple who had provided the references for him and his wife when they applied for the job. Mr Luty called at the couple's house to find if they knew Stephenson's new address.

'No, but he did get in touch with us, think it must have been yesterday. Quite a surprise hearing from him. Told us he was going to bring us a present. That's because we spoke to the Cleavers to get him and his wife work. Must have been him that left the things on the doorstep.'

'What things?'

'Well, a television and a video. Good ones too. Not new, but look as if they're working.' The television and video set were quickly identified as coming from Burgate House.

Stephenson was on file at the National Identification Bureau. His photo was on file in the West Midlands. The day after the murder his picture was on national television and in all the daily papers.

'The public are advised not to approach him. Police say he is violent and extremely dangerous.' The receptionist at the car hire firm recognised him as the man who had presented his driving licence when hiring the Rover. The Dalys were quickly traced through George's cheque and were arrested that night. Stephenson made plans for the sustained lie that he hoped would clear him of any knowing participation in the murders. He went back to Hampshire and surrendered to police. He did not surrender immediately, but spent the evening drinking in a pub where he met two girls who were camping nearby. He went back with them to their tent where they discussed how much he looked like the man whose picture was in all the papers. Finally he walked to a public phone box, dialled 999 and waited for the police to come for him. From the moment he was arrested it was hard to stop him talking.

It was all down to the Dalys. They were driving round Hampshire when George Daly asked, 'Didn't you used to work in a posh house round here somewhere? Let's go and have a look at it.' So they drove to Burgate House. Stephenson did not want to go in because of his past problems with the owners. But the Dalys were keen to look round. He was horrified to see they were wearing masks. They came back to the car after about fifteen minutes, put some things in the boot. (He hadn't even got out, you could open the boot from inside.) They didn't tell him what they had done in the house. They took the ignition keys from him and left him sitting in the car, coming back twice more to put things in the boot. They drove back to Coventry with the two Dalys laughing and drinking from the bottles which they must have taken from the house. He had heard about the murders on the news.

'I loved the Cleavers. I would never have hurt any of them.' He decided to give himself up to the police and say exactly what he knew about the brothers. The brothers already in custody were a little more forthcoming in their statements to the police. Stephenson had been the instigator. John admitted his part in the rape and robbery. The three were charged and committed for trial. Stephenson continued to talk in prison, and that's where I came in.

I'll tell you how I came to know Erroll Walker later on. What you need to know at the moment is that he was on remand in the same prison as Stephenson. He wrote to me.

Hi, Mr Herridge,
   I do hope when this reaches you it may find you in the best of health. you may know by now that i am doing time in scrubs and I would like to see you as soon as possible. how is all the other boys and say hi to them all for me. I stop eat (doughnut) only ice bun (Joke). Ha Ha. in the meantime i wait to see you. from Errol

I've kept the letter. It is the only letter I've ever had from a murderer serving a life sentence. I went to see Erroll. You have to put a request to the Commissioner to visit someone in prison and give a good reason for it. Then the Commissioner signs a form 612a which is a request to the prison governor to allow you to speak to the prisoner. Erroll had been speaking to George Stephenson during association. He was one of the few prisoners to whom Stephenson ever spoke. Stephenson wanted to know about the killing in which Erroll had been involved.

Then one day he told Erroll what he had done himself. He had gone with two brothers to a country house at which he knew there were some antiques worth stealing. He was going to keep out of the way because he knew there was a chance of being recognised. He also had it in mind to steal a particular picture which he understood was worth a lot, but did not want the brothers to know he had taken it. He was recognised by one of the family, and knew that they would all have to be killed. He poured petrol all over the house and put a match to it. It was necessary that all the evidence that they had been in the house should be destroyed. The two brothers had been drinking and could not remember properly what had happened.

Stephenson also told him that the two brothers had confessed to everything, but he had tried to persuade them to retract their confessions. He had persuaded a prison officer to let him share their cell at a remand hearing and told them to say that their confessions had been made up by police, and to say that he had nothing to do with it. He could then go free and arrange their escape from prison.

'So when they let him go,' Erroll had written in the note he made about the conversation, 'he then say when he get them way from jail he would destroy them.' They did not know anything about the picture he had stolen. Erroll was willing to attend court and give evidence of his conversation with Stephenson.

He gave evidence. It supported that given by the two

Dalys; Stephenson was sentenced to a minimum of twenty-five years, with the brothers receiving similar sentences.

Erroll took the opportunity to clear himself of a number of other matters. He'd used me as a confessional before. But that's a separate story.

# Supergrass

I had never expected to meet Erroll Walker again. I had first come across him in 1982 when he had been arrested taking part in a raid on a post office. He'd been captured redhanded, and gave us no trouble at all. He accepted that he'd been caught, and would spend time in prison, but he had obviously been well at it. This was not the first raid in which he had taken part, but he would not open up about any other jobs. I interviewed him several times. We got on well, but he wouldn't say anything. We'd got over the black/white business. I hope I treat everybody the same: black, white, or Asian. Erroll had to overcome his distrust of police officers, of white police officers. We could talk straightforwardly to each other.

'Erroll, you've got the sense to work this out for yourself. You go inside for the one job. We get evidence about other jobs you've pulled, and you get nicked when you come out, and start all over again. You put your hands up now, and all your sentences will be concurrent. We'll tell the judge that you've been cooperative. You might do a few years longer but you'll have a clean sheet when you do come out.'

'But I'll have to put my mates away. That'd be grassing. I ain't no grass.'

'It's your choice, Erroll, but just ask yourself this. They're your mates now. But say one of them gets nicked after you're sentenced. Someone like me is going to make him the same offer. Do you think they'll stick by you in the same way? Do you think they'll say that they couldn't grass on their mates? Just think about it.'

He thought about it for a few days, had a word with his solicitor and decided to tell us all.

'Since 1980, about December, I've been working security vans, snatches and robberies like that. I've been working with Winston, Livingston, Bongo, Ronnie and Bernie. We've used all sorts. Hammers, machetes, shotguns, handguns, baseball bats and coshes. I only carried stuff for show. I never used them. One or two of the others did. First job we did, we bought an old car for. We all chipped in £60 each. It was jeweller's shop that Livingston had sussed out. The man was a big Indian man. We went in at closing time, and he took no notice of Bongo with his knife and tried to push us all out. He got cut and fell down the cellar steps, but he came back up. We broke open the display cases and grabbed trays from them and from the window. We all ran out dropping stuff as we ran back to the car. We took it over to a bloke who worked in Hatton Garden. I waited outside in the car while the rest went in. We got three grand. My share was about £700 . . .'

And so it went on. Fifteen or more robberies, and about eight other men who had worked with him in small groups. A security van – 'Bongo put the gun in the guard's mouth, and his mate in the back of the van threw the bags out to us.' An Indian warehouse – 'We did it three times. I got £5,000 for my share the first time, about £1,000 the second time.' Then there was the parcel trick. They would go to a post office at closing time with a parcel, persuade the staff to open the door to accept the parcel, and rush in waving guns and knives when the door was opened.'

They often used guns. His mates sometimes fired them as a warning . . .

'We kept the two guns in Bernie's mum's washing-machine.'

Not everything went as they planned it.

'We were going to wait and get the guards as they walked past, but we arrived late, and missed the drop.'

Then the reason for his change of mind.

'I used to go clubbing, spending about £100 every night. I saved up £7,000 and lent it to Livingston just before I was nicked. He used it to buy a house and now says I never gave it to him so I'm not going to get it back . . . I want to get everything cleared up so that I can start a new life with my wife and kid.'

He went to court in 1982, was sentenced, and was back out in 1985. I heard nothing of him until Christmas Day. I was down in Devon with my family and had just finished a traditional Christmas dinner when the phone rang. The only people who ring policemen at Christmas dinner are other policemen who are working on Christmas Day and need help urgently.

'Roy. We've got a siege on. There's a bloke with a knife who's holding a child hostage. File says he's one of your snouts, Erroll Walker, and he's spoken to you in the past. What's the chances of you coming up to see if you can talk him out?'

He knew the chances were good because there was a local police car at the door before I'd put the phone down. Jean, my wife, knew the chances were good too. She knows the job comes first, Christmas or not.

'Better put a tie on, Roy. Can't go out in a police car looking informal.'

I was at the scene in about five hours. The Devon car dropped me off in Hampshire; the Hampshire car took me to the Met borders, and a Met car took me to the block of flats in Northolt where Erroll was holding his hostages in a first floor flat.

He had arrived at the flat at about 10.00 a.m. on Christmas morning. His wife Marlene and their 6-year-old daughter were there as well as his sister-in-law Jacqui and her daughter Carlene. There was sudden anger on the part of the two women at Erroll coming round on Christmas Day. Erroll was equally angry at their insistence that they didn't want the presents he had bought.

He drew a knife and stabbed Jacqui in the neck. She

staggered bleeding from the flat calling for help, and had died before an ambulance called by a neighbour arrived.

When police arrived in a van, Marlene and her daughter managed to get out, but Erroll, holding Carlene with one hand, and brandishing a knife with the other, made it clear he would kill the little girl if the police came any nearer. The flats either side of his were cleared and Erroll was under siege, striding in and out of the front door of the flat onto the narrow first floor balcony with a long knife in one hand and his young hostage with the other. The local uniformed police had, by 1.00 p.m. been supplemented by the armed men of PT17, the specialist firearms squad. They were there to kill him if he showed any sign of attempting to harm the girl.

In the middle of Christmas afternoon, while most of the nation was watching the Queen's speech, Erroll was dangling 4-year-old Carlene over the edge of the balcony, shouting incoherently. Marlene volunteered to try to talk him into surrendering. She got within four or five feet of him, and then had to be dragged back by police as Erroll made a jump to try and grab her. All the time that he was outside the flat he had Carlene in one hand and the knife in the other.

When I got to the flat, it was dark, Erroll had gone inside, and the waiting police settled down for the night. A phone link had been set up, but I was unable to speak to Erroll. As it was not my operation, I was not able to go to the door and tell Erroll who I was. He may have talked to me, or he may have become even more disturbed. There was no point in taking the slightest risk where Carlene's life was concerned.

Just after 9.00 a.m. the next day, he was seen again at the door with Carlene. A neighbour volunteered to cook breakfast for him and the girl. It was left on a tray, and when everyone was out of reach, he came out and took the tray in. The fire brigade arrived and set up a safety net beneath the balcony. Erroll again held Carlene over the edge. Most of the time police with guns and riot shields were within ten yards of him.

I was waiting for an opportunity to start negotiating with

him. This can be done, face to face, but is more usually carried out by phone, or at the very worst, by loudhailer. The philosophy is that if you can build up a relationship with the hostage taker he is less and less likely to carry out his threat to kill his victim.

Erroll, to be fair, was behaving very irrationally, walking in and out of the flat with the little girl in his arms, and shouting unintelligible demands. It would have been difficult to get him to a negotiating stage.

The siege area was now also the focus of television cameras which could, and did, cover every move made on that short stretch of balcony. At 3.45 p.m. Erroll made a dash along the balcony to pick up a riot shield that had been dropped by one of the siege officers. You might have seen what happened next on the evening television news.

The waiting officers chased after Erroll but he reached the flat door before them and slammed it in their face.

'I'm going to kill her,' he shouted at them from inside. 'You're stupid. I told you not to. I'll kill her now.'

The waiting officers seemed to be in some doubt, then one smashed a window with the butt of his revolver, and threw two stun grenades inside. Even after the grenades had exploded, another officer, attempting to break through the front door with a sledge-hammer, had still not been able to open it. Two armed officers climbed through the window. There were three shots, and then one of the officers ran from the flat carrying the little girl. Erroll had cut her twice with the knife, but her wounds were not serious. Waiting ambulance men rushed in, and Erroll was brought out, unconscious, in a wheelchair. He had been hit twice, one bullet entering his head and grazing his brain. He survived, pleaded guilty to the murder of his wife's sister, and was sentenced to life imprisonment.

He wrote from prison to tell me about Stephenson. He also told me about what he had done since coming out of prison in the middle of 1985. He went back on the robbery bandwagon.

'We run in this post office with masks. The women there scream and rush about. One presses the bell. They slam the drawers shut and we can't get at the money. So we come running out. He's more disappointed than me. He thought we might take about forty thousand and then he buy this restaurant.'

He hadn't changed much, until that Christmas Day when the man who took weapons on robberies but never used them, stabbed his sister-in-law in the neck and killed her.

Erroll's still in prison, permanently brain damaged from the police bullet. I didn't ask him what had happened to Carlene.

# A Man Who Buys And Sells

The minicab driver had bought this clock from a girl who looked down on her luck. He was one of these kind-hearted naïve drivers who abound in the capital, and when the girl told him about her misfortunes, he believed her. She was hard up and hungry, and she had this clock that a friend had given her. Would he like to buy it so that she could get some money to buy food?

The driver, a simple man, decided to help her out. He went back to her house, looked at the clock, decided it was worth about £150 and offered her £50. She hadn't told him the clock was stolen, so why should he think it had been? People are offering each other clocks in the street every day of the week. She took the £50, and off he went to a shop in Westbourne Grove that might be interested in buying a £150 clock for, say, £100? This is how Larry, the minicab driver, described the next part of his day when he later made a statement to police.

'Before I got to the shop I noticed a gentleman coming from the shop with the look of a man that buys and sells. I approached this person and mentioned the clock to him, and we settled that he would buy the clock for £110 which he paid me there and then in £10 notes.'

'The look of a man who buys and sells? . . . I mentioned the clock to him?' Sounds more like Dickens than a modern London street doesn't it? Perhaps things haven't changed that much.

The following day, Larry, our well-intentioned friend, was approached by two younger men, who told him that the

clock had been stolen, that the girl who had sold it to him
wanted £200 for it, and that if he did not hand over £200, she
would report him to the police as a fence. Larry, righteously
indignant, said that he had no idea that the clock had been
stolen. And anyway, he had already sold it. And what's more
they might like to know that it was worth nowhere near £200,
and they weren't getting any money off him. So there.

'They abused me and went away.'

Larry, recognising his duty as a citizen, went to Notting
Hill Police Station, told us all about the clock and brought an
end to a burglary enterprise that had begun a year earlier when
a Viscount had allowed a prostitute to shelter from the rain.

There are a number of small squares round the Bayswater
Road used unobtrusively by prostitutes. They pick up customers in cars and take them to one of the roads in Hyde Park
where they indulge in what is euphemistically known as 'hand
relief'. Even clients who want something more intimate find
themselves being massaged while driving to the park, and
often have climaxed before the car even stops.

'What a pity you came so quickly,' says the girl sympath-
etically, one eye on her watch. 'We could have had a lot more
fun if you had been able to hold on.' Do that ten times in an
evening and you're making money. If it rains, of course, a
girl doesn't want to be walking around, and there are fewer
punters on the prowl. Most of the girls working in that area
know Viscount Blank. He never uses their services, but his
house has a deep porch, and he has made it clear that he has no
objections to the girls sheltering there. So Jasmine and Sandra
were in the doorway on this wet July evening, waiting for the
rain to stop so that they could get out and earn.

'You know that Jimmy, you know the black lad with that
sort of pigtail, he got lifted last week. Being done for a whole
load of burglaries.'

'Didn't think he was that sort. Don't look violent or
anything.'

'He ain't violent. Nice quiet thieving with no one around
is what he does. Showed me how he did it once. Dead easy on

the right doors. All you need is a piece of plastic. Just stick it in the crack and it sort of slides the lock back.'

'Don't be daft. Can't open a door with a piece of plastic. You got to know about keys, and locks. Stuff like that.'

'No. Honest. Look I'll show you. This old bloke never locks his door properly until he goes to bed. See if I can do it with an Access.'

Sandra rummaged in her bag for an Access card, slid it into the crack of the old-fashioned Yale lock, and the door swung open. They pulled it to in a panic.

'He comes out, he'll think we're trying to thieve from him. Easy though, isn't it?'

And the next day Sandra and Jasmine experimented first on their own door, and then on a neighbour's door. Dead easy.

They went to a local café, and over coffee decided on a change of occupation.

'Just small stuff that we can put in our pockets. Nothing that you have to carry in bags.'

'And not miles away from here either.'

'How we going to get rid of it?'

'That Jane bird. One who keeps the hotel at the back of the Tube.'

'Hotel? More like a doss house. She pay properly?'

'Long as you're one of her regulars.'

And that's how they started. Two young women, smartly dressed, no one would see anything suspicious about them. And when, now and again, there was someone in the house they intended to burgle, it was, 'We've come about the room to let', followed by pretended confusion at mixing up addresses. They quickly found that they needed something better than an Access card for most doors, so they experimented with long strips of heavy plastic which could be thrown away once they had been used. They also learned to avoid doors which had frames that protruded more than a quarter inch over the surface. And they quickly realised that many of the tall Paddington houses were divided into bed-sitters and flats from which the tenants were absent all day.

So for between three or four hours in the middle of the day, Jasmine and Sandra wandered round Notting Hill, noting likely houses, watching them in the morning to see how many people left, and then opening the simple front door locks with their lengths of plastic. Once inside, they stood in the hallway.

'Anyone in?' When there was no answers, and usually there were no answers, they went from room to room, looking quickly through drawers and cupboards, putting rings, watches, jewellery, and small ornaments in their pockets and handbags, and stopping as soon as they had no more room to carry anything else. Then over to Jane at the Balmoral Guest House to sell the stuff immediately.

The life suited them. They were no longer working in the evenings. There was less danger – angry or disappointed punters can become violent and attack the prostitute when the experience has not been what they expected – and they had moved a few stages up their particular social ladder. Their boyfriends treated them with more respect. Then they stole the clock, broke their pattern, and got themselves arrested.

Perhaps it was over-confidence. Perhaps it was greed. So far they had been careful, prudent even. Too often they had left property behind because they did not want to carry it through the streets. Once or twice, when there had been expensive coats, they walked out wearing them. But in this flat just off the Bayswater Road there were a few pieces of jewellery and what even to them looked like a beautiful clock.

'Bet that's worth a bit. Jewellery's a bit old-fashioned, sort of antique. Bet the clock's an antique as well.'

'Don't want to walk through the streets carrying something like that. We always said we didn't want to be seen carrying things.'

'Suppose you're right, pity though . . . Here, tell you what, there's a suitcase here. We could stick it in there. No one's going to notice us with a suitcase. Place is full of people staying overnight and going to Paddington.'

'OK then. But if we're taking a suitcase, might as well fill
it.' So they took the clock and a video-recorder as well as
two jewel boxes. Jane at the Balmoral did not share their
enthusiasm about the clock.

'Sorry love. You know me. No antiques. Don't know
nothing about them, and you get caught too easily paying out
for rubbish. Give you a hundred for the video. That's all I've
got. You'll have to come back with the Tom another time.
Try me at the end of the week. I'll have cash by then.'

'Knew we shouldn't have gone for the clock,' Jasmine
muttered as they walked back. 'Don't know anyone else
likely to take it.'

'What about that Larry down at the minicab place? He's
always up to something.' So Jasmine sold the clock to Larry,
and the two girls told their boyfriends about it.

'Bastard's seen you off. Bet it was worth more than that.
Clock on the *Antiques Road Show* other week. Reckon it was
worth two grand. Let's see if we can screw another few quid
out of him.' You know now that they couldn't screw another
few quid out of Larry. Larry's caution was greater than
Larry's greed. This clock was becoming a talked-about item.
Larry's philosophy had always been to tell us about things
before we asked him about them . . . if he was absolutely
certain of course that we would get to hear of them.

So when Larry came to Notting Hill, he was sent up to see
me. I was looking for any information on local burglaries,
especially those that might involve two girls. There had
been a dozen or so burglaries on the ground in the last
six months which had been linked with a couple of good
looking girls. We were lucky at Notting Hill to have some of
the old-fashioned types of copper who didn't see their job as
dashing from one call to another. They asked questions, and
when they had asked questions at the houses next to those
which had been burgled, they had been told about the two
girls, seen close by, around the times of the burglaries.

On Monday there had been a burglary in which a carriage
clock had been taken. A street cleaner had seen two girls in the

road whom he had noticed about before. So did Larry know anything more about the girl from whom he had bought the clock?

'Well, Mr Herridge,' (always told them my name – it helps to establish confidence) 'I can point the house out to you. She had a funny name, sort of foreign, Jasmine, something like that. Fancy her stealing it though. I would never have bought it in a million years if there had been anything illegal about it. I was just feeling sorry for her.'

So I went with Larry, and he pointed the house out. But we had a few more inquiries to make yet. Much too early to make a move yet. First check our own collator's records. Yes, there was a Jasmine at that address, few previous for soliciting, but nothing for thieving. Among her associates, Sandra, also with previous for soliciting. They were still friends. A PC who had once arrested Jasmine for soliciting had stopped her a week ago in Queensway. She was with Sandra at the time.

Next a check with CRO. Jasmine and Sandra were on bail to St Albans Crown Court accused of planning a burglary with a man who was being held in custody. Then as accurate a description of the clock that Larry could provide, and a quick comparison with the description of the clock stolen in Monday's burglary. Enough now to justify a search warrant.

The courts were closed so I swore out the information for the warrants in front of a JP in his front room. He fitted me in during the commercial break of *Coronation Street*. Then it was time to give instinct a little run. We had known about Jane at the Balmoral for a long time. But arresting a receiver requires a bit of finesse. Most of them are in occupations in which they can give a plausible account for being in possession of any property found. Dealers who make their living from buying second-hand goods can produce an excuse for anything found on their premises. Jane, at the Balmoral, could easily claim that anything found at her hotel had been left by a guest who was expected to come back. The way to arrest a receiver successfully is to make it clear that thieves are being arrested at the same time. Jane, arrested on her own, would say nothing. Jane, arrested when it was clear that local thieves were being arrested, would be eager to drop everyone else in it before they did the same to her.

So at 7.30 a.m. the next morning I went to Jasmine's flat with two DCs. Another squad went to Sandra's and a third to the Balmoral.

Jasmine would not answer the door, so it had to be forced. I showed her the search warrant.

'You won't find nothing here.'

We found jewellery everywhere.

'It's all mine.'

A television set that was not being used. 'Bought it off a bloke in a pub. Didn't ask too many questions.'

Then a piece of plastic in the pocket of one of her coats. 'Shit. Thought I'd thrown that away.'

We took her to the station. Jane was already there. Sandra came shortly afterwards. Jane wasted no time. 'Bought a video off them on Monday. Paid 'em a hundred quid.'

Sandra and Jasmine were not going to answer any questions until their solicitor was present. They were put into separate cells.

Sandra called Jasmine, when they thought the cell corridor was empty, 'Have the one we did on Monday, that old cow has put us in it. Don't admit anything else.'

When their solicitor came, I told them what we knew about the Monday burglary, including the clock.

'All we took was a video,' Sandra said. 'We got a hundred nicker for it from Jane. That's all we took.'

They had enough street sense to know that without the clock, and relying only on Larry's evidence, we hadn't much to go on. They knew also that we had found the jewellery they had taken, but took a chance on the owner not knowing the pieces well enough to identify them.

So I laid out all the jewellery taken from both flats on the table between us and went through it bit by bit with each in turn. There was a lot more than the contents of the two boxes taken on Monday. It was hard work, very hard work. I started with Sandra.

A pair of earrings – 'My gran's. She's dead now.'

A gold chain – 'Bought it in the Portobello two years ago. Think it was a Friday.'

A watch, – 'Boyfriend asked me to look after it. Haven't seen him about for a bit.'

And so on, for twelve pages and fifty items.

Same routine with Jasmine. Same sort of answers.

'Little shop off the Mile End Road . . . Girl called Gilly left it when she stayed one night . . . Got those as a present from a punter who wanted to marry me.'

Silly really. They must have known that a lot of the stuff could be identified, and that had we gone through the list a second time they would not be able to remember what they had said about each piece the first time. Within a week we had organised an exhibition of the jewellery recovered for the dozens of people who had been burgled in the area. Many of the pieces were identified, and we could put a full case together against the two lady burglars. They got two years apiece, suspended. I don't know which of their two professions they now follow.

My only disappointment in the whole affair was being unable to trace the man 'with the look of a person that buys and sells'. Had I been blessed with Larry's supposed gift of being able to identify that type of person on sight, the rest of my police work would have been so much easier.

# A Hole In the Wall

The two prisoners in Pentonville's B32 cell had been working on the bricks for six weeks. They had started almost
idly, finding a mailbag needle which had been hidden in
the brickwork of the cell by an earlier prisoner, and had
picked away casually at the cement holding the bricks in
place. It was soon clear that it would be fairly easy to remove
a complete brick.

So they started to work methodically. Wait until the screw
had checked the cell, last thing at night, then take turns
scraping away at the mortar. Get rid of the dust at slopping
out in the morning, or during exercise periods. Much like
Steve McQueen in *The Great Escape*. Alieu and Billy took
turns in scraping, and watching and listening for the screws
by day. During the night the prison officers never physically
checked the cells. The two prisoners worked at the bricks
beneath the air vent, prising them loose with a bolt which
they had taken from another part of the prison. Each day
they replaced the mortar with a papier-mâché paste made
from scrap paper, and painted over with powdered milk.
On December 23, they were ready to go.

At 9.00 p.m. the prison officer on their wing made a
physical examination of the cells, that is, he looked through
the spy hole on each door, and checked that each cell had its
correct quota of prisoners. Cell B32 was correct. The wing
would be checked at intervals throughout the night, but
with everyone banged up in their cells there seemed little
need to check each cell again. The night duty dog-handler
checked the yard outside B wing at 4.00 a.m. The checks

were made conscientiously, but without any great belief that there would be an attempt at escape. Most of the prisoners on this wing were awaiting trial, many of them hopeful of being found not guilty, or of being given a short sentence. There was no point in any of them escaping.

Alieu and Billy, having found a way to get out, may well have thought it a waste of a good opportunity not to take advantage of it. They knew the routine, waited until after four, removed all the bricks, and stacked them neatly in a box under a bunk. Bricks lying about on the floor would immediately give the game away if a screw looked in, but hiding them away could give them a few seconds extra when the screw made his 6.00 a.m. check. Their bunks were made to look as if they were still asleep, and the hole under the air vent would not be immediately obvious. Once they were sure that the dog handler had finished his routine check of the yard they pulled out the air vent and then crawled through into the exercise yard.

The outer wall had scaffolding against it so it was not difficult to cross from the exercise yard into the work yard. There was a wooden ladder chained to the scaffolding; Alieu freed it by using a scaffolding shoe to break the runner to which the chain was attached. Although the sound seemed monstrous to them, there was no response from the warders. They then put the ladder against the outside wall, and Billy impetuously swarmed up and immediately trapped himself in the razor wire on top of the wall. Alieu had to leave him there in the wire which was cutting into his face and hands, and put the ladder alongside him so that he could get to the top and help him. He had to pick the wire out piece by piece, a nerve-racking task on top of a prison wall with the chance of their absence being discovered at any time. When Billy was free of the wire, he jumped onto a light standard, and then to the ground. Alieu just jumped down. He stayed with Billy all day until the latter found friends who would look after him. He could have left him there as soon as Billy was stuck in the wire. He could have abandoned him as soon as they were outside the prison. Alieu was black, Billy was white. They had never met before they shared a cell.

Alieu Cessay had been on remand in Pentonville awaiting trial. Dale Morris, 21, had been out for six months. He was philosophical about his latest, and his many previous imprisonments. You commit an offence. You get arrested. You go to court. You get sent to jail. That's it. All over, finished. You should have no more to worry about. If an employer wants to know what you were doing during your time in jail you can tell him, or invent a trip abroad, or even claim to have been unemployed. Dale, his sentence behind him, was entitled to feel he had been given a new start. Unfortunately the only trade he knew was selling cannabis. That's what he had served his six months for, and that's how he told other prisoners he intended to earn his living when he came out of prison.

'I had a mate in prison, and told him that when I got out I was going back to trying to sell "puff" again because I didn't know how else to earn a living . . . I think he must have talked about me,' he said afterwards. Quite a few people had called on Dale since his release on the assumption that he had gone back to dealing. But Dale had taken up with a new girlfriend, and was making a genuine attempt to go straight. The callers were told that Dale was not dealing in drugs any more and left in search of a new source of 'puff'. Just after Christmas Dale had two more callers who were not willing to accept that he was no longer a dealer. One of them was Alieu.

Dale was living with Pauline and her 4-year-old son in a council flat in Battersea. It was after midnight, the television film was over and Dale was getting a meal ready in the kitchen while Pauline chatted with a neighbour in the lounge. Pauline answered a knock on the door thinking it was Lloyd, her neighbour's husband. A black man, six foot two inches tall, with a knife in his hand, and an even taller white man pushed into the flat. Imagine that happening to you. It's Christmas. You're sitting at home, talking to friends, and within seconds you're facing death or injury from a total stranger carrying a knife with a four-inch-long blade and a knuckle-duster handle. When you read on and start thinking 'Why didn't she do something?' or 'I wouldn't have let him do that' put yourself in that flat a few days after Christmas, talking to friends, having had a couple of drinks. All of a sudden there are two very big men with knives feet away from you.

The black man went straight to Pauline in the lounge and the white man, also carrying a knife, grabbed Dale by the hair and started punching and headbutting him.

'You know what we've come for.'

Dale managed to stammer that he was no longer selling drugs, but the white man kept hitting and punching him. The black man kept Pauline and her friend in the lounge. They screamed and wept, but Pauline had the presence of mind to stamp on the floor to attract the attention of friends in the flat below. The white man after ten or so minutes tired of hitting Dale, and told him he would have to steal whatever else was worth having in the flat. Then there was a knock on the door. Four friends from downstairs had heard the noise and had come up to help.

'You bastard!' the white man leapt at Dale across the bed. 'I'm coming back for you.'

The two intruders left, pushing the four men at the door to one side.

'Next time, we'll carve you up.'

The threat was to Dale, but the danger to everyone was clear.

'Better come downstairs with us, and bring anything you don't want nicked,' his friends told him. They knew the two men. The white man was Foxy. Alieu Cessay they knew was on the run from prison.

'They're bad news,' his friends told him. Within minutes there was a knock on the friends' door. Foxy and Cessay were back.

'Give them the keys to your flat,' his friends urged him,

'Let them take anything they want. We'll sort it all out later on.'

Dale gave the two robbers £100 and some cannabis. They left. Dale didn't tell the police about it.

'I was frightened and I'd never made a police statement against anyone before.' Dale who had been before a court every year since he left school, for offences ranging from burglary to carrying an offensive weapon and dealing in drugs, was not the type of man who would willingly go to the police for any reason at all. His friends eventually told them that it had 'all been sorted out' and he wouldn't be bothered again.

It could not have been a high quality sorting out. Foxy and Cessay came back early in January. Dale, his brother Vance, and a friend from the downstairs flat, Lloyd, had been out to the pub. When they got back to the flats, they saw Foxy near the garages at the back of the flats. Lloyd went over to speak to him, and then Dale and Vance joined them, having been told by another friend that Cessay was waiting at the end of the road in case Dale tried to run away. There was no doubt that Dale was the target.

That's what a reputation for violence can do. There must have been ten able-bodied men capable of dealing with Foxy and Cessay who knew they were waiting for Dale, but who felt unable to protect him.

As soon as Foxy saw Dale he grabbed him by the hair, held a knife at his throat and told him he wanted everything in the flat. Dale, knowing that Pauline was asleep there with her son, wanted as little disturbance as possible. Lloyd and his brother made some token display of resistance, but Dale was dragged to the lift, where Cessay was waiting. At the flat, Foxy took the keys from him and opened the door. Foxy again was the one who displayed violence. Cessay's role seemed to be that of a back-up.

Pauline was asleep on the settee. Dale woke her up.

'They've come to take everything,' he told her. 'You'll be OK if you don't make a noise.'

Cessay kept watch over Pauline, Vance and Lloyd in the lounge while Foxy took Dale into another room and subjected him to another beating. He punched him about the face and body and when he fell to the floor he kicked him between the legs.

'Show me what you've got. We want everything.' he said, punching and kicking Dale dispassionately. Cessay unplugged the TV, the video, and a record-player.

'We've got to take it all,' he told Pauline. He was speaking quietly, almost as if he was apologising.

'It's not enough. I want more stuff.' Foxy was shouting at Dale. Punch and kick, punch and kick again.

Pauline curled up on the settee hiding her head between her knees, took off her rings and hid them beneath a cushion. When Foxy came in and demanded gold from her, she gave him two bracelets from her wrist and a ring which she kept in the kitchen. Foxy brushed them aside.

'Load of rubbish. You better find something better. I'm bored.' He drove the knife through the wood of the lounge door, leaving the blade protruding from the other side. He came back with some earrings.

'You didn't tell me about these. You're trying to hide stuff.'

'They're not worth anything,' Pauline told him. He hurled them across the room. It was now clear that Foxy was drunk, and was arguing with Cessay.

'Black bastard.'

'Honkie cunt.' Their prisoners kept quiet, terrified of provoking more violence. Dale was being punched into unconsciousness.

Then Cessay and Foxy started spraying aerosol cans and lighting the sprays. They had already sprinkled lighter fluid on a bed. To their prisoners it appeared that a single wrong word would provoke the two men into setting the flat alight. Cessay and Foxy spent an hour piling together what they wanted to steal, with Foxy pausing now and again to beat Dale. Eventually they loaded their loot into the lift;

a television, a video recorder, a phone, a cassette-player, some jewellery and £10 they had taken from Pauline. Five minutes later they came back to cut the phone wire.

This was a strange community. So many people knew Foxy and Cessay to be violent men who would not hesitate to rob their neighbours. Just as many knew that Cessay had escaped from prison. No one thought it their business to tell the police until Dale decided that he had had enough and called the police to report what had happened to him.

I took over the investigation which was not the formality that it looked. We knew the suspects, but not where to find them, and we knew that witnesses who had been afraid to give evidence before, could still go back on their statements. The two men were clearly known to all the witnesses. Cessay was on the run and therefore unlikely to be given a lot of help. But we began to get all sorts of information that we did not expect. Possible addresses. Who might be handling the few pieces they had stolen from Dale and Pauline. The number of the car they were using. It had been stolen a week after they had attacked Dale. Current information like that was a good indication that there was a full commitment on the part of the minor local villains to put these two trouble-makers away.

The number of the car was circulated to all police in south London. Early in February a uniform police sergeant saw the car parked in a cul-de-sac. He could have been a hero, and steamed in himself, risking a beating, and the escape of the wanted men. But he used his head. He drove to a point where he could watch the end of the cul-de-sac, called for plain-clothes assistance, and then drove away in case one of the wanted men, walking back to the car, might be warned off by the presence of a uniformed police officer.

The car was kept under observation. Cessay came out of a block of flats opposite, and was allowed to drive away. We had a list of all his friends, and the flat was already being watched, with a search warrant ready for immediate use. When he was clear of the road, he was stopped. He locked all the doors of the car and an officer had to break a window with a truncheon before he could be arrested.

While he was being taken to the station, his girlfriend at the flat he had just left was also arrested. She had a letter from him, and a newspaper cutting describing his escape from prison. She also had property that had been stolen in local burglaries. Alieu had given her most of it.

'I knew it was nicked. It had to be with him on the run.'

In between the beating up of Dale Morris and his arrest, we discovered that Cessay had been involved in a bizarre attempt at rape. Jill Small, a 20-year-old secretary living in Battersea, woke up about 7.30 a.m. to find a man in her room. Her flat was one of a number being repointed and there was scaffolding outside her window. Her first thought was that one of the workmen was playing a joke. Then the intruder pushed her back in her bed, and put his hand over her mouth.

'Not a sound,' he said, 'or I'll put you in intensive care.'

Jill tried to scream, but couldn't tell how loud the noise she was making was. She realised that she had her duvet stuffed in her mouth as well as a hand across her face. The man, it was Cessay of course, lay on top of her for two or three minutes. Then he stood up and Jill started talking to him. She told him about her flatmates, what time they would be going out, what work she did, how she might be sacked if he kept her and made her late. After thirty minutes she went out to the corridor, told him there was no one else around, and he walked out of the front door. At the front door he was stopped by one of Jill's flatmates, Nicholas, whose attention she had managed to attract. He spoke to Nicholas for two or three minutes making no attempt to hide his face.

Two days later, armed with a knife, he robbed a television shop in Lavender Hill. Again he made no attempt to disguise himself, and although he was violent in his language, no one in the shop was harmed. He was easily picked out on a later identification parade.

When he was interviewed about all these offences, he was open only about the escape from prison. He excused himself for the attack on Dale Morris by saying that they had just gone to collect electrical equipment for a man to whom Dale owed money.

'I was just being helpful.' No one was assaulted. The car had been given to him by a man he didn't know. He hadn't robbed the television shop. The witnesses who had identified him must have recognised him from his picture in the local paper. He did not try to rape the girl in the flat at Battersea. He was staying with someone in Fulham that night. He was not prepared to give his name.

'I don't want to say his name because it will lead to other things. But if it comes to court you can speak to him in the witness box.' He was asked about six other burglaries at each of which a footprint had been found with markings identical to the trainers that he had been wearing when he was arrested.

'The burglaries ain't got nothing to do with me.'

'Why are you smiling?' he was asked.

'Can't I smile? I just got a good sense of humour.'

For a man who had made a well-planned and success-ful escape from Pentonville Prison, Cessay made some terrible errors once he was out. He came back to the area in which he was known; mixed with the people he had mixed with before going into prison and made no attempt at all to disguise himself. Almost as if he wanted to go back inside. He sounds almost a gentle giant. Six foot two, on the run, and no physical harm to anyone.

So what was he in Pentonville for in the first place? Well, he had raped a 16-year-old girl while she slept in the next room to her parents. Five weeks later he went back to the same block of flats and raped a 23-year-old woman living on her own, threatening her with a two-foot machete. Jill, who found him in her room at 7.00 in the morning lived a few blocks from those two rapes. I don't know if she ever realised what a lucky escape she had had.

# Sin In The Sticks

Adultery is with us all the time. I don't say this in a censorious way: adultery is nothing to do with the police, but we have to be aware of it. When we appeal for witnesses, we have to recognise that the 'couple in the red Sierra who stopped to help the victim and then drove off' might have very good reasons for not wanting anyone to know that they were in that area, or that they were together. As soon as a wife or husband is reported missing, we need to know as tactfully as possible if the spouse reporting him or her suspects that there is a lover involved. Men and women injured in quite vicious attacks or alleged robberies may not want any police inquiries at their own addresses. Even criminals sometimes need to keep adultery a secret.

'Look, Mr Herridge. If I plead to the motor, can you keep shtum about the bird. She didn't know it was bent, and if my old lady finds out . . .'

When Jeff Browning found that his wife was in legal terms 'committing adultery', or in secular terms 'was over the side', he did not accept it as normal. It took him a long time to accept it at all, and when he finally realised what was going on, he could not work out how he felt. He was not particularly well educated, but he was intelligent and earned good money on catering shift work at Heathrow.

Working irregular hours he was not too upset on those evenings that he returned home late to find that his wife was out with friends from work, playing badminton perhaps, or attending night-school. They had been married for twenty years. Both children were away at universities. Betty had a good job with a solicitor. They both had cars. She enjoyed night-school. He thought he remembered her saying that she was studying sociology. He had not taken much interest in what she was doing, but he knew she got on well with her fellow students.

'Nice lot of people. Jeff. We all go off for a few drinks after the lesson. Learn more at the pub than we do in class.'

It was, after all, only once a week. It was only once a week at first. One Friday Jeff realised that Betty had been out four nights running. Then he realised that they had not made love for four or five months. He sat at the kitchen table, the beans on toast that he had prepared for his own supper going cold in front of him, as he began to come to terms with a truth that he had been pushing to the back of his mind. Betty, always a smart dresser, had been spending more time on her appearance. Every Saturday morning now, she had a hairdressers' appointment. She had taken to wearing stockings and suspenders.

'Thought you always said they were too much trouble, Bets. Always told me you preferred tights.'

'Fancy you noticing. Ages since you took any notice of what I'm wearing.' Betty had been amused rather than angry. 'I'd rather wear tights. They're a lot easier. But stockings are quite fashionable. Some of these modern dresses, they don't hang properly with tights.' He pushed the plate away. He knew it had been a weak excuse at the time, but he had not wanted to pursue it.

Jeff started spying. He came home early from work one evening and waited outside the school at which the night-classes were held. At 9.00 p.m. the caretaker was locking up. At ten past the school was in darkness.

'Normally goes on 'til 10.00.' Betty had told him once. 'Woman could get killed in the rush to the pub.'

Still he said nothing. Ask the wrong question, show that you doubted her when there was no good reason for it, you'll never hear the end of it. She might be able to explain it all.

She might be able to explain why she hadn't been to the local badminton club for six months.

'Sorry mate,' the club barman told him over the phone, 'not seen her about since, probably Christmas.'

One night, he went into a pub by accident. He was not spying. He'd given a workmate, whose car had been stolen from the airport, a lift home.

'Get a call from the police telling me it's just been driven off Beachy Head, if I'm lucky,' his friend told him philosophically. 'Insurance will have to look after it. Least I can do is buy you a pint. Nice little pub on the corner of the road.'

Jeff sat at a table in the corner while his friend went to the bar. They were half-way through their pints when Jeff saw his wife on the other side of the pub going to the ladies'.

'Obviously with her night-school mates,' he told himself, refusing to examine the reason for his wife being so far away from the school.

She went back to her place without seeing Jeff, who finished his pint, said good-night to his workmate, and walked to the door. The pub was crowded. At the door he turned and looked at the other side of the room. His wife was standing with her back to him. There was a heavily-built man talking to her, not the idle chatter of someone passing the time, but the intense conversation of someone who is sure that his audience is listening. The man had a glass in one hand, and with the fingers of his other hand he was quite deliberately tracing the outline of his wife's knickers round the top of her thigh. She made no attempt to stop him. Jeff drove home, sat down at the kitchen table and waited.

It was past 11.00 before he heard her car in the drive. She looked surprised to see him up.

'What a night,' she said, taking her coat off. 'Even the lecturer came for a pint tonight. He . . .'

'I saw you in the pub, Betty. Saw the fellow with you. What's going on?'

She looked directly at him.

'What's all the fuss? That must have been Bill. He's the lecturer. We all went over to this pub, because Doreen wanted a change. Why didn't you come over. Fancy not making yourself known.'

'Knock it off, Bets.' Jeff was calm. This was something serious to be sorted out without a row. 'There was only the two of you, and he was having a real grope. Checking to see that you weren't wearing tights.'

Betty took her coat to the hall and hung it up, then came back to the kitchen and sat down opposite Jeff.

'All right then. It's true. I was trying to make up my mind to tell you. It's serious, Jeff, not just a bit of slap and tickle. He's left his wife. Seems silly at our time of life to talk about love. That's what it is. Not just an affair. We love each other. We can't help it.'

'You been to bed with him?'

Betty looked down at the table, pushed her handbag to one side, fiddled with her wedding ring. Finally she answered.

'Yes.'

'When? Where?' Jeff was still calm.

'Not here. I wouldn't do that to you. A hotel. We took a day off. You were off fishing. A few other times. But not here, Jeff. Jeff, look no good saying I'm sorry. You've always treated me well, but we can't give each other up.'

'You mean you're going off with him?'

'We've talked about it. It will come to that. It's got to. I don't care about anything else. It sounds, well, cruel. But I just want to be with him.'

'You thought about the kids?'

'They're grown up now, Jeff. They know what life is all about. I'd have told them. Sooner or later. But I've made my mind up. I'm leaving. I'll go tonight. Get a hotel room or something. We better get a solicitor and sort things out properly.'

Jeff was still sitting at the table as he had been when Betty first came in.

'You've been thinking about this for a long time. How long you been seeing him?'

'Six months. I think.'

Each of them was surprised that the other was so calm.

She was thinking, 'It's going to be all right. He's not angry. He's not going to shout. It's going to be all right.'

He was thinking, 'Has she been that unhappy with me? I must be thick not noticing.'

She went back to the hall and got her coat.

'I'll go to a hotel. I'll just pack a few things. We'll have to meet to talk things through.'

'No point in going to a hotel. I'll sleep in the spare room until we sort something out. What's he going to do for you? He got somewhere for you to stay?' There was the first sign of doubt in Betty.

'This is all a bit quick, Jeff. We know we want to be together. He's still trying to sort things out with his wife. You've only just heard about it. We hadn't talked about this in detail.'

Jeff got up from the table.

'Can't sort anything out unless we know just what he's got in mind. You going to tell me his name? We should get together. The three of us. See what's going to happen. If this is what you really want, there's nothing I can do about it. But I'd like to know just what he's got in mind.'

'You mean he should come round here and talk it all over?'

'Soon as possible. Seems sensible. No point in putting this off. We'll all talk it out, and you might change your mind. I don't want you to go, but I don't want to hang around like a spare prick if you want to be somewhere else.'

Betty went up to the bedroom thinking, 'It's going to be all right. It's going to work out. I wish I'd told him sooner instead of him finding out. It'll be all right.'

Jeff sat for a long time on the edge of the bed in the spare room.

'I should be feeling something. Can't feel anything at all.

No point in being angry. She's set her mind on going. Wish I could feel something. Sooner I see whoever he is, sooner I'll be able to feel something.'

So Bert came to tea. Jeff felt slightly ashamed that his wife had a lover called Bert. He would have perhaps felt better about someone with a slightly less working-class name, but that was his only emotion. He seemed to himself to be working in a space in which certain actions had to be carried out before feelings could be allowed to enter.

It was only a few days after Jeff had found out. Betty, in some sort of panic, had insisted on making sandwiches, and providing cake.

'Now it will be no good if you start rowing. No point in shouting at each other. We've got to talk this through calmly.'

'It was my idea in the first place,' Jeff reminded her. He had not shouted or raised his voice in anger since he had first confronted Betty. There was a knock on the door. Betty answered. Jeff stayed in the sitting-room with the table laid for the formal tea.

'Jeff, this is Bert. Bert, Jeff.' They shook hands formally. Jeff was five foot ten, Bert considerably taller and heavier. He was obviously determined to try to get through what promised to be a traumatic visit by making forced jokes.

'Nice to meet you at last, Jeff. Heard a lot about you, of course. Nice to meet you in the flesh, so to speak.' The first of many laughs spluttered out. Jeff smiled slightly.

'Thought it was better to sort all this out face to face like civilised people.'

'Quite right. Quite right. Lot of things to be discussed. We're all adults. These things will happen. Glad you're taking it like this.'

Betty, clearly nervous, got them to sit down at the table, then, obviously signalling that she expected them to arrange details without her being present, went into the kitchen to make tea.

'Well, Jeff. OK if I call you Jeff? Suppose we've got to sort

out things like maintenance. I obviously got to look after my
family. Betty needs somewhere. We were thinking perhaps
you move out . . . take your time of course . . . seems sense
that Betty has somewhere for the kids when they're home.
Place'll be too big for you on your own.'

Bert was quick and awkward in his speech. Jeff recognised
that he was going through a script that Betty had prepared
for him.

'Thing is, know it sounds daft, but we're in love. Like a
couple of kids. I haven't been getting on with my missus for
years, and she's got a fancy man, so we're separating. She's
got to have the house 'cos there are still kids at school. Bet
tells me that she earns a fair bit. I got to support my own
kids of course. So we can manage OK. No point in making
a definite arrangement until the kids are off our hands.'

'My kids are off my hands,' Jeff pointed out quietly.

'Course they are. I was talking about my own. They're
going to like Betty. We want to tell them as soon as we've
got things sorted out. You should be able to get a flat
somewhere.'

Jeff stayed silent, looking straight at Bert, Bert kept
glancing at Jeff but wouldn't hold his eyes.

'Look,' he stumbled on. 'Know that you're angry. Understandable when everything's said and done. You want to take
a smack at me. Go ahead. You're entitled. I won't stop you.'
He half rose from his chair and pushed his chin towards Jeff.
He was still in his half joking mood.

Jeff stood up. Bert, half up, lifted his chin a little higher.
Two seconds later he was dead. Jeff took the kitchen knife
that Betty had left on the table, and in one quick blow drove
it directly between the protecting ribs into and through
Bert's heart. Bert's body fell forwards and sideways with
the knife fast and deep in the trunk. Jeff, who had not let go
of the knife fell with him. He stayed there, lying partly on
top of this man he had met five minutes ago and whom he
had just killed. He was in no doubt that Bert was dead. He
had no experience of death or violence, but the easy way that

the knife had slipped into Bert's chest up to the hilt, coupled with the way the life had flicked out of Bert's eyes as they fell to the floor together meant that he was in no doubt that he was dead.

Betty, hearing the noise, ran back into the kitchen. All she could see was her lover lying on the floor on his side, and her husband lying on top of him with his hand on the handle of a knife that was deep in the body beneath him. She had the presence of mind to run to the kitchen to call for an ambulance, keeping her eyes fixed on the door in case her husband should now want to kill her.

Police and ambulance arrived together.

'I killed him,' he told the young constable, the first police officer there. 'He was going to go off with my Betty, and I just couldn't stand the thought of it.'

There was no need for a lengthy investigation. Jeff made a statement admitting the killing, although all he claimed to remember was being found on Bert's body holding the knife that had killed him. His fingerprints were on the knife. Bert's blood was on his clothing, and we had Betty's evidence of what had happened immediately before she had gone to the kitchen, and what she saw when she came back into the dining-room. He had said to her in the presence of the constable, 'I love you Betty. I wouldn't have killed him if I didn't love you.' He was charged with murder, and six months later appeared at the Old Bailey where he pleaded not guilty to murder or manslaughter.

That only left him with the defences of accidental death or self defence, and he could not remember anything other than Bert asking to be hit. The death was clearly not an accident, as Jeff had admitted killing Bert.

'I didn't mean to kill him,' he had told me in one interview. 'But I was in a blind rage at what he had done and what he was asking for.' I had hoped to prove that he had himself placed the knife, a carving knife on the table himself, but Betty told us that she had put it there.

'I just wasn't thinking straight. There was a lot of stuff

on the table that I wouldn't dream of putting there just for tea.'

That was true enough, I had had the items on the table listed as soon as it was clear that the killing had been with a kitchen knife.

The jury were told that they could only find Jeff 'not guilty' if they were satisfied that he had acted in self defence. The twelve good men and true and similarly gifted women of the jury found him not guilty. I think he was as surprised as the judge and the lawyers. He left the court, and went straight back to the house where he had killed Bert. Betty, of course, had been living there while Jeff was in custody. I wonder what they had to say to each other that evening. As far as I know they are still living together.

One thing more. Jeff came to the station to ask for the knife back. I suppose that he was legally entitled to it, but returning it just did not seem right. So I refused to let him have it and that's the last I heard of him. The knife went off to the police property store and was later destroyed.

# Something In The Attic

They had mugged about eight people already that year. Not old women, not kids. Their victims were all men, most of them fit and young. They may have had a pride that prevented them picking on the weak, but they certainly had an instinct that told them that a fit young man was likely to be carrying more cash than an old woman. But you couldn't really call them friends, not even a team. Lennie, 25 years, a skinhead, around five foot ten inches, had been living in squats around London for three years, after leaving a wife and baby in Birmingham. Sam, the same age, about the same height, had been squatting for five years. The first time they met had been in a squatted block of flats at King's Cross. They had each taken over rooms on the first floor. Lennie had forced out a 17-year-old girl with a baby.

'Council should be looking after you,' he told her, pushing her and a plastic bag with her clothes out onto the landing. Sam looked out from his room to see what the noise was about. He recognised that life with Lennie as a neighbour would be easier if Lennie was a friend.

'Fancy a pint?' he called across to Lennie as the girl's sobbing and her baby's crying faded down the stairs. That's how it started. In the pub, Lennie told Sam that he took most of his money from other people.

'Reckon you got to help yourself. No other fucker's goin' to.'

They stayed in the pub until Sam's money ran out.

'Time we was earning,' Lennie said, putting his glass down. 'Take you to a right place.'

They went to York Way at the side of King's Cross Station, waited for a man on his own, one of the Australians or New Zealanders going up to the Backpacker. When one appeared walking briskly Lennie stepped out in front of him, Sam stood behind.

'Scuse me mate. Need a couple of quid to make up the money to get a ticket home. Can you help out?' Lennie's stance, blocking the young Australian's way, made it clear that a refusal would certainly offend. The Australian reached into his back pocket to pull out his wallet. Sam grabbed his arm and pulled the wallet from his hand. Lennie kneed their victim in the groin and as he fell to the pavement kicked him dispassionately in the face. They walked back into the station, not even running. They took the £30 in the wallet, before throwing it under a train.

As soon as they had shared the money, they split up, agreeing to meet in a week's time at a pub in Kentish Town.

'Keep changing places is the trick,' Lennie told him. 'Old Bill might be looking for us at the Cross if that Aussie makes anything of it. No one in Kentish Town's likely to give a shit about us.'

So a week later they met, had a drink, and mugged another youth in another side road. They developed the pattern: meeting for a drink, selecting a victim, splitting the money, arranging the next meet in a different area. They knew London well between them, knew the squats, knew the pubs where they could sell their victims' credit cards. They weren't friends, just business partners, but in the first pints that they drank together each meeting, they found where each other was living or squatting that week, where fellow squatters that each knew were living that week. Then they met at Clapham, at the Nightingale, just before 8.00 in the evening. It was late May, still warm.

'Easy tonight,' Lennie said. 'Common's crawling with these queers looking for pick-ups. Come from all over; fucking pansies. Sort out a right one, no problem.'

They finished their drinks and walked onto the Common. Three minutes later they saw a middle-aged man in a white T-shirt and blue jeans walking slowly towards them along the poorly lit path looking into the bushes where possible partners sometimes waited. Lennie did not even go through the preliminary of asking for money. He stepped in front of the man and headbutted him without warning. The victim groaned in shock and put his hands up to his already bleeding face. Lennie grabbed him with two hands behind his head, pulling his face forward and bending him over until he was in a position to bring his knee up sharply into the man's face.

The man was now moaning to himself conscious enough to recognise that if he screamed or shouted he might attract police attention, and police attention could be worse than the beating he knew he was going to have. Lennie held the man's head locked in his arm while Sam went quickly through his pockets.

'Got it!' he told Lennie when he had found the wallet, preparing to move away. But Lennie was not finished. He punched the man deliberately across the throat, and when the latter fell gasping for breath at his feet, started to kick and stamp on his face. Sam pulled him away.

'Knock it off, Lennie. Let's clear out.'

Lennie kicked the man deliberately between the legs.

'Fucking pansy!' he spat. 'Fucking disgusting.'

They walked quickly towards Clapham North tube.

'Bit over the top, there, Lennie. Might have killed the silly bleeder.'

'Might have done, yeah. Forget meself sometimes. Killed a bloke about three weeks ago in a bit of a temper. Forgot meself then too.'

Sam paused for a half-second in their walk to the tube. Lennie never boasted. If he claimed to have killed someone, he probably had. They paid for tickets at the ticket machine (no good attracting attention for fare dodging and then find yourself weighed off for the mugging) and went down to the platform.

'How you come to top someone then, Lennie?'

'You know that Acton squat? Been there about two months, even getting the DHSS posting stuff there. He nicked my dole. Wouldn't have it. So I bricked him. Wrapped him in an old carpet and stuck him up in the loft. Still there far as I know. Squat's empty now. They cut off the water and stuff.'

They travelled to Embankment and split up, Lennie off to a room in the East End that he had frightened someone into letting him have, Sam back to Fulham. But Sam decided that the time had come to do something about his increasingly violent partner. He walked to Scotland Yard.

Now, Scotland Yard in Victoria Street is one of the few buildings in London to have a twenty-four hour police guard. Two armed officers patrol outside the building all the time to ensure that terrorists do not leave a car bomb in any of the four streets that surround the building. Sam got to the Yard just after 10.00 p.m. and found an officer at the corner of Broadway and Victoria Street.

'I think my mate's killed a bloke.'

'Oh, yes. What makes you think that?'

'He's just told me. It was about three weeks ago. Says the body's still there. Wrapped in a carpet. Up in the loft of an empty house.'

'Where's this body supposed to be then?'

'Acton. I know where the house is.'

'Acton? Nothing to do with us then, is it? Better get yourself over to Acton and tell them about it.' Now and again you get some very stupid policemen, who don't think thoroughly, and regret it later. Unfortunately Sam had come across one of them. But he persevered. He went to Acton. They treated him more seriously, went to the empty house just before midnight, climbed up into the attic on an old ladder that was still in place from the landing to the loft, and found the rolled-up carpet. Shining a torch into one end they saw the top of a head, at the other end, a pair of feet. They left the attic, put a guard on the house, and called me out.

So at one in the morning I was climbing up a ladder into the loft of a house that had been empty for months. The windows were broken, the plaster had fallen away from the walls, it was like something from a horror film. If the body had been there for three weeks, it would be looking like something from an even worse horror film. The only people to come into the loft with me were the photographer, who would take a picture of each step of the proceedings, and a Detective Sergeant who would have to be responsible for the routines of dealing with a murder victim.

The loft was not boarded, and was completely in the dark, so we had to make the best of things with torches and other temporary lights until we could get the proper equipment there. We also had the common problem in unboarded lofts of having to look carefully every time we took a step. But the most important thing was to make certain that we were dealing with a corpse rather than a shop dummy. I unrolled as little of the carpet as I needed to, to convince myself that this really was a body. It was a corpse, the corpse of a young black man, and the same thought came into my head as came at nearly every murder victim I've examined.

'Wonder if your poor mum and dad ever thought you'd end up like this?'

The following morning the carpet was unrolled carefully, with each stage being photographed in much more suitable light. Inside the carpet the young black man with a deep wound in his skull looked as if he had died only hours ago. The draughts in the attic had helped to preserve the body. The next stage, moving the body, identifying it, collecting witnesses in the street, checking local and national records, was the DS's responsibility. But before that happened I went back from the loft to Acton to speak to Sam.

He did not know exactly where Lennie lived, but he knew the name of the street, so at three in the morning I took a couple of DCs over to Limehouse to see how much further we could get with tracking down Lennie. We went into Limehouse nick and found ourselves in luck straight

away. The home beat officer whose beat covered the street
that Lennie was living in was on duty. Home beat officers
rarely work after 10.00 p.m. This PC had been helping the
night duty CID. Yes, he knew the street that Lennie lived
in. Quite a short street. Lennie had frightened someone into
giving him a room.

'Granny Schmidt. Told me about it last week. Young
bloke got talking to her at the supermarket. Found out that
she had a spare room and just moved in. Told me all about
it, but didn't want to do anything. Afraid the bloke would
come back if we threw him out. Room looks right onto the
street. Take you straight there if you want, Guv.'

Was there a WPC on nights? Yes. Could we borrow her?
They looked puzzled at my wanting a WPC to help to arrest
a violent male skinhead, but it was a technique that I had used
before. I told her to get back into plain clothes.

The street was an old-fashioned East End row of terraced
houses. The home beat PC pointed to Granny Schmidt's
house, and indicated the front ground-floor sash window
as belonging to Lennie's room. I had told the WPC what
I wanted her to do. She tapped on the window.

'Lennie. You there? It's Jean.' There was some movement
in the room. She tapped on the window again.

'Come on, Lennie. The old man's thrown me out. I need
somewhere to kip.'

Now, I didn't know Lennie, but I was willing to gamble
that a man like him would be unable to resist offering a
bed to a girl who knocked on his window at three in the
morning. She might have mixed him up with someone
else, but that could be sorted out later. It worked. The sash
window was pushed up and Lennie leaned out.

'Who you then? What you want?'

'You remember me Lennie. It's just 'til morning, 'til I can
get my things together.' Lennie leaned out a little further
to get a better look at her face, and the DCs on either
side of the window grabbed an arm each and dragged
him forward so that his feet came off the floor inside,

and they had little problem handcuffing his hands behind his back.

'You're being arrested in connection with a murder in Acton. You don't have to say anything, but anything you do say will be taken down and given in evidence.'

'It was just a fucking accident,' Lennie snarled.

I gave him the caution as he was pulled bodily out of the room and walked across to the waiting police van. The WPC and one of the DCs crawled through the window, and collected the few clothes that Lennie had. The arrest had been carried out so quickly and quietly that Granny Schmidt had not been woken. The home beat officer who had been waiting a few doors away in case she had been alarmed, promised to come back the next day and tell her the good news that her lodger had left her.

Lennie stuck to his story that the dead man, Barden, had died when he slipped and hit his head on a protruding brick in the kitchen. He had panicked and hidden the body in the loft, because he knew that if police found out, he would be blamed. We took him to the house. He was vague about where the brick was in the kitchen against which Barden had fallen. He had no explanation for the splashes of blood on the wall above a mattress in one of the bedrooms. Near the mattress was a brick with bloodstains on. The post-mortem showed that Barden's skull had been stationary when the injury had been caused. (The brain is bruised in a different area when an injury is caused through a fall than that in which the injury is caused by a blow.)

I told Lennie that Barden had been killed by being hit on the head with a brick while he was asleep on the mattress. He gave up, and admitted it. There had been a quarrel over dole money delivered to the house. Barden had denied taking it. Lennie went out and got drunk. When he came back, Barden was asleep. Lennie hit him on the head with a brick and saw almost immediately that he had killed him. He rolled him up in an old carpet, lifted him up to the loft, and left the house immediately. He pleaded guilty to manslaughter, and got twelve years. Sam, because of his help to police, got two years for the muggings that he had admitted.

The house in Acton has been rebuilt and looks quite smart now. I wonder if the present owners know what was once in their attic?

# A Man On The Run

It took us a lot of time to find Carvel O'Brien after he escaped from prison. Anyone who believes that the police have an easy time tracing details of people they want to interview should read through the file on O'Brien and just see how much effort is involved in tracing one man who is almost certainly living in the area in which he has always lived.

When I took over the job of finding Carvel, we had few pieces of solid information. We had a photograph of him, knew that he always dressed well in dark clothing, was a bit of a loner, and a very, very, good liar. We knew the addresses of six families with whom he was very close, and we knew that he always worked alone, and that therefore there would be little or no chance of a fellow criminal grassing on him. So one team started with the known addresses, the second with possible addresses. And as we also had the name of the married woman, Rosemary, who had left home to live with Carvel, all the inquiries had to be duplicated.

The possible address team first checked the Police National Computer. Then they checked what was in those days the C11 index which held information about criminals' movements and whereabouts, and the A7 index which held miscellaneous information about any women coming to police notice. Next they checked the DHSS to see if either was claiming the dole or was paying National Insurance. After that they checked the Driving Licence and Vehicle Registration computer at Swansea. They checked the Family Allowance department in case there was a child.

Later in the inquiry when there was more information from the known addresses, they checked all the doctors in the area that either could have registered with. They checked opticians who may have supplied Rosemary with spectacles. They checked bingo clubs for lists of employees when it became known that Rosemary had been employed in such a club, and they asked VAT inspectors from Customs and Excise to check shops at which she might have been working. We knew what Carvel was doing for most of the time, but we could never find him. We found plenty of people who 'had seen him last week'. We tried estate agents, debt collectors, and milkmen. We asked the Post Office Investigation department to search their records to see if either Carvel or Rosemary had ever come to their attention, and we sent photos and descriptions of each to every prison, in case Carvel ever visited friends who were still inside.

We knew that he did make such visits in spite of being an escapee himself. A prison officer at Wandsworth had seen Carvel and had not recognised him.

'I had just transferred to Wandsworth,' he told us later. 'I was walking across the public car-park which was quite busy. It was the weekend, and there were a lot of visitors about. I saw this smart-looking bloke, tall, well-dressed, and I knew his face right off. You know how it is, you recognise someone, but you can't place them immediately. He recognised me too as he was getting into his motor. Gave me a big smile and said something like, "You over here now then? Be seeing a bit more of each other then. See you." And off he drives. I put him down as another PO. Didn't click for hours over who he really was. He'd been on my wing at the Scrubs. Even then I didn't realise that he was an escapee.'

What the prison officer did not realise was that Carvel had been using the car-park to sell stolen goods. And if you're wondering why so much effort was being put into tracing a single escaped prisoner, it was because Carvel O'Brien was establishing a record as a burglar that would put him into *The Guinness Book of Records*. Carvel O'Brien was a one man mobile crime wave.

One of the problems of this intensive form of checking is not only the time taken to make inquiries, it is also the time wasted in making inquiries about the wrong persons. One of the hospitals checked did have records of three C. O'Briens, all living in the north London area. Their last addresses were checked, and inevitably they had all moved on, and their new addresses had to be found. Nor each time was it simply a matter of knocking on a front door and asking, 'Does someone called Carvel O'Brien live here?' The address has to be checked beforehand at the local police station; neighbours tactfully asked about who lives there. Officers would pose as bill collectors, marketing surveyors, or even estate agents to ask such questions, before finally calling at the house itself. But none of the three C. O'Briens traced this way was Carvel.

The inquiries at the known addresses were more profitable. There were ten of these, houses or flats at which relatives or close friends of Carvel lived or had lived. The neighbours of the woman Rosemary, who had left her husband, had not liked the family at all. They described the family as 'dirty'. There was a daughter, Julie, who had liked neither her mother Rosemary, her father, nor Carvel, but who was believed to be in touch with Rosemary. She was put under surveillance.

Another friend of Carvel's, a petty criminal called Boylan, agreed to assist police. He had worked with O'Brien once or twice before the latter went into prison, but had since fallen out with him. O'Brien had sent him an extremely threatening letter before he came out of prison, so threatening that the prison authorities refused to release it. Boylan saw it in his own interests to help police to catch his former friend. He was able to confirm that O'Brien was still in the area.

A few weeks previously, O'Brien had quarrelled with

a quartet of criminals in a pub near King's Cross Police Station. He had run from the pub, pursued by the gang, into the police station. They, thinking that he would call police to them, had then run off. Carvel, buying time for himself, had reported the loss of a pair of spectacles. When we called at King's Cross, there was an entry in the lost property book at the relevant time, with, of course, a false name and address.

We were given the names of pubs which Carvel used, even the names of hairdressers which Rosemary went to. We did what we could about watching the pubs, but such a surveillance took up too many resources to make it a practical proposition. We were able to to get a VAT inspector to check the hairdressers' books to see if there was a past or future appointment in Rosemary's name. He could find no trace of her. There were many other seemingly helpful clues to Rosemary's or Carvel's whereabouts, including an address in a caravan park in Northamptonshire. They were all followed up, some causing embarrassment to entirely honest people who just happened to have the same names or descriptions, but none of them took us any further.

All the time Carvel was burgling away at a rate that would have won him a Queen's Award for Industry had he been following a lawful occupation. He burgled between 6.00 p.m. and 11.00 p.m., confining himself to houses that could be reached from wasteland adjoining a railway line or through a cemetery and which had louvred windows at the rear. Unless such windows are professionally secured, they are very easy to remove by pushing the individual louvres backwards out of their sockets until there is a hole big enough to scramble through. He sat on the railway embankment at dusk and watched as the lights were switched on. If the lights in a house had not gone on an hour after dusk he saw it as a fair target. And he rarely wore gloves. His fingerprints kept turning up in every London suburb. One of his idiosyncrasies was to drink milk from the fridge during the burglary; he left clear prints on glasses and bottles. It was almost as if he was challenging us to find him.

He could burgle two or three houses in a night, and then go, the following night, to the other side of London and carry out three or four more. He was undiscriminating in what he took. Some houses lost as little as £2, others over £1,000. He burgled factories, going back to them three or four months running, until they had taken the hint and replaced the louvres with more secure windows.

We tried to predict a pattern, but there was no pattern to follow. Ealing, then Enfield, Wandsworth followed by Woolwich. The one constant was the railway track. We were lucky once and predicted accurately where he was likely to strike, saturating the area with police in plain clothes. There had been a number of break-ins in the area before, and if Carvel had a weakness, it was for going back to a place he had broken into to see what more he could get. This time we assume that he came along the railway line, made his way over waste ground and climbed over the fence at the back of a house, before the householder spotted him. Officers keeping watch in the area had heard a dog bark, and had gone straight to the house where they heard the noise. It had been burgled a month before.

'Yes, I saw him.' The owner was quite pleased at being the centre of police attention. 'Oh yes, I saw him all right. Climbing over the fence he was. This dog, must have been next door's, he barks, and the geezer goes back over again.'

'Why didn't you phone the police ?' The owner paused. This was obviously a novel idea to him.

'Phone you? Well, didn't seem much point. I knew you was all over the place, so I thought you was bound to catch him.'

In the end our plan was born out of desperation. He had burgled so many houses and factories in so many areas that there were no new places to go. We knew that he was likely to come back to a house that he had burgled already. But where? We had made so many inquiries around Islington where we knew he had been living, that we were certain he would have moved away, so we picked on one area and decided we would wait there until he turned up.

We knew what he looked like, we knew what his girlfriend looked like, we knew that he preferred Minis to any other car. And that was it. We picked on Thornton Heath as it was six weeks since he had burgled a house there. So the fifteen officers in the team started to patrol Thornton Heath, not in the hope of stopping a burglary, but in the hope that they would meet Carvel, Rosemary, or even sight a suspicious Mini. And within days we struck gold. Two officers saw Rosemary, or rather they saw a distinctive green leather coat which had been reported stolen in a burglary in north London, and then they realised that the woman wearing the coat was Rosemary. They were able to follow Rosemary back to a house in a side road. One of them stayed watching the house, the other radioed in with the news.

We had a hurried conference. No point in bursting in there if Carvel was not at home, so we set up an observation post from which we could watch the front of the house without having officers in the road itself. Once more we were lucky, the house was within view of the Traffic Patrol garage in Thornton Heath, so we were able to take over a room there and watch the house to which Rosemary had gone.

About 9.00 p.m. a Mini drew up outside the house, paused and drove off. It did this about three times. I reckoned that if it was Carvel he was making a routine check to ensure that he was not being followed or watched, and that to attempt to follow him in the Mini would be to risk losing him. After the third stop, we saw a man get out of the car and with night binoculars it was possible to see that it was Carvel. We let him get into the house, made sure that the back was properly covered, broke down the door and raced up to the flat on the first floor. I would not pretend that he was pleased to see us, but he accepted that the game was up and made no attempt to struggle or fight. It may sound a bit old-fashioned, but

I shook his hand and told him how pleased I was to meet him at last.

'You've been a very good burglar, Carvel,' I told him, 'but it's all over now.'

And it was all over. Carvel admitted over 2,500 burglaries, many of which we knew nothing about. He had a remarkable memory and could almost tell us to the day when he had burgled a particular house. He gave us addresses at which a lot of the property he had stolen was stored. In one case he told us that he had left property wrapped in a plastic bag in a water tank in a house that he had stayed in for two weeks. When we looked, the property was still there. We took over a complete floor of an East End police station to store and catalogue everything that he had stolen. His only regret, he told me, was that he had never come across a Victorian £5 piece.

I had a letter from him when he was in prison. Rosemary had left him for another man, and he had no one to write to to bring in a small parcel of clothes that was about all he had left. Could I arrange it for him?

'No policeman has ever treated me as properly as you did, Roy,' he said. 'You are the only one who has ever helped me.'

# The Wrong Sort Of Knife

Police attitudes towards domestic violence have changed a lot over the last ten years. So has the attitude of women who have been the victims of domestic violence. The police attitude used to be . . . 'We'll help you if you agree to make a statement, come to court, and give evidence against the man'.

The victim's attitude used to be an amalgamation of, 'I just want him to stop attacking me. If he knows I've called the police he'll just become more violent. If he goes to prison who's going to pay the mortgage?'

Police practice was based on the cynical belief that women did not really mean it. In the morning they would repent of their call for help, and refuse to attend court. Everything was black and white. Either you wanted your husband to stop beating you up, so you gave evidence against him, or you were prepared to put up with it. Police rarely saw themselves as having to examine the reasons that battered women would not go to court. Hopefully we are now much more considerate, and understand the pressures on the woman.

Some forces have an immediate arrest policy. If a man is accused of a serious attack on his partner he is arrested immediately and kept at the police station for a minimum of four hours to enable the woman to get professional advice on what she should do next. Many police stations have domestic violence units manned by experienced male and female officers to whom wives and partners can come for advice without revealing their identity or having to involve themselves in legal proceedings. Sometimes that understanding can go too far. Remember the case at Stoke Newington in which a battered wife came to the station for help and was followed in by her husband. There seemed to be a chance of reconciliation and the officer in charge of the case left them alone, at the wife's request. The husband then stabbed her to death.

But even with these advances, with advisory services, with hostels for battered wives, women continue to suffer, often in silence. One wife, in the last twelve months, having been beaten almost daily for a year by her husband, finally had to go to hospital because he had broken her jaw. Even then she would not tell the hospital staff what had happened. Her jaw had to be wired to allow the fracture to mend. Her husband thought that this reflected badly on him, and physically pulled out the wires with a pair of pliers. When she screamed, he punished her by putting a hot iron to her breast. Only at that stage did she decide that she had suffered enough, and called in the police.

It is sometimes hard to explain why women continue to put up with beatings. Quite often, they receive no affection, little financial support, and lead lives of permanent misery. But they never go to the police.

Tina Morland was one of the battered women who did take action. Tina, a single mother with a 3-year-old son, lived in a first-floor flat. She was a very good-looking girl, and had done some modelling work, but not enough to be noticed and to move into the high earning field. She was only 5 feet tall, and so, however attractive she looked, the model agencies, who wanted girls at least 10 inches taller, put little work her way. She was 29, and the model agencies wanted girls at least 10 years younger.

Early in 1985, Tina met Andrew Czernik at a friend's party. They began going out together, when Tina could get a babysitter, and Andrew spent more and more time at the flat. Tina would not commit herself to a more permanent relationship.

'Come on, Andy. We've only known each other for six months.'

Czernik showed increasing signs of jealousy and possessiveness.

'It's another bloke, isn't it? You've got someone else in the background, and you ain't telling me. Bet he comes round when I'm not here.'

Once he hit her across the face. She told him to get out, but he apologised, saying he was crazy about her, and it would never happen again. The next time he punched her, and threw her against the wall. There were more apologies, but in October he beat her quite badly, and told her he would kill her if he found her with another man. Tina called the police, agreed to give evidence, and went to court. Czernik admitted everything, told the police that he was ashamed of himself, and promised that he would never see Tina again. He was bound over to keep the peace. Binding over is a procedure used by magistrates to deal with a defendant who is unlikely to repeat the offence of which he is accused. They can impose conditions. In Czernik's case the conditions were that he made no attempt to contact Tina.

Her friends told us later that he continued to phone her, threatening to kill her. Tina told police nothing about the calls. Presumably she thought that the hassle of Czernik at the end of a phone line was preferable to the hassle of going back to court. Three weeks before Christmas he met her and her son in the street, apparently by accident. He wished them a happy Christmas, but Tina made it clear that she did not want to see him over the holiday. She was not unpleasant to him, but she was firm.

On December 20 he called at her flat. Czernik was a printer and had been working through the night, so he arrived at the flat around 10.00 in the morning. Tina was still not dressed and was wearing only a dressing-gown. She did not want to see him, but a mother with a young son at that time of the morning does not want to become involved in an argument. Nor did she want any of the neighbours hearing raised voices. She let him in. An hour later, neighbours did hear raised voices, or rather they heard a scream and came out to the stairwell. They found Tina lying dead on the stairs. The walls and steps were smeared and splashed with her blood where she had put out hands to support herself. She had a deep knife wound visible in her chest, and blood still flowing onto the concrete stairs showed that there were more wounds on her back. Her little boy could be heard calling for her in their flat on the floor above.

When I arrived at the scene just before 1.00 p.m., the first steps of the investigation had been completed. Tina's son had been taken away while we tried to trace a relative who might look after him. Tina's body had been photographed and was put in a plastic bag awaiting removal to the morgue. Her flat was being examined thoroughly and also photographed. Samples had been taken from many of the fresh blood stains in the kitchen. It seemed clear that Tina had been stabbed a number of times in her flat and had then staggered down the stairs presumably in the hope of getting help. Statements were being taken from all the neighbours not only about what they had heard and seen that day, but also about what they knew of Tina and her friends. And a weapon had been found. A kitchen paring knife. It was lying near the front door of the flats, and it had blood on the handle. But it did not take great detective powers to realise that this was not the knife that killed Tina Morland. The stab wounds that I had seen on her body had clearly been made by a flat two- edged weapon. The wounds on Tina's hands showed that she had grabbed at a flat two-edged weapon. The paring knife was single-edged and curved.

It may have been nothing to do with the murder at all. Ignoring the possibility of a coincidences is a certain way of fouling up an investigation. Just because there's been a murder with a knife, and just because there's a knife nearby, does not mean they must be connected. So for the moment, we could take notice of the paring knife but not accept with certainty it had anything to do with the murder. We really wanted to find a flat two-edged weapon, a sharp weapon; again it might have been a coincidence, but the telephone wire outside Tina's flat had been cut cleanly with a sharp knife. Now what we wanted was a suspect. And it was not long before Czernik was squarely in the frame.

The local collator's records told us about his October attack on Tina. One of Tina's neighbours knew all about it. Within the next twenty-four hours, friends had told us of Czernik's threatening phone calls. One neighbour thought he had seen 'a young man very like the young man who used to spend some time at the flat earlier in the year' going up the stairs as he took his milk in, and Czernik was missing from his own flat and from his job.

Two days later he came to Acton Police Station with his solicitor and admitted the killing, and that, you may think, was that. But the story that Czernik told was rather different to what I knew had happened. According to Czernik, Tina had invited him to call in to see her and her son to make plans for Christmas. He had brought a Christmas card for them. But when he arrived, having worked all night before, she made it clear that he was unwelcome. She had no intention of spending Christmas with him. She had a new boyfriend. When he handed her the Christmas card, she had not even opened it. She just sneered and threw it on the floor. She told him that the court had said he was not to call at her flat. Well now she was going to phone the police. She'd see that he would spend Christmas in prison.

'I just snapped. There was this knife lying on the kitchen table. I grabbed it without thinking. I just stabbed and stabbed at her. She tried to take it off me. I ran out in a panic. I didn't know she was dead until I read the papers. So I ran away. I spent one night sleeping at the factory in my car, and then another night in a hotel. Then I decided to give myself up.'

I asked him about the knife. I didn't tell him we had already found it.

'I threw it away when I ran out of the flats.'

'Are you sure that you didn't use a flat knife? Didn't you once own a flick knife?' (That was in Tina's statement in October.)

'Yes. I had a flick knife once, but this was a paring knife. I picked it up in the kitchen.'

'This was a two-edged knife that killed Tina. Are you sure you did not use a flick knife? A paring knife is like a potato knife.'

'No. It was a paring knife. I picked it up in the kitchen.' And that's all he would say.

What Czernik was hoping for was a charge of manslaughter. You can argue for twenty-four hours and then start all over again about what manslaughter really means. The easiest explanation is a killing resulting from an assault that was never intended to kill. So manslaughter is less serious than murder which is committed with the intent to kill someone. Lawyers will have a great night out contradicting those statements, but for the sake of Tina Morland, these explanations will have to do. Czernik wanted to plead guilty to manslaughter, and would claim that Tina had provoked him into the attack.

However, there were a number of things that indicated that Czernik had planned the murder, and had not been provoked into a frenzied, uncontrolled attack. The telephone wire had been cut. We could not prove that Czernik had cut it, but it was unlikely that anyone else would have done it. The murder had not been carried out with the paring knife. Czernik was insistent that it had been and was quite open about where he had thrown away the knife. That meant that he wanted us to find a weapon that had been readily available in Tina's flat. There was the Christmas card. He said that Tina had thrown it on the floor. But when he attended the station, he handed over the Christmas card stained in blood. Why would a man in a jealous frenzy stab a woman repeatedly, pick up a Christmas card from the floor, and carefully preserve it for three days, unless he wanted to prove his version of the killing. But there was another piece of evidence which we kept until his cross-examination.

At his trial he pleaded not guilty to murder, and we refused to accept a plea of guilty to manslaughter. One of the first witnesses was the pathologist who described the seventeen wounds he found on Tina's body; sixteen of them were in her back, and one was in her chest. Most of them were three inches deep. People pay little attention to the pathologist after his opening sentences, and the prosecution asked him very few questions.

'Yes. There were wounds to both of the deceased's hands, indicative of the victim trying to seize the knife.'

'Was there any indication of cuts to the victim's hair?'

'None at all. Most of the cuts were to her body. Two were through her dressing gown. Her hair had not been cut.'

Reading now about a killing you would think that every word about how it was done would be heard in silence with the full attention of everyone in the court. But after the first few lines of evidence, the court became numbed; even the defence paid little attention to what was little more than a routine description.

'Now, would you look at photograph no 7 in the album. This shows what?'

'This is a group of three wounds delivered, I would estimate by the same weapon, a sharp-edged instrument with two sides about three inches in length. The wounds are each about three inches deep and bruising on the skin indicates that the handle of the weapon had prevented the blade entering any further.'

'These wounds are identical to those described in photographs numbered 5 and 6?'

'They are.'

'And caused by the same instrument.'

'I believe so.'

Gets dull after a while, doesn't it? Just a list of wounds and opinions almost divorced from the horror of the killing itself.

When Czernik came to give evidence his counsel took him through his version of his 'frenzied' attack. He had gone to the flat in good faith. He loved Tina very deeply. He had been thrown into a blind rage by her treatment of him. He grabbed a knife, he thought it was the paring knife as that was in his hand when he ran from the flat. He had never meant to kill her.

Prosecution counsel concentrated on the wounds. Most of them were to the victim's back.

'Yes. I didn't know what I was doing. I was just stabbing wildly.'

'Were you not holding Miss Morland down on the bed when you inflicted these wounds?'

'No. She was standing up.'

'Why didn't she just run away?'

'I don't know. I was just stabbing at her.'

'Was she not lying face down on the bed?'

'I don't think so. I can't remember.'

'Many of the wounds were three inches deep. Would they have been so deep had she been standing up?'

'I don't know. I just know I lost control.'

'Would she not instinctively have moved away had she been standing up?'

'I can't remember.'

Then the real questions.

'May I ask you to look at the photographs of the body. You will see that there are a number of photos which show stab wounds. Would you look at photos 12 and 13. They show wounds to the back of the neck.'

'Yes. I did those as well.'

'Would you agree that those cuts are slashes rather than stabs?'

'They could be. I had just gone mad.'

'May I also draw your attention to photograph no 2. This shows that Miss Morland had rather long hair, certainly longer than shoulder length.'

'Yes. She had very long hair.'

'Can you therefore explain how, if Miss Morland was standing up, and you were slashing at the back of her neck, can you explain how it is there were no cuts to her hair.'

'I can't remember.'

'Is this not the truth of what happened. If the jury would look at the photos of the bedspread, and then the photos of Miss Morland taken from the back, does it not appear that Miss Morland was lying face down on the bedspread when many of these injuries were inflicted. And is there any other explanation for the lack of damage to her hair, other than you holding her down, holding her hair away from her neck with one hand, and slashing at her neck with the knife.'

'I can't remember.'

'Can you remember holding Miss Morland face down on her bed? Can you remember holding back her hair with one hand to enable you to cut the back of her neck?'

'No. I can't remember. But I know it wasn't like that.'

'Mr Czernik. Are the facts not these? There was no frenzied attack. You went to that flat with the deliberate intention of killing Miss Morland. You took with you a knife for that purpose. You deliberately arranged for the police to find a knife from the flat suggesting that this was an impromptu killing. And before you stabbed Miss Morland to death, you tortured her. You kept her face down on the bed, you lifted her hair from her neck and you repeatedly slashed at the back of her neck with the intention of causing her great pain, before you deliberately stabbed her to death.'

'I can't remember.'

The jury did not believe Czernik. He was sentenced to life, which means he's probably already out of prison.

Police recruits, taught the new approach to domestic violence, are also reminded of another pertinent statistic. Almost 80 per cent of murders in this country involve people who know each other. If you go to a 'domestic' today, you could be a witness in a murder trial next year.

# Operation Shampoo

One of the most successful operations against organised crime in London was brought to a sudden end without an explanation. Over 150 participants had been arrested for crimes varying from the importation of drugs, demanding money with menaces, to widescale and systematic frauds on building societies and insurance companies. A small, committed squad of never more than twenty men and women had taken eighteen months to break down an international organisation which had connections in Europe and North America and which thrived on threatening potential witnesses. Its centre was in Southall, and its membership was drawn from one of the most honest, respectable, minorities in the UK, the Asian community. But before the Squad's work was finished, or even nearly finished, it was closed down.

We had no idea of the protection rackets, the frauds, the drug dealing that involved a tiny minority of Asians until we started to investigate the strange all-Asian gang fights in Southall. We knew there were two gangs, the Tootinungs and the Holy Smokes who were recruiting members from local schoolchildren. There is no real English translation of Tootinung, the nearest is a cross between Les Miserables and The Worthless Ones. The only explanation for the Holy Smokes' name is that the families from which they came had connections with Hindu temples. The fights were not just street battles with six of one gang picking on four of the other side met by chance in the street. These fights were arranged in advance with forty or fifty on each side.

Those fighting were armed with knives, machetes, swords, and axes, and fighting only for the honour of the gang. There were no religious differences, no territory disputes, no battles for control of drugs or any other form of crime. They met just to fight.

There were injuries, of course: stabbings, beatings, some gang members crippled. We arrested over fifty people after one fight, all Asian youths aged from 14 to 25, and charged them all. None of those injured would make statements about what had happened. We were left in the position that police are often in. We knew what had happened, we knew who was concerned, but we just could not prove it. We had to withdraw all the charges.

But when the respectable Asians saw that police were determined to stamp out this particular form of violence, they began to provide evidence of what else was going on. Nothing concrete, just hints of 'You should speak to so and so . . . Ask yourself where "X" gets all his money from.'

So we started speaking to the people who wanted to speak.

We found out about the postmen. A number of gang associates had quite deliberately taken jobs with the Post Office. Once they were employed as postmen they kept a look-out for the fairly distinctive letters in which banks send out service cards and credit cards. They kept these letters back and a few days later abstracted the follow-up letter which contained the PIN number. That gave them about a fortnight to milk the banks before either the bank contacted the client about the overspending, or the customer asked the bank why there was a delay in sending out the card. The goods bought were sold immediately for cash, and the cash in many cases used to buy hard drugs which were sold for the highest profit of all.

In one case, in Brixton, where gang associates had taken over a sub-post office, the Asian postmaster and his family were raided by a West Indian gang who threatened them with shotguns, poured petrol over the wife, and demanded that the safe be opened. Over £117,000 was stolen in the raid, and no suspects were ever arrested. Six months later the postmaster was seen around in a brand new car. The investigation was reopened. There had never been a robbery. £100,000 of the money taken from the post office had gone to finance drug deals, the rest the postmaster decided to spend on himself and his family.

We found out about the bogus insurance agents. It is not generally appreciated that an insurance agent gets a considerable commission on arranging an endowment insurance. Remember also that we are talking about prosperous days in the house market when the value of a house could increase by £1,000 a month. So prospective house buyers would arrange an endowment mortgage and pay the first three months mortgage before defaulting. That gave time for the insurance agent to claim his commission. The house then had to be repossessed and resold. That could take as long as twelve months, by which time the house had increased considerably in value and the profit (often around the £20,000 mark) would be handed back to the purchaser by the building society after they had recovered their costs. There were over twenty agents involved in the scam, so many that the major insurance companies formed their own department to cooperate with us in launching prosecutions. We think that at least £2 million had been stolen in this way.

We found that there was a very sophisticated forgery operation which could produce passports, driving licences, even visas for illegal immigrants, as well as photostat copies of birth and death certificates. There was even a refinement for those who wanted to live in Canada. They were provided with the documents and tickets to board an aircraft in the UK, destroyed the documents in the aircraft toilet once the plane had taken off, and then declared themselves to be political refugees in Canada.

There were the stolen cars. Both gangs fancied Ford Capris, and ran complicated networks stealing cars in one part of the country to sell them cheaply to gang members in another city. Some of the younger gangsters adopted the fashion of having two new cars, each for their personal use. Cars were not only status symbols. Once stolen they were easily sold for cash, and the cash used to finance drug deals. One man we arrested for his part in car stealing had £100,000 in notes beneath the floorboards of his sitting-room. He claimed they were his life savings. We, to say the least, were suspicious about its origins. Two years later the Metropolitan Police is still locked in a civil action in relation to the money

Then there were the protection rackets; shopkeepers forced to hand over money to gang leaders or risk having their premises burnt down. The threats were the hardest to prove or to act on. Some threats were so subtly implied that it would have been very difficult to prove there was a threat. One shopkeeper described what had happened to him.

'These three youths, they come to my shop in a big car and park outside. One comes in and buys a tin of coke. Says nothing, but just looks hard at me. He goes back to the car. The second one comes in, does the same. The third buys cigarettes. "Must make plenty of money in a shop like this. You wouldn't miss a few thousand pounds." A week later they come back, do the same. Soon you're scared enough to give them the money.'

It was a shopkeeper, Mohinder, who gave us our major breakthrough. Up to that point we had talked to a number who had been attacked, had their premises damaged, or whose deliverers had been scared off. They had nothing to tell us. The beatings were 'just family matters', the damage to their shops – 'You know what the local kids are like, some of their parents are very racist'. The delivery drivers – 'some confusion over invoices'. Then Mohinder was asked to pay out £20,000.

Mohinder had an off-licence in Greenford. One afternoon two young Asian men came into his shop telling him they had some business to talk over with him. Would he just come outside and speak to their partner who was in a car outside?

He went out to the car. There were two other men in the car. Their business was very simple. One of them pointed a gun at the shopkeeper.

'We are from Tootinung. You know how powerful we are. We want £20,000. It is a simple choice. You pay us the money, or we will shoot you and feed you to the dog.' The man nodded towards an alsatian which one of the first two callers was holding on a chain. 'We will be back next week.' Besides the clear and obvious threat, Mohinder had another fear. He had £20,000 in a deposit account. Was it a coincidence that they had asked for that amount, or had someone told them just how much he had in the bank?

They came back a week later, took him to his bank where he withdrew the £20,000 and handed it over. They drove off and left him to walk back to his off-licence. As he walked he realised that he had not finished with the gang. As soon as he had saved more money they would be back. He had heard that there was a police squad anxious to talk to any shop-keeper or businessman who had been threatened. So he rang Ruislip and asked to speak to me. He was able to identify the two men who had come to his shop. When they were arrested they had £95,000 in cash between them. Despite this news in the local papers, no one else came forward to give evidence against them. Mohinder's testimony was enough to put them each away for four years.

By now you'll be wondering where you heard these stories, or something like them, before. Sounds like the Mafia, doesn't it? A minority controlling the majority through fear, making money by direct theft, or by illegally manipulating legitimate businesses. Small businessmen in fear, money collected for protection, and strong widespread family con-nections among the gangsters. During the eighteen months of Operation Shampoo we learned a great deal about these extended criminal families. We learned of the links between Southall and major cities outside London, links to Germany, France, Canada, and Pakistan, and we learned that, unlike the Mafia, the Asian gangs had no single godfather. There were many apparently genuine businessmen running their own particular parts of the conspiracy, and often taking an active part rather than delegating work to younger, lesser gangsters. Which is how we came to arrest a number of prominent Asian businessmen.

We arrested one property developer for the offence of conspiracy to pervert the course of justice, after a witness in another case had been offered a large sum of money not to appear at court. He was sentenced to three months imprisonment. The information gained from the arrest of this man resulted in the arrest of another member of the local community, Barkat Kahn. Kahn was one of several rich men who had come to notice because of information gained through using a variety of electronic surveillance methods: phone intercepts, video surveillance, long range microphones. We gained enough evidence to arrest him for conspiracy to import £500,000 worth of heroin. He had actually contacted the sellers and importers face to face, rather than employ intermediaries. He had set up the sales links himself, rather than broker them out to associates. We had evidence on tape, on film and in writing. He was later convicted and sentenced to four years imprisonment. But almost as soon as he had been tried, I was told that Operation Shampoo was being closed down, the technical facilities we had been able to use freely were being withdrawn, and the squad was to be broken up.

We had only gone half-way towards achieving the wholesale breaking down of the gangs; there were dozens more people to be arrested, just as many leads to follow. Violent crime in Southall had been reduced by 50 per cent but there was still a lot of work to do. Operation Shampoo was the last job I did for the Metropolitan. I had given a report to a meeting of senior officers from all over the Met on the success of the operation. I was able to show that there had been a massive reduction in crime in the Southall area through the arrest of dozens of active and often violent criminals. The squad was on an understandable high, much had been achieved and there was still much to do.

One of the Met's continuing objectives is the reduction in organised crime, and, however glamorous or newsworthy murder investigations might be, it is campaigns like Operation Shampoo that really provide the community with value for money, that really clamp down on the everyday crime that can alter the quality of life in a particular area. After the report I was assured that there were sufficient funds available to carry on with Shampoo and other similar operations. My squad and I were justified in seeing the operation as a success.

However, without any warning, a short time after Kahn's conviction, I was called before a senior detective and told that my squad officers would be returned to normal duties and I should close the report on Shampoo. To say the least, I was shocked by the decision.

'May I know the reason for this, Sir?'

'No. Just close the operation down.'

I had no other option than to tell the equally surprised members of my squad that Shampoo was over, that they would be returned to their own stations, and that I had no explanation for it. I submitted the final report. I have never been given a reason for the decision.

Six months after Kahn had been convicted, I retired from the job I loved so much.

# Epilogue

## by Brian Hilliard

You will have realised from the last sentence of the last paragraph that Roy Herridge did not leave the Metropolitan Police a completely happy man. *Believe No One* has only been half the story of his achievements. In his thirty-two years' service he received thirty-three commendations, the highest number ever awarded to a Metropolitan police officer. He had a unique career – even though he began and was promoted as a uniform officer, his investigative talents resulted in him being invited to join the Criminal Investigation Department. Everyone else who wants a career in the CID asks to join. When he was awarded the Queen's Police Medal, officers of every rank and from most of the stations at which he had worked cooperated in a 'This is Your Life' presentation to him which showed the enormous respect he enjoyed throughout the Metropolitan Police.

So what went wrong at the end? Why did Roy not carry on for another five years? Did, in fact, anything go wrong? Roy, with a deep and continuing loyalty to the Metropolitan Police, denies that anything out of the ordinary took place at the end of Operation Shampoo. But other officers who worked on the Shampoo Squad are still puzzled about its abrupt end. It is known that as soon as Barkat Kahn was arrested, Roy had a number of enigmatic phone calls from detectives serving in other areas. Roy, who can talk for hours about his jobs, is reluctant to talk about the calls, but officers working with him were surprised at the interest taken by detectives unnconnected with the investigation into a man who was a comparatively minor criminal. Roy, through no other motive than a reluctance to believe that Kahn had some form of influence with other police officers, does not willingly talk about the operation which should have been one of the highlights of a successful career.

I found myself in the position which he had occupied so often, dragging answers from a witness.

'When Barkat Kahn was arrested, did he seem surprised? Did he think he was immune from arrest?'

'Well, yes, but I suppose most people are surprised when they are arrested. Most people think they are safe.'

'Yes. But he took it rather personally, didn't he? Almost as if he thought he was exempt.'

'Well he certainly thought he was not going to have to go to court. He seemed to think that we hadn't enough evidence to get him to court.'

'Yes, but didn't he give the impression that he thought you were naive in thinking that you would get him to court.'

'Certainly, he did. But so do a lot of defendants. But he seemed a bit bewildered by the whole thing.'

'Did he ever make any sort of approach to you?'

'He rang me while he was out on bail, asking to meet me. I had the impression that he was taping the call in the hope that I would say something foolish. All his questions were deliberate, rather as if he was reading from a prepared script. I agreed to meet him, but told him that we could not say a single word about his case. That was not what he wanted, so he rang off.'

'Did he offer you a bribe?'

'Never, not the hint of it. But that phone call was certainly funny. It was as if someone had told him what questions to ask.'

'What sort of evidence did you have; witnesses, that sort of thing.'

'A few witnesses, but we had a fair amount of electronic surveillance. We knew what he had been saying, what the deal was that he was arranging, where he was sending messages. It was a cast-iron case, a stone bonker.'

'Apart from his own personal surprise, I think that a number of police officers were disturbed that this sort of person had been arrested.'

'There were a few calls from police officers who knew him. I suppose it was the usual business/round-table connections. I'm told that he had contributed to some police charities.'

'Were they asking you to go easy on him?'

'No. Nothing like that. They were just sort of surprised that a respected businessman had been involved in drug dealing. One or two might have suggested that I should be a bit careful, that I might have made a mistake.'

'So almost as soon as he was arrested, the operation was stopped?'

'Immediately after the end of his trial.'

'Did you think it had come to an end?'

'No way. There were dozens of people still to be seen. I reckon that had we gone on, we could have nicked another hundred people. But when I put in requests to continue surveillance on Kahn's associates, it was refused. Remember that he had only come into the picture because of information from another arrest. When we looked at his records, it became clear that there were a number of other people who would warrant our attention. But Kahn was convicted, and I was told to close the squad down.'

Now there are many reasons for closing down an operation of this sort. The first is that it is failing consistently to achieve its targets. That certainly could not be said of Shampoo. During its eighteen months' life there had been nearly 150 arrests with a very respectable 80 per cent conviction rate, and the Asian business community, which was being squeezed by Asian criminals, was gaining enough confidence in the police to report crimes to them which they had never previously talked about, and to agree to give evidence at court. A number of old unresolved investigations had been reopened with positive results.

'Was there any indication that Shampoo was being viewed in some quarters as racially motivated? After all it was dealing almost exclusively with Asian defendants.'

'I got on very well with the leaders of the Asian community,' says Roy. 'I worked with them for a long time, especially over Mrs Bhatti's murder in 1988. While Shampoo was running, we were getting a lot of praise from Asian businessmen for dealing with the people who were preying on them. Anyone who knows the community there, would know instantly that Shampoo was never seen as a racist operation. I still have a number of good friends in the Asian community. They've commented more than once on the delicate and sensitive way our inquiries were carried out. There was absolutely no racist element. In fact, the people I got to know during Shampoo still ring me up with information that I pass on to the local police.'

'Perhaps in these days of overtime restrictions there was no money available to keep it going?'

'No,' says Roy, 'I spoke to the Deputy Commissioner about this shortly before I retired. He told me that there was plenty of money available to keep Shampoo running.'

'Had Shampoo outlived its usefulness?'

'Not at all. Look at the figures. Since Shampoo closed down, three Asian businessmen have been killed and the killers have gone undetected. Asian friends tell me that the protection racket has returned. Some of the gangs are now so organised that they hire white villains for particular jobs. They are increasingly involved in counterfeit money, even counterfeit credit cards. Most of the work that Shampoo did is having to be done all over again, because we had to leave many of the principals untouched. This year, the Met has opened Operation Wichita to take over the work left when Shampoo was closed down.'

So an operation which had the support of the community, which was reducing crime, which had further criminals in its sights, for which there were sufficient resources: why was that operation closed down after the conviction of a man in which other officers appeared to have an unusual interest?

None of the routine reasons apply. If there had been dissatisfaction with Roy's leadership, he could have been replaced in twenty-four hours. That happens all the time in the Met.

There seems to be only one reason left for the closure. Someone above Roy must have had a personal interest for ensuring that the investigation into organised Asian crime went no further.